Towards Reading Freud

Towards Reading Freud

SELF-CREATION IN MILTON, WORDSWORTH, EMERSON, AND SIGMUND FREUD

Mark Edmundson

THE UNIVERSITY OF CHICAGO PRESS

CHICAGO AND LONDON

The University of Chicago Press, Chicago 60637
© 1990 by Mark Edmundson
All rights reserved.
First published by Princeton University Press.
University of Chicago Press edition 2007
Printed in the United States of America
16 15 14 13 12 11 10 09 08 07   1 2 3 4 5

ISBN-13: 978-0-226-18461-6 (paper)
ISBN-10: 0-226-18461-7 (paper)

Library of Congress Cataloging-in-Publication Data
Edmundson, Mark, 1952–
   Towards reading Freud : self-creation in Milton,
Wordsworth, Emerson, and Sigmund Freud / Mark
Edmundson.
      p. cm.
   Originally published: Princeton : Princeton Univer-
sity Press, ©1990.
   Includes index.
   ISBN-13: 978-0-226-18461-6 (pbk. : alk. paper)
   ISBN-10: 0-226-18461-7 (pbk. : alk. paper)
   1. English poetry—History and criticism. 2. Mil-
ton, John, 1608–1674—Knowledge—Psychology.
3. Wordsworth, William, 1770–1850—Knowledge
—Psychology. 4. Emerson, Ralph Waldo, 1803–
1882—Knowledge—Psychology. 5. Freud, Sig-
mund, 1856–1939. 6. Literature—Psychological
aspects. 7. Psychoanalysis and literature—United
States. 8. Psychoanalysis and literature—England.
9. Psychology in literature. 10. Self in literature.
I. Title.
   PR508.P9E36 2007
   821.009′353—dc22
                                        2007015646

For Elizabeth Denton

_____

CONTENTS

PREFACE

THIS BOOK offers a redescription of some of Sigmund Freud's major writings on the nature of the self. I try, in the pages to come, to persuade the reader to conceive of Freud in a somewhat unaccustomed way. The Freud I present has two sides, what might be called the normative and the Romantic. These two aspects combine with each other in the most intricate and changing ways, but for introductory purposes—and only for that—I consider each in isolation.

The normative Freud is a therapist whose objective it is to acquaint his readers and his patients with the causes for their sufferings and to show them the way to psychological health. Freud the therapist demonstrates repeatedly how small the area is in which reason can hope to hold command. Again and again, he affirms the vast powers of the unconscious. This Freud operates in the tradition of conservative ethical thought that reaches back at least as far as Montaigne. He insists upon human limits. He teaches that the best sort of life eschews overreaching, and that the most salutary changes for which a human being can hope occur gradually and, because they depend upon "sublimation," demand that one renounce immediate pleasures. This is the Freud who undermined the pretensions of culture to have brought men and women beyond the claims of their instincts. He is the "rational voice" Auden mourned in his elegy and the moralist brought to life in the pages of Philip Rieff's brilliant early work.[1]

But there is, I argue, another Freud as well. This Freud is best conceived of as a Romantic writer, one whose objective is symbolic self-reinvention. Freud the self-creator places very little stock in the normative standards of the devoted therapist. His objective is originality. Not only does the Romantic Freud aspire to displace his culture's favored modes of description and explanation for nearly everything that matters in human experience, he also aspires to produce images of himself, as creator and authority, that are so dramatic that they qualify as symbolic rebirths. Like the Romantic poets, like Shelley and Blake and Emerson, Freud is drawn to images of self-overcoming that are sudden, dramatic, and sometimes rather violent. "Sublimation"—the process of gradual change—is for others. Freud figures his own self-transformations in the rhetoric and imagery of crisis.

The normative side of Freud's work has been effectively documented.

[1] *Freud: The Mind of the Moralist* (Chicago: University of Chicago Press, 1979).

Rieff's *Freud: The Mind of the Moralist* opens up the practical implications of Freud's therapeutic philosophy; the work of Richard Wollheim
lays out the conceptual development of Freud's normative thinking.[2]
Numberless other studies, particularly those written by currently practicing analysts, proceed in this tradition. The perception that Freud is in
some dimension of his work a "literary" writer is itself of course not a
new one. It was crudely anticipated by Karl Kraus, who viewed psychoanalysis as nothing more than a deceptive fiction, and by the medical col-
league who called Freud's work a "scientific fairy tale." Perhaps Freud
affirmed the view himself when he referred to the drives as "our mythology." Closer to the present, claims for Freud's literary status have been
made by Stanley Edgar Hyman, by Harold Bloom, and, with certain qual-
ifications, by Shoshana Felman.[3] What is missing in the studies of these
fine critics, it seems to me, are the kinds of extended demonstrations of
Freud's literary affinities that would make them truly plausible to readers.
In this book I try to prove Freud's literary status by pointing out the analogies that exist between him and various "imaginative" writers. My objective is to show that Freud belongs in the company of Shakespeare and
Milton and Sophocles, writers who provide supreme fictions for the nature of reality.

Over the past fifteen or so years, most of the attention devoted to
Freud's "literary" designs has been offered by deconstructive readers, by
Jacques Derrida and those who have been influenced by his work.[4] These
critics seem to be drawn to Freud chiefly for two reasons. They find his
text ripe for deconstruction: self-reflective and self-subverting, illuminatingly at odds about the status of its own authority. They also find, particularly in books such as *The Interpretation of Dreams* and *The Psycho-
pathology of Everyday Life*, intimations of their own mode of
interminable analysis. Freud's sense that the interpretation of a dream or
of a slip of the tongue is, theoretically speaking at least, never completed
foreshadows the deconstructive polemic against claims to the final appre-
hension of Truth. The deconstructors' Freud is the one who, to use Allan

[2] See Wollheim's *Sigmund Freud* (New York: Viking, 1971).

[3] See Hyman's *The Tangled Bank: Darwin, Marx, Frazer and Freud as Imaginative Writers* (New York: Atheneum, 1962); Bloom's *Agon: Towards a Theory of Revisionism* (New
York: Oxford University Press, 1982) especially pp. 91–144; and Felman's *Jacques Lacan
and the Adventure of Insight* (Cambridge, Mass.: Harvard University Press, 1987).

[4] See Derrida's *The Post Card: From Socrates to Freud and Beyond*, trans. Alan Bass
(Chicago: University of Chicago Press, 1987); Jane Gallop's *The Daughter's Seduction:
Feminism and Psychoanalysis* (Ithaca, N.Y.: Cornell University Press, 1982); Neil Hertz's
The End of the Line: Essays on Psychoanalysis and the Sublime (New York: Columbia
University Press, 1985); and Leo Bersani's *The Freudian Body* (New York: Columbia Uni-
versity Press, 1986).

Megill's distinction, taught us not "how to live" (the "modern" Freud supposedly did that), but "how to read."[5]

The following pages do not make extensive use of Derridean modes of reading; I am far more beholden to the kind of pragmatic approach to interpretation that is epitomized by Kenneth Burke. Where I am indebted to deconstructive thinking, though, is in my concern with the ways that Freud's writing dramatizes its own quest for authority. Deconstruction has taught us to be attuned to the claims that texts make for influence over us, especially if those claims are particularly subtle or seductive. It has also encouraged us to be aware of those moments in which texts seem to move beyond their own overt patterns of accommodation. The dialectic of the normative and the Romantic that I develop here is far different from the dialectic that Derrida locates (which of course he claims is not a dialectic, not a tension, not an opposition, etc.) between the "metaphysics of presence" and *différance*, but both approaches are attuned to the issue of how a text achieves the power over readers that it does. The fact that this book is overall more affirmative than it is demystifying ought to distinguish its spirit unmistakably from that of deconstruction.

I depart here from deconstruction, too, in the extent to which I make overt reference to the social context. I argue in the Introduction that a study like this is worth undertaking in part because the normative effect of Freud's work has become, over time, stultifying. At present, the therapeutic Freud deprives us of more human possibilities than he opens up. This at least is my view, one in which I follow such writers as Hannah Arendt, who was frequently writing in opposition to Freud without saying as much; Michel Foucault, whose work from *Madness and Civilization* to *The History of Sexuality* can fairly be read as an extended polemic against, among other things, the ethos of psychoanalysis; and the later Philip Rieff, who develops his critique of "psychological man" in *The Triumph of the Therapeutic*.[6] I should add that this view on the limitations imposed by a culture of psychoanalysis is not one that can be proved empirically. It relies on judgments of value: what to one observer looks like tranquil contentment is pure inertia to another. In the pages to come, I describe my own resistance to the ethos of normative psychoanalysis and ask my reader to share it, but I do not try to ascribe a scientific status to my position.

The major task of the book is to reflect on the relations between the two Freuds, the normative and the Romantic. Yet, after this prefatory word, I do not pose the situation in terms of a simple dualism or, as Blake

[5] *Prophets of Extremity: Nietzsche, Heidegger, Foucault, Derrida* (Berkeley and Los Angeles: University of California Press, 1985).

[6] (New York: Harper and Row, 1966).

might call it, a "cloven fiction." Part of what makes Freud's major writing on the nature of the self so fascinating is the play between the two tendencies, their power to engender, animate, transform, and defend one another. For Freud's writing at its most formidable does two things simultaneously. It provides persuasive myths of normative human development, and it records, as symbolic action, Freud's overcoming of all normative standards. It is upon this paradoxical achievement that *Towards Reading Freud* continually reflects.

. . .

This book took a long time to write and in the process accrued many debts. I am grateful in particular to William Kerrigan, J. Hillis Miller, and Michael Pollan, who gave crucial support, both practical and intellectual. Many others contributed as well. Thanks to Megan Benton, Harold Bloom, Gordon Braden, Leslie Brisman, Robert Brown, Ralph Cohen, Lars Engle, Virginia Germino, James Guetti, Geoffrey Hartman, Daniel Kinney, Holly Laird, Rob Leventhal, David Levin, Louis L. Martz, Richard Poirier, Richard Rorty, Murray Schwartz, Susan Schweik, Kevin Taylor, Chip Tucker, and Tony Winner.

Judith Belzer, Nancy and Peter Devine, and Max MacKenzie and Rebecca Cross gave me their invaluable friendship throughout. Debbie Shea and Ida Garrison lent generous aid in preparing the manuscript. The University of Virginia provided a term of research leave and four summer grants, for which I am most grateful. Material from chapter 2 was first published in *The Kenyon Review*, New Series, Spring 1988, Vol. X, No. 2. Reprinted with permission of *The Kenyon Review*. Material from chapter 4 is reprinted by permission from *Raritan Quarterly Review*, vol. VI, no. 4 (Spring 1987). Copyright © 1987 by *Raritan*, 165 College Ave., New Brunswick, N.J., 08903.

Towards Reading Freud

READING FREUD

"THERE IS an inducement to say, 'Yes, of course, it must be like that.' A powerful mythology": thus Ludwig Wittgenstein reacted to reading the work of his contemporary Sigmund Freud. What is needed, the philosopher said, is "a very strong and keen and persistent criticism in order to recognize and see through the mythology that is offered or imposed on one."[1] And yet, even if one does not seek the Enlightenment-style penetration that Wittgenstein's remark seems to endorse, the challenge of coming up with an authentic reading of Freud is a considerable one. For we live, at least according to numberless commentators, in the Age of Freud, a cultural moment in which the critical and descriptive terminologies readiest to use sound with unmistakably Freudian resonances. Freud's influence, says George Steiner, "is enormous, all-pervasive." For Philip Rieff Freud's work brought on the birth of "psychological man," an entirely new character type in the West. Jacques Derrida writes that "we inhabit psychoanalysis, living with it, in it, around it, or beside it."[2] Accordingly, despite Derrida's drive to exceed the discourse of metaphysics in which he sees Freud's text for the most part implicated, deconstruction tends often to resemble nothing so much as an attempt to psychoanalyze the Western tradition, an effort to liberate thought from its fixation on the center, the Word—the Father.

It is well known that Freud played a crucial part in the development of modern literary criticism. Seminal figures on the Anglo-American scene during the 1930s and 1940s, writers such as Lionel Trilling, William Empson, and Kenneth Burke, found that contact with Freud's writings did a great deal to release their interpretive energies.[3] It was not just Freud's terminology that inspired them, for they tended to use that with restraint. What mattered more, I think, was the sense Freud gave that one

---

[1] *Lectures and Conversations on Aesthetics, Psychology and Religious Beliefs*, ed. Cyril Barrett (Oxford: Basil Blackwell, 1966), p. 52.

[2] Steiner's remark is from *Voices: Psychoanalysis*, ed. Bill Bourne, Udi Eichler, and David Herman (Nottingham: Spokesman/Hobo Press, 1987), p. 11; Rieff's phrase is used in *Mind of the Moralist* and *Triumph of the Therapeutic*; Derrida's observation is from *The Post Card*, p. 262.

[3] See for example William Empson's *Some Versions of Pastoral* (London: Chatto and Windus, 1935); Kenneth Burke's *The Philosophy of Literary Form* (Berkeley and Los Angeles: University of California Press, 1973); Lionel Trilling's *The Liberal Imagination* (New York: Scribner's, 1950).

could penetrate literature in a new way. To put it crudely, the critic inspired by Freud was in a position to say things about the work of art that were closed to earlier critics, and—more important—that the author himself could not have said. Freud made a major contribution to a shift in power relations between critics and artists.

Marx and Nietzsche were key figures in precipitating that shift, but Freud, I believe, was more influential, in part because of the implicit analogy to literary interpretation that psychoanalytical therapy provided. It was not only the idea that the interpretation of literature could be carried on in certain respects analogously with the analysis of dreams and neuroses that inspired early Freudian criticism. There was something else as well. The notion that the critic's relation to the literary work might be comparable to the analyst's relation to the patient was rarely stated directly. No critic of the time was willing to make so grand a claim about his own priority over art. But the idea does take hold, it seems to me, however implicitly, in the work of the earliest criticism influenced by Freud, and it has only become stronger over time. It is common knowledge that a great deal of the terminology used in contemporary literary criticism, particularly criticism of the more "advanced" sort, is owed to Freud. But it is also the case that critics are in many ways indebted to him for the status they claim alongside the works that they analyze. I have more to say on this subject at the close of the book. For now, though, I simply offer the point that part of what makes the task of reading Freud so difficult is that our standard critical terminologies, and the standard critical attitude toward the text, are in many ways already Freudian. To use some currently established critical mode to read Freud is thus likely to be a circular exercise. Standard Freudian readings of literature are by now commonplace enough, but the prospect of another one of those is positively invigorating as compared to that of a Freudian reading of Freud.

But Freud's influence is not limited to the realms of high culture. What one might call a commonsense Freudianism has become pervasive in the West. Without thinking much about it, people have come to believe in the determining power of childhood; they take the child's relations with her parents to be archetypes, or models, for future love relations and relations with authority. Even readers of supermarket tabloids know something about the perils of the Oedipal complex. It is understood that dreams are fulfillments of repressed wishes and that they are susceptible to analysis, as are slips of the tongue and the pen. Few now will deny that "repression," which Freud called the "cornerstone" of his theories, is a large part of what determines any individual character. People speak serenely of infantile sexuality, neuroses, and narcissism. In many ways, it is Freud's vocabulary and Freud's concerns that make the world available to us. One might even say that we are "commonsense Freudians" in something like the way that Chaucer's more worldly contemporaries were commonsense Christians.

This sort of day-to-day immersion in Freud's vocabulary combines with his determining status within literary criticism to make Freud's a difficult text to see freshly, to "defamiliarize," as the Russian formalists would say. Reading of the analytical sort is, in one of its dimensions, comparable to metaphor making. One attempts to illuminate the text at hand in terms of something that it both "is" and "is not." To achieve a critical "perspective by incongruity" (Kenneth Burke's phrase) is to achieve a certain double vision. It is to describe the text in a contemporary vocabulary that affirms the text's current significance while sustaining the sense of "the pastness of the past." (Metaphor "gives you two ideas for one," as Dr. Johnson said.) But if we do live in an Age of Freud, in which one cannot readily locate a critical discourse subtle and comprehensive enough to apply to Freud's text but alien enough to record some disengagement or detachment from it, then an exceptional approach to the task of reading Freud is necessary. But what method shall one use? How does one, at the present time, interpret the century's master interpreter, read its most formidable reader?

To answer this question it is worthwhile to back up somewhat and to consider some preliminary issues. Why should the critical exercise that Wittgenstein recommends be worth undertaking in the first place? Granted (for the moment) that Freud's text promulgates a mythology, suppose that it is a useful one, one that gives us effective orientation in the world and good cues for action (to invoke the pragmatic criteria of William James). And if there are reasons to read Freud critically, one needs to begin to develop a sense of why his discourse has so completely penetrated received cultural vocabularies, making the search for a metaphorical translation (or transvaluation) of the Freudian text as difficult as it is. Such questions obviously defy comprehensive or final response, and yet some consideration of them is a necessary first step. In the pages that follow I look at the ways that Freud's discourse lends itself to being—again I borrow a term from Burke—"bureaucratized," functioning socially to affirm and enforce normative standards.

.   .   .

They have the press, they have the stock exchange, and
now they also have the subconscious.
—Karl Kraus

A casual reader of the *New York Times* not long ago might have encountered a story that served less to inform than to remind her of a well-known condition. The story was entitled "A Case Study on Wall Street," and one revealing sentence observed that "the Street has focused—to the point of fixation—on interest rates, and a 'very strong' economy implied that rates would be driven higher." By using the terms "case study" and "fixation" and referring to "drives" and resistance to drives, the story exploits the easy commerce that exists between the rhetoric of psychoanalysis and that of investment finance.

When Freud formulated his economic theory of the drives, he posited that we each have a finite and more or less constant quantity of libido, or psychic energy, at our disposal. This quantity we invest (*besetzen*), first internally or narcissistically, to establish and ensure our own egos. With what remains after this initial commitment of psychic funds, we may invest in "objects" in the world. In a passage that has taken on some notoriety, Freud explained the necessity for such secondary commitments:

> Here we may even venture to touch on the question of what makes it necessary at all for our mental life to pass beyond the limits of narcissism and to attach the libido to objects. The answer which would follow from our line of thought would once more be that this necessity arises when the cathexis of the ego with libido exceeds a certain amount. A strong egoism is a protection against falling ill, but in the last resort we must begin to love in order not to fall ill, and we are bound to fall ill if, in consequence of frustration, we are unable to love.[4]

All love, in Freud's severe diagnosis, begins as self-love and remains so even when it appears to be directed at external objects.

The narcissistic ego's situation reminds us, as it probably reminded Freud, of a national economy in which the governing powers are compelled to invest and reinvest their capital surpluses, often at some risk, to preserve the system from destructive inertia. The center of individual governance, the ego, seeks for (and by no means always finds) moderately safe and reliable investment opportunities for its reserves of disposable libido. Even in the best of markets, this is a high-risk activity. And for some of us, the process is fated always to go awry. We repeatedly select a kind of object that consumes our surplus then draws on the reserves at a frantic rate, or another kind that suddenly declares that it is bankrupt of our funds, or that it never requested or received them.

In time we may take our portfolio of libidinal disasters to an analyst or

---

[4] *The Standard Edition of the Complete Psychological Works of Sigmund Freud*, trans. James Strachey et al., 24 vols. (London: Hogarth Press, 1953), 14:85. Subsequent references will be cited in the body of the text by volume and page number.

investment counselor, most of whom are rigorous supply-siders. The analyst's task will be to bring our investments into line with our true goals and interests, allowing us to break even, or perhaps in time to operate at a profit. Surely calculation never made a man great, as Cardinal Newman said, but it may sustain an economy through threatening vicissitudes. Depression is, in any case, to be avoided. So too is that mood of exultation (which so often precedes or follows a crash) in which the burdens of self are lifted, and which Freud and Longinus name so differently. "The therapy of all therapies, the secret of all secrets, the interpretation of all interpretations, in Freud," Philip Rieff says, "is not to attach oneself exclusively or too passionately to any one particular meaning, or object."[5] For Freud, romantic love is wild speculation: "we are never so defenseless against suffering as when we love, never so helplessly unhappy as when we have lost our loved object or its love" (21:82). Even culture, the blue-chip opportunity par excellence, reveals its precarious standing in the face of war and the abiding fact of human aggressivity. Work is the only salvation ("Travailler comme une bête" was Freud's personal motto), and the image of the machine informs Freud's model of the psyche nearly as often as, and in complicity with, the image of an economic system.

A younger Philip Rieff, more at peace with the ascendancy of "psychological man," brilliantly defended Freud's model against the tendency to historicize it as a reflection of reigning economic theory:

> Any notion that Freud's doctrine of scarce satisfaction in some way reflects the economic doctrine of scarcity representative of the best social thought in his era is to render trivial Freud's point. His use of a quasi-economic metaphor to discuss sexuality gives no warrant for treating the insight frozen into this metaphor as dated. Nature still seeks a state of balance. Freud's is a theory of the equilibrium toward which the emotional life tends after every disturbance. Sexuality is subject no less completely to Freud's first law of the emotions than any other element of human existence. Only one way lies open to escape the dissatisfactions inherent in every satisfaction, and that is to grow equable. When the inner life is not easily disturbed it has achieved what is to Freud as nearly ideal a condition as he can imagine. There is something Oriental in the Freudian ethic.[6]

This is potently argued, invoking with authority the biological base that Freud felt would eventually confirm his entire enterprise. And where is biology more absolutely determining than in the realms of sexuality?

[5] *Triumph of the Therapeutic*, p. 59.

[6] *Mind of the Moralist*, p. 342. Rieff is writing here in critical response to David Riesman's fine articles, "The Themes of Work and Play in the Structure of Freud's Thought" and "Authority and Liberty in the Structure of Freud's Thought." Both are reprinted in *Individualism Reconsidered* (Glencoe, Ill.: Free Press, 1954), pp. 310–64.

The ethical appeal of Freud's economic metaphor is considerable as well; with it Freud joins the tradition of humane pessimism that descends from Epictetus and Marcus Aurelius to the Montaigne of "Experience": "I bid my soul to look upon pleasure and pain with a sight equally well-balanced—'for the dilation of the soul in joy is as blameworthy as its contraction in sorrow' (Cicero)—and equally firm."[7] Both Montaigne and the Freud of the unpleasure/pleasure principle compel one to ask if the uncalculated life is worth living.

The urge to live without waste, within a perfect ecology of the spirit, brought Thoreau to Walden and to the profession that he "wanted . . . to drive life into a corner, and reduce it to its lowest terms, and, if it proved to be mean, why then to get the whole and genuine meanness of it."[8] A comparable impulse often sparks the pursuit that characterizes current literary criticism at its most persuasive. Geoffrey Hartman describes "the search for an exemplary text: a text to be used against the wastefulness of living without concentration."[9] In saying this he almost seems to speak to William Empson's famous expostulation in the essay on "Proletarian Literature" that begins *Some Versions of Pastoral*: "And yet what is said is one of the permanent truths; it is only in degree that any improvement of society could prevent wastage of human powers; the waste even in a fortunate life, the isolation even of a life rich in intimacy, cannot but be felt deeply, and is the central feeling of tragedy."[10] The desire to redeem that waste or to mourn it authentically is a major preoccupation of some of the tradition's greatest writing, including much of Freud's.

Yet from the peak of their aspirations, the great Romantic poets would have looked down on "economizing," Freudian and otherwise, as a spiritual form of double-entry bookkeeping. Rieff's Freud is right only if biology has absolute priority, and libido in its various transformations motivates every human pursuit. Imprudently perhaps, the High Romantics ascribed priority to the visionary power and posited a version of love that transcends the pressures of a limited selfhood, the love that Shelley characterized as a total "going out of our own nature and an identification of ourselves with the beautiful which exists in thought, action, or person, not our own."[11] Though the Romantic poet begins in some version of Keats's "habitual self," his urge is for a vision that preserves erotic inten-

---

[7] Michel de Montaigne, *Essays*, trans. S. J. Trechmann, 2 vols. (New York: Oxford University Press), 2:595.

[8] *Walden*, ed. Owen Thomas (New York: Norton, 1966), p. 61.

[9] *The Fate of Reading and Other Essays* (Chicago: University of Chicago Press, 1975), p. 255.

[10] *Some Versions of Pastoral*, p. 5.

[11] *Shelley's Prose*, ed. David Lee Clark (Albuquerque: University of New Mexico Press, 1954), pp. 282–83.

sity (and thus cannot be encompassed within the category of "sublimation") but, because it is the product of a redeemed imagination, is continuous, beyond the "economic" vicissitudes of merely mortal desire. From Wordsworth to Wallace Stevens, Romanticism has provided us with strong hopes for a life beyond the governance of mere quantity, as well as with compelling resources for putting those aspirations into doubt.

It would be fruitless here to attempt to arbitrate a dispute between the "sublime" and the "economic" in absolute terms. For one thing, the two tendencies coexist, as much in Freud as in the major Romantics (with the possible exceptions of Shelley and Blake), and in many of the modern poets. When Robert Frost writes, in "The Constant Symbol," that "strongly spent is synonymous with kept,"[12] he is not unaware of any of the valences of "spent." It is not a matter of the relative correctness of either system of self-representation, but one of their immediate applications here and now—not the meaning but the use, to follow Wittgenstein.

The reciprocity or symmetry that I have lightly sketched between the discourses of libido theory and of finance capitalism involves only one of the major filiations of Freudian representation. One might have spoken of Freud's military tropes (*besetzen* also means "to occupy"); of the concord between the "laws" of libido and those of thermodymanics; or of Freud's (originally Platonic) figure of the city-state to represent the action of the psyche. But it is tempting for the socially minded critic to focus on the fact that the rhetorics of Wall Street and Central Park West are not only compatible but mutually reinforcing. In their reciprocity they may help to validate or authorize each other. Such authorization would guarantee that a system of representation—which is also always a system of power, potential or realized—is perceived as "natural," beyond the vicissitudes of history. The theory of repression, which produces the idea that there is a sense in everything and thus "that everything is past and there is nothing new,"[13] is a proper ally for an economic theory that, as Marx often pointed out, posits itself as the "natural" fulfillment of human material strivings.

This alliance of figurative systems bears directly upon us. It contributes to our tendency to forget that Freud's economic representation of the psyche is a trope, one descriptive possibility among many, not literal fact (if one may confidently speak of that now). As Kenneth Burke says, "We seem somehow to have got so turned around that, if you treat man as a sheer machine, you are thought to be literal whereas, if you draw a distinction between a machine's motions and the machine maker's actions,

---

[12] *Selected Prose of Robert Frost*, ed. Hyde Cox and Edward Connery Lathem (New York: Collier, 1977), p. 24.

[13] J. H. van den Berg, *The Changing Nature of Man: Introduction to a Historical Psychology*, trans. H. F. Croes (New York: Delta, 1961), p. 176.

you are more likely to be called figurative."[14] When we uncritically or involuntarily employ the tropes of loss and profit in a calculus of the drives, we are being created by Freud. The text of Freud reads and interprets us. It does not evoke our situation so much as produce it: "Great is he who imposes the metaphor," Frost said, and Freud has imposed many of the figurative constellations by which we set our bearings and chart our futures.

Like Freud, the major nineteenth-century American writers responded to the pressures of finance capitalism around them. For most of them "economy" was a commanding rhetorical category: Wordsworth's prompt dismissal of commerce as an out-and-out opponent of vision— "getting and spending, we lay waste our powers"—was rejected by the American Romantics. Emerson figured his own slow accretions of insight, followed by inspiration, then by spiritual emptiness or vastation in the terms of investment, booming profit and bankruptcy. The dynamics of the depression of 1837 (as well as Emerson's inheritance of the second installment of the Tucker estate in that year) are manifest throughout *Essays: First Series*. Whitman, of course, was the great spender, playing Keynes to Emerson's Adam Smith, affirming "perpetual payment of the perpetual loan." Whitman's image of himself as a source of ceaseless reception and circulation—"To me the converging objects of the universe perpetually flow"—figures an economy under continual expansion. These images of internal economy are no less metaphorical than Freud's, yet when we map our own "energies" for ourselves, the form that seems to rise spontaneously is not that of Emerson or Whitman, or even of Melville or Thoreau, but of Freud, "no more a person / now," as Auden put it, "but a whole climate of opinion."

Surely we are still in a position to be moved by Peter Gay's simple tribute to Freud, that he taught us "that there was more to know and less to judge than most thinking people had imagined."[15] Yet more and more Freud's text knows and judges us. Perhaps we need to reclaim some of our ignorance, to "see . . . again with an ignorant eye," as Stevens commends. It is tempting to begin this process by observing that Freud's text has been "literalized," and to recommend a "figurative" or "literary" restitution, which reawakens the excess of meaning over mere denotation, allowing Freud's text to respond to any interpretive effort as the canonical literary works do, with "and yet, and yet." But we need to begin by describing more specifically the resistance to being read that Freud's text currently offers.

[14] "A Theory of Terminology" in *Interpretation: The Poetry of Meaning*, ed. Stanley Romaine Hopper and David L. Miller (New York: Harcourt, Brace, & World, 1967), p. 93.
[15] *Freud, Jews and Other Germans: Masters and Victims in Modernist Culture* (New York: Oxford University Press, 1978), p. 73.

It is difficult to feel reconciled to the term "ideology" as a description of this resistance, even as the term is sophisticatedly deployed by such theorists as Pierre Macherey and Terry Eagleton.[16] The category is entwined necessarily with the notion of an absolute "science" and a subject who "knows," amidst a mass of humanity that is correspondingly mystified. It is difficult, though not impossible, to divorce "ideology" from a Marxist/Hegelian teleology of revolution, which appears now to have as much in common with astrology as with science.

If we need a term for Freud's literalization as a social text, I suggest Kenneth Burke's deliberately ungainly "Bureaucratization of the Imaginative": " 'Bureaucratization' is an unwieldy word, perhaps even an onomatopoeia, since it sounds as bungling as the situation it would characterize. 'Imaginative' suggests pliancy, liquidity, the vernal. And with it we couple the incongruously bulky and almost unpronounceable."[17] Burke refers to a situation in which an imaginative text has been put into action by institutions. The institutions' need for clear and coherent administrable policy often results, according to Burke, in isolating one possibility in the imaginative work and putting it into practice. Thus the text is literalized socially: "An imaginative possibility (usually at the start Utopian) is bureaucratized when it is embodied in the realities of a social texture, in all the complexity of language and habits, in the property relationships, the methods of government, production and distribution, and in the development of rituals that re-enforce the same emphasis."[18] Surely there is an idealized sense here of imagination as conceivable prior to and independent of social force,[19] yet Burke's characterization seems particularly apt in regard to the contemporary uses of Freud's imaginative achievement, down even to the therapeutic ritual of reinforcement.

As Michel Foucault has often indicated, no text can be significantly literalized, becoming a law, a limit, a boundary, without being allied intricately with administered power. Although the institution of medical psychoanalysis has gained nothing in prestige over the past two or three decades (even inveterate maligners of psychoanalysis will probably spare some compassion for the Balzacian cast of characters that Janet Malcolm found associated with the Freud archives),[20] Freud's rhetoric, often de-

---

[16] See Pierre Macherey's *A Theory of Literary Production*, trans. Geoffrey Wall (London: Routledge and Kegan Paul, 1978) and Terry Eagleton's *Criticism and Ideology* (London: New Left Books, 1976).

[17] *Attitudes Toward History* (Los Altos, Calif.: Hermes, 1959), p. 225.

[18] Ibid.

[19] Frank Lentricchia takes this kind of criticism of the term further than I would. See his fine and sympathetic reading of Burke in *Criticism and Social Change* (Chicago: University of Chicago Press, 1983), pp. 60–63.

[20] *In the Freud Archives* (New York: Alfred A. Knopf, 1983).

based far below Strachey's *Standard*, has infused social service, health care, and even government and business. Freud has become his (often unwitting) admirers. Job retraining for the recently laid-off employees of a major U.S. steel company, for instance, included a speech by a psychologist, who acquainted them with the repressed truth that the plant had served them as a mother surrogate. With the plant's closing, the workers were told, it was time for them to be weaned.

Rarely is the authority of psychoanalysis in such ludicrous complicity with the "lucrative patterns of frustration." Yet the concept of the "bureaucratization" of psychoanalysis takes us to what I think is the crucial dialectic within Freud's text. As a therapy psychoanalysis is concerned with the normative, defining the healthy person as one capable of love and work beneath the reign of the Reality Principle. Psychoanalysis's grounding in the normative is hardly absolute, of course; the "normal," as Philip Rieff says, is established in part by its resemblance to illness— there is continuity, not a gap, between Freudian sickness and health. Moreover, it is often clear that normality is an ideal and not a statistical average: "We are all sick," Freud famously said. Yet Freud's invocation of the norm, no matter how critical, places psychoanalysis with the other "sciences of man" that rose at the beginning of the modern period. All were informed by the conviction that, as Hannah Arendt puts it, "men had become social beings and unanimously followed certain patterns of behavior, so that those who did not keep the rules could be considered to be asocial or abnormal."[21] Arendt contrasts modern behaviorism with the classical veneration for action—the deed or word that transforms a public situation. Classically, action is always competitive. The politician, the soldier, and the athlete strain to make their contemporaries forget past deeds and enshrine their own. If men come and go like the leaves, as Glaukos says in book 6 of *The Iliad*, it is the classical poet's vocation to draw out the leaf of resplendent hue from the brown scatter of passing generations. Even if Freud's writing is in its argument sometimes behavioristic, the text itself is an action. It seeks the first place. Though Freud's work quite often meshes noiselessly with our ideologies of getting and spending, our hunger for conformity, and the bland exigencies of an administered society, it also, I think, works as a Romantic drama of self-reinvention, for Freud and for him alone.

To most of us, Freud is best known as the theorist of the Oedipal complex. The narrative of the child's passage from autoeroticism, to desire of the mother, through the vale of the castration threat, and finally into an acquiescence to the father's law probably stands as Freud's major theoretical achievement. For Freud every dream, neurosis, and parapraxis, but

---

[21] *The Human Condition* (New York: Anchor, 1959), p. 39.

also every instance of "normal" experience in which meaning is concentrated, carries the imprint of the Oedipal struggle. The Freudian subject, whether "normal" or "neurotic," is always susceptible to a more or less definitive representation in terms of his experience of the crisis.

But there is another aspect of Freudian self-representation. Part of Freud's genius, I think, lay in his ability to formulate moments of self-transformation that could function within persuasive myths of human development *and simultaneously* as emblems for his own self-remaking *as an author*. The Oedipal conflict might thus be seen (as I show in more detail later) both as a generalizable myth of childhood passage and, as it is narrated by Freud for the first time in *The Interpretation of Dreams*, as an image for Freud's "self-recreation." The Oedipal passage, I believe, represents Freud's personal struggle for authorship of a discourse that exceeds, and threatens to render irrelevant, previous literary forms. This book considers two such crises in which Freud, while propounding a new version of general human subjectivity that is normative and delimiting, is simultaneously undergoing a "symbolic pass"[22] of his own in which he figures the "freshness of a [self-]transformation" (Stevens). Freud's second self-genesis, which is associated with a crisis of authority, is manifest in the essays "On Narcissism" and "Mourning and Melancholia" and in the 1911–1915 papers on therapeutic technique. There Freud extemporizes a new version of the psyche, including a hitherto unmentioned principle of internal authority, the "ego ideal." This new configuration, I argue, is at least in some measure a precipitate of Freud's own struggle for authority, which is associated with his fears about the continuity of psychoanalysis.

Thus this book speculates continually on the internal dialectic in Freud's work between the normative Freud and Freud the sublime author. The normative or therapeutic Freud is bent on the salutary humbling of his audience—and implicitly of himself. He would demonstrate the tight boundaries in which reason and consciousness can hope to hold command and introduce us to the intractable powers of the "id" or "it." His aim is to diminish the perpetual cause of self-destruction in men and women. What the classical dramatists called hubris Freud renames "narcissistic self-regard." And yet, even in the act of representing our limitations and imposing the doses of therapeutic humiliation that are implicit in his formulation of the Oedipal crisis (the reduction of the gloriously tragic *Oedipus Rex* into the mundane Oedipus complex),[23] Freud is representing himself as an author comparable in certain ways to Sophocles

---

[22] The phrase is from Burke's essay "Freud and the Analysis of Poetry," which appears in *Philosophy of Literary Form*, pp. 258–92.

[23] The formulation is Philip Rieff's.

and Shakespeare. Thus Freud is on the one side a normative, behavioral physician, devoted to the law, the aesthetic of the beautiful (as it is exemplified in "the cure"), culture, and the given dispensation. Yet a reading of Freud also suggests that he is simultaneously (and paradoxically) committed to the imagination, and that he holds in reverence no traditions or forms but instead sees in the sum of established "facts" a system of relations merely "vehicular and transitive," in the words of Emerson.

Take as another instance of the double nature of Freud's writing the vision of grief and restitution set forth in "Mourning and Melancholia." "Mourning and Melancholia" is a great achievement, not only because it has so much to teach us about human loss, but also for its implicit critique of certain aspects of the elegiac tradition. In fact, "Mourning and Melancholia" yields what appears initially to be a condensed poetics of the Romantic elegy. Consider, for example, the critical applications of this paragraph—in which Freud describes the process of crossing over from grief to tranquility—to, say, "In Memoriam" or "Adonais":

> Reality-testing has shown that the loved object no longer exists, and it proceeds to demand that all libido shall be withdrawn from its attachments to that object. This demand arouses understandable opposition—it is a matter of general observation that people never willingly abandon a libidinal position, not even, indeed, when a substitute is already beckoning to them. . . . Normally, respect for reality gains the day. Nevertheless its orders cannot be obeyed at once. They are carried out bit by bit, at great expense of time and cathectic energy, and in the meantime the existence of the lost object is psychically prolonged. Each single one of the memories and expectations in which the libido is bound to the object is brought up and hyper-cathected, and detachment of the libido is accomplished in respect of it. (14:244–45)

The final sentence makes a fine commentary on the episodic bursts of recollection and grief that structure Tennyson's and Shelley's elegies. The form of the elegy, its brief forays of "yet once more" into the "memories and recollections" by which the mourner is "bound" to his lost love, receives a dignified account and justification here. In the sentences that follow, Freud faces an authentic difficulty in his own analysis of object love: why does the psyche prolong painful attachments to the departed objects when new possibilities beckon?

> Why this compromise by which the command of reality is carried out piecemeal should be so extraordinarily painful is not at all easy to explain in terms of economics. It is remarkable that this painful unpleasure is taken as a matter of course by us. The fact is, however, that when *the work of mourning* is

completed the ego becomes free and uninhibited again. (14:245, emphasis mine)

The passage seems initially to respect the mystery inherent in the crisis of mourning: though prolonging our attachments to objects that are lost may be, in strictly economic or practical terms, inefficient, we also accept it as a natural part of being human. Freud's remark recalls the volatile paradox at the center of elegy: death is a matter of course, ineluctable; but death is also an outrage. Yet consider the essay's key trope, which in its deep simplicity is apt to elude us: mourning is "work" (*Trauerarbeit*), not unlike a piece of socially productive labor in daily life. The ethical injunction submerged in the trope is that "normal" mourning strives for complete resolution of the crisis, as swiftly as possible, economically. Again we encounter social filiation in the imperative to invest efficiently, curtail our losses. Here Freud and the poets part company.

The easing of sorrow over time is a secondary source of grief for the Romantic elegists. Recall Tennyson:

> O sorrow, then can sorrow wane?
> O grief, can grief be changed to less?[24]

Or Shelley:

> Alas, that all we loved of him should be,
> But for our grief, as if it had not been,
> And grief itself be mortal![25]

The stakes here involve more than the dignity of human attachments. Both poets, one feels, are in a complex drama of self-sacrifice and gain, in which they offer their own sufferings for the power to write superlative verse. The self-lacerating tendency often remarked in elegy may arise from the attempt to keep the verse flowing. The idea that grief can give intensified access to experience is an article of Romantic faith impressively challenged by Freud's implicit critique of the elegiac tradition.

But one needs to look further into Freud's text to understand its bearing on, for instance, the authority of the physician in psychoanalysis. What difference does the patient's commitment to an ethos of mourning make in the struggle for power that takes place within the transference? What effect would the onset of the Romantic affliction that Freud called melancholia have there? For Freud is not only giving us a normative treatise on loss and grief in "Mourning and Melancholia." He is also reimag-

---

[24] *The Poems of Tennyson*, ed. Christopher Ricks, 3 vols. (Berkeley and Los Angeles: University of California Press, 1987), 2:391.

[25] *Shelley, Poetical Works*, ed. Thomas Hutchinson (London: Oxford University Press, 1967), p. 436.

ining himself as a figure of therapeutic authority, not just for his patients but for Western culture at large.

Consider, as another example of this critical approach to Freud, the submerged literary affinities of the "super-ego." This agency of the psyche is first discussed in Freud's 1914 essay that invents new terms for representing the human subject, "On Narcissism," an essay that makes no mention of Ovid or any of the versions of the Narcissus myth in the Western tradition. A look at Ovid and at the text of Milton's *Paradise Lost* (a poem Freud loved)[26] allows us, however, to see the textual filiations that Freud's essay ignores. "On Narcissism" proposes that the "ego-ideal" (the preliminary version of the harsher "super-ego") originates at the resolution of the crucial scene of Freudian self-remaking, the Oedipal complex, which brings the child's "primary narcissism" to an abrupt close. It is then that the child internalizes the father's prohibition against possessing the mother. The "ego-ideal" exerts itself, Freud says, "by the medium of the voice" (14:96). The essay indicates that the "discovery" of the "ego-ideal" was a clinical matter, arising from the treatment of paranoiacs—those whose efforts to liberate themselves from authority activate their internalized (and previously unconscious) voices of prohibition.

A look at Ovid and Milton demonstrates that the prohibitive voice of the "ego-ideal" was not first disclosed in the consulting room. With Narcissus far gone in the raptures of self-love, the Ovidian narrator suddenly intervenes:

> O fondly foolish boy, why vainly seek to clasp a fleeting image? What you seek is nowhere; but turn yourself away, and the object of your love will be no more. That which you behold is but the shadow of a reflected form and has no substance of its own. With you it comes, with you it stays, and it will go with you—if you can go.[27]

Narcissus, of course, cannot hear a word. In Milton's rewriting of the scene in book 4 of *Paradise Lost*, Eve is in the place of Narcissus. Thus she describes her first moments of life staring at her reflection in a pool:

> A Shape within the wat'ry gleam appear'd
> Bending to look on me, I started back,
> It started back, but pleas'd I soon return'd,
> Pleas'd it return'd as soon with answering looks
> Of sympathy and love . . .

[26] See Ernest Jones, *The Life and Work of Sigmund Freud*, 3 vols. (New York: Basic Books, 1953–1957), 3:422.

[27] *Metamorphoses*, trans. Frank Justus Miller, 2 vols. (Cambridge, Mass.: Harvard University Press, 1977), 1:155.

The narrative of Eve's infatuation is similarly interrupted by a commanding voice of indeterminate origin:

> there I had fixt
> Mine eyes till now, and pin'd with vain desire,
> Had not a voice thus warn'd me, What thou seest,
> What there thou seest fair Creature is thyself,
> With thee it came and goes: but follow me,
> And I will bring thee where no shadow stays
> Thy coming . . .[28]

Eve does hear the voice and follows it to Adam, and thus she is saved, presumably, from the fate of Narcissus or, in Freudian terms, of the "narcissist."

The genealogy of the "ego-ideal" hastily uncovered in these scenes from Ovid and Milton opens a number of possibilities for critical development, to which I will return. Overall, though, the result of even this brisk historicizing is presumably to expose the authority of Freud's trope, the "ego-ideal," to an ironic reappraisal, if indeed a certain form of irony results from perceiving a continuity between two ostensibly different realms. In a fine passage Shoshana Felman meditates on this kind of encounter between literature and psychoanalysis:

> There is one crucial feature which is constitutive of literature but is essentially lacking in psychoanalytical theory, and indeed in theory as such: irony. Since irony precisely consists in dragging authority as such into a scene which it cannot master, of which it is *not aware* and which, for that very reason, is the scene of its own self-destruction, literature, by virtue of its ironic force, fundamentally deconstructs the fantasy of authority in the same way, and for the same reasons, that psychoanalysis deconstructs the authority of the fantasy—its claim to belief and to power as the sole window through which we behold and perceive reality, as the sole window through which reality can indeed reach our grasp, enter into our consciousness.[29]

To ask that Freud's Narcissus myth receive the account of its literary debts is perhaps to initiate the process that Felman describes.

Scrutiny of the "ego-ideal"/"super-ego" need not stop here, however. One might consider how the figure stands in relation to Freud's reflections upon his own act of writing. Might the relation between authoritative voice and self-infatuated subject dramatize Freud's sense of his relation to his readers? And might not the "ego-ideal"/"super-ego" be Freud's im-

---

[28] Merritt Y. Hughes, ed., *John Milton: Complete Poems and Major Prose* (Indianapolis, Ind.: Bobbs-Merrill, 1957), ll. 461–71.

[29] "To Open the Question," in "Literature and Psychoanalysis / The Question of Reading: Otherwise," *Yale French Studies* 55/56 (1977): 8.

age for his own voice at its most authoritative? If so, what aspect of himself, his readers, or his patients does Freud aspire to discipline with it? Finally, what can the refiguring of Freudian authority tell us about the dynamics of domination, acquiescence, and resistance as they are symbolically (and actually) enacted in contemporary political and social life?

If Freud's text possesses the strange property of being both normative and transgressive, therapeutic and (symbolically) self-overcoming, with the "disjunctive" tendencies being always in some sense embedded within the normative design, then an effective approach to the difficulty of reading Freud might be developed from the strategy I have been practicing in rather abbreviated form thus far, a reading by way of extended *analogy* with major "imaginative writers" who have made "self-creation" a central concern. If Freud's discourse has thoroughly infused contemporary critical vocabularies, then it may be worthwhile to take the anomalous step of seeking access to his work by way of the texts of writers who came before him, and whose achievement was as large, or larger.

The text of Freud is so comprehensive and varied and Freud's cultural presence so subtly pervasive that to attempt a "reading of Freud" in the space of a single given volume would be ludicrous. I have thus limited my focus to the issue of self-representation in a handful of writings that Freud produced over a relatively short period, from 1900 to 1917, comparing them with relevant works by Sophocles, Milton, Wordsworth, and Emerson. Another criterion for my choice of Freudian writings is social and political. I have tried to select works that have major cultural bearing, those that have been the most influential in the modern construction of the self. The Oedipal ego and the narcissistic ego are very much with us. Most literary critical approaches to Freud have at least something—and usually much more than that—to say about *Beyond the Pleasure Principle*. This book does not, for the reason that the mythology Freud develops there never succeeded in taking hold. In general people simply do not talk about themselves as the battle grounds of Eros and Thanatos, nor do they respond to the authority of those few who do so.

My major topics are two moments of Freudian "self-reinvention," the invention of the Oedipal self, which is the subject of a critical passage in the 1900 text, *The Interpretation of Dreams*, and that of the narcissistic ego, which is first comprehensively delineated in the 1914 essay, "On Narcissism, An Introduction," but which is significantly foreshadowed and then elaborated in the papers on therapy and technique published between 1911 and 1915. Freud's great essay of 1917, "Mourning and Melancholia," further develops (and perhaps completes) the vision of the self set forth in "On Narcissism." Readers weary of "Freudian analyses" of literary texts may thus find something of interest in what will work initially as a reversal, a literary reading of Freud's "reading" of Sophocles and Shakespeare, a Miltonic reading of "On Narcissism," a Wordsworthian parallel to the papers on psychoanalytic method, and an Emersonian response to Freud's piece on loss, grief and restitution. As the book progresses I attempt to move this dialogical approach one step further by allowing for something of a Freudian rebuttal to the Romantic writers.

My descriptions of Freud and of the "literary" writers make continual use of Kenneth Burke's term, "symbolic action." Readers of Burke, even admiring ones, have complained that he never quite gives a succinct definition of the concept. This is true, but the omission is, I think, a strategic one. What Burke seems to mean, first of all, is that one ought to see texts as actions and as acts. One ought to recognize that most writings that matter have dramatic qualities; they present images of transformation. They are not full of inert "symbols." Rather they provide images of change taking place, whether that change be intellectual or spiritual, private or public, comic or tragic. The actions that imaginative writing dramatizes are symbolic. They require interpretation because it is never entirely clear how they might be applied to the life of the reader. Pragmatic reading in Burke's mode entails asking what effect this or that work would have for one's way of living. The answer will not always be obvious, of course. What *is* one to do or think differently after having read *King Lear*? Keats's sonnet on the subject anticipates exactly this oncoming difficulty.

To read texts as symbolic acts is to ask what kinds of changes they commend, or subtly prepare, or even determine for the subject. Looking at Freud's work as "symbolic action" means trying to see the sorts of behavior it enforces, or would enforce, and also how it dramatizes Freud's own personal desire for change, his desire to make himself. The word *symbolic* qualifies our sense of how immediate a work's bearing on experience is, or can be. The word *action* reminds us that literature exists in the world. It can have material effects. There is a tension between the two terms that is significant of the tension between imagination and fact, between literature and life. Burke does not submit a simple definition that favors either one of these poles. He keeps his key critical term as dramatically alive as the works he uses it to characterize.

Having said something about my method of approach, there remain two questions I want to consider before setting out. Why have I chosen the writers I have and not others for the purposes of analogy with Freud? Yes, Freud obviously read Sophocles and Shakespeare and Milton, but why include writers to whom he never makes reference, Wordsworth and Emerson? Second, what is meant in the present context by the term self-representation? Given the copious literary critical and philosophical debate that has gone on around the issue of "the self," this is surely not a term that one may use naively.

By "self" I do not mean a solid and substantial entity, a fixed, continuously identical "I." Rather, following Richard Rorty, I tend to see selfhood in relation to various fields of terms that are applied in attempts to describe human subjects.[30] (The words *human subjects* themselves naturally constitute such a descriptive attempt.) Selfhood, for the purposes of this enquiry, might be conceived of as a habitual discourse, a linguistic weave, not an object in the world. As a linguistic potentiality, self is thus susceptible to ideological and social determinations—it has no necessary autonomy or transcendental value. At the same time the verbal field of subjectivity is one in which trope may exceed, undermine, or otherwise prove inconsistent with received discourse, with what Shelley called "impressions blunted by reiteration." As Jerome McGann writes, "In a capitalized world, all work may be abstracted and objectified. But some works resist the process more vigorously than others, and may offer positive alternative forms of communicative action, may suggest these forms even to criticism."[31] And yet, though criticism must be responsive to the invention of new and potentially transforming terminologies (Johnson's remark that the essence of poetry is invention may still be, as Eliot suggested all of Johnson's views were, dangerous to disagree with), it must also try to record their costs.

Rorty's conception of cultural life as a process in which vocabularies displace one another—much in the way that "paradigms" do in Thomas Kuhn's vision of scientific change—is one that I draw on continually in this book, albeit critically. Where I depart from Rorty is in his confidence that old sets of terms inevitably give way when some new and more "useful" metaphors make their way into circulation. Rorty's view, as I see it, underestimates the extent to which discourses are solidified and defended by social interests, and particularly by class interests. The fact that people who are now prosperous and powerful may derive some advantage from a doctrine that inevitably finds the ultimate horizon of meaning to be the psyche and not the social situation helps make that doctrine as resilient as it is. Though the relations between class interests and bureaucratized vocabularies are never simple ones, they do exist.

Rorty's position, put into artful practice in his book *Contingency, Irony, and Solidarity*, is that given any set of terms, one can simply use what one needs and discard the rest. This is an attractive idea, but I think that it ignores the strong links that exist between discourses and established social practices. Certain ways of putting things contribute to making us what we are; they help to create our characters. To pass beyond

---

[30] See "The Contingency of Selfhood" in *Contingency, Irony, and Solidarity* (Cambridge: Cambridge University Press, 1989), pp. 23–43.

[31] *Social Values and Poetic Acts: The Historical Judgment of Literary Work* (Cambridge, Mass.: Harvard University Press, 1988), p. 49.

vocabularies that have been literalized socially frequently requires not only the invention of "useful" alternatives, but the negative work of ridding ourselves of the superannuated forms, something that Emerson, as the fourth chapter shows, knew painfully well.

Rorty's sense that some vocabularies succeed because they happen to catch on, happen to be "better" than the ones that are current, makes culture into a zone of free play and brackets off the facts of social conflict. This much becomes immediately perceptible when one turns to Foucault, who is himself interested in the effects of vocabularies. *Vocabulary* is of course too neutral a term for him. He prefers to use the word *discipline*. Michael Walzer has accurately remarked that in a sense Foucault's work can be understood as an elaborated play on the double sense of that word.[32] It denotes on the one hand a discrete area of knowledge, on the other the practice of molding subjects, of keeping them in line. To Foucault, "disciplines" or "discourses" are means of sizing up, describing, limiting, in fact Foucault will even say "creating," subjects. I do not believe, as Foucault seems to, that every developed method for understanding human life qualifies as a "discipline" in the strong sense of that word, but I do think that normative psychoanalysis has, over time, evolved into something very much like the sort of confining structure Foucault describes. But Foucault's sense of the tenacity of disciplines seems to me altogether too severe. If they were not amenable to being changed through criticism why would he write so scathingly, and with so much ostentatious show of labor, against them to begin with? Yet Foucault offers a necessary antidote to Rorty's idealizing view of cultural change. Similarly, it is necessary to confront Foucault with Rorty's American pragmatic belief that invention is possible and that it can and does change the way society goes about its business. Thus this book combines the pragmatists' faith in the potential powers of imagination with Foucault's sense of how perdurable the disciplines can be.

My position between the two writers informs my belief that negative critique is necessary (what is debilitating in a discourse will not always go away on its own); that criticism can have social effects (we are not imprisoned in ideology); and that imagination—the power to come up with fresh modes of perception—is an authentic faculty that provides potential for change. Only on such premises does a critical reading of Freud like this one make sense. These beliefs also determine the way that the book takes up the issue of "self-creation." This book focuses on moments in writing when a relatively new way of representing the self seems to be

---

[32] See Walzer's chapter "The Lonely Politics of Michel Foucault" in *The Company of Critics, Social Criticism and Political Commitment in the Twentieth Century* (New York: Basic Books, 1988), pp. 191–209.

coming into existence, a way that is achieved against the pressures of prior forms. At these moments of "self-creation" a set of terms can be seen as giving way to, or being displaced by, another. Thus the acts of self-renaming considered here are inseparable from symbolic acts of destruction visited against prior vocabularies and perhaps against the allegiances those vocabularies enjoin. This "regeneration," moreover, is in many cases as symbolically destructive of social concern and of others as it is antithetical to the existing verbal construction of the self. The book's focus, then, is on moments of some violence, on imaginative acts of self-destroying self-invention.

As to the first question, on the issue of Freud's juxtaposition with two writers who apparently meant nothing to him, one might begin an answer by briefly considering Freud's much-debated reading of Nietzsche. On this matter I am persuaded by Samuel Weber's adroit paraphrase of Freud's conflicted claims about his relations with the philosopher: "No, I haven't read Nietzsche—he is too interesting. No, he hasn't influenced my work and I know nothing of his. Moreover, he has completely failed to recognize the mechanism of displacement."[33] Nietzsche, as Stephen Donadio has shown, himself maintained a critical debt to Emerson—one that, as I try to demonstrate in the fourth chapter, he never quite succeeded in discharging.[34] One might go on, then, to speak of Emerson's own reliance on Wordsworth and Coleridge, and their responsiveness, in turn, to the tradition of German Romanticism that meant so much to Freud.[35] As Eric Heller has written, "Our imaginary historian of literature would show that there is a compelling logical development from German Romanticism, the fountainhead of so many currents in modern literature, to the works of Sigmund Freud."[36] (Peter Rudnytsky has gone on, accordingly, to play the part of Heller's historian, demonstrating the continuities between Freud's version of Oedipus and variations on the

[33] See Weber's essay, "The Debts of Deconstruction and Other, Related Assumptions" in *Taking Chances: Derrida, Psychoanalysis, and Literature*, ed. Joseph Smith and William Kerrigan (Baltimore, Md.: The Johns Hopkins University Press, 1984), pp. 33–65. This quotation is from p. 41.

[34] See Donadio's *Nietzsche, Henry James, and the Artistic Will* (New York: Oxford University Press, 1978), pp. 40–42. Donadio bases his observation upon Charles Andler's *Nietzsche, sa vie et sa pensée*, vol 1, *Les précurseurs de Nietzsche*, 2d. ed. (Paris: Editions Bossard, 1920).

[35] For reflections on the imprint of German philosophy on the English Romantic movement see Thomas McFarland's *Coleridge and the Pantheist Tradition* (Oxford: Clarendon Press, 1969) and *Romanticism and the Forms of Ruin: Wordsworth, Coleridge and Modalities of Fragmentation* (Princeton, N.J.: Princeton University Press, 1981).

[36] See "Observations on Psychoanalysis and Modern Literature" in *Literature and Psychoanalysis*, ed. Edith Kurzweil and William Phillips (New York: Columbia University Press, 1983), pp. 72–84. This quotation is from p. 84.

theme by Schiller, Hölderlin, and Kleist.)[37] Despite the appearance of complete separation, there are a number of legitimate historical connections that one may draw between Freud on the one hand and Emerson and Wordsworth on the other.

And yet such genealogies of the literary imagination can be taken too far, until everyone is linked by a progress that runs "past Eve and Adams, from swerve of shore to bend of bay" (Joyce). I am more intrigued, for instance, by the motive that arises from Stanley Cavell's perception that certain tendencies in Freud's text have been called into cultural eminence for their ability to circumscribe or to reduce the potentially refractory energies that emanate from particular works of art.[38] Romantic writers— and particularly Wordsworth and Emerson—have shown themselves to be especially susceptible to this sort of critical disciplining, and thus perhaps have as their due some rebuttal and defense. (On this issue, the Conclusion will have much more to say.) Finally, though, the only justification for the use of a critical approach lies in its capacity to illuminate the works at hand and the cultural and political situation in which the critic and his audience find themselves. And this is an enterprise whose success only the interested reader can judge.

[37] See *Freud and Oedipus* (New York: Columbia University Press, 1987), pp. 93–149.
[38] See "Freud and Philosophy: A Fragment," *Critical Inquiry* 13 (Winter 1987): 386–93.

Chapter One

FREUD'S FIRST SELF-GENESIS:
THE INTERPRETATION OF DREAMS, 1900

FREUD'S first major psychoanalytic work, *The Interpretation of Dreams*, is concerned in two ways with the issue of self-representation. The book, of course, provides a fresh terminology for normative representation of the self. (Though it is true that any number of the terms used there had been in circulation for some time, Freud took them up and inflected them in a new way.)[1] But the *Traumdeutung* is also an autobiography, a work of self-reflection.[2] As Carl Schorske puts it, "Imagine St. Augustine weaving his *Confessions* into *The City of God*, or Rousseau integrating his *Confessions* as a subliminal plot into *The Origins of Inequality*: such is the procedure of Freud in *The Interpretation of Dreams*."[3] Beginning with this book, Freudian writing, at its most formidable, tends to perform a double task. It provides a normative account of psychic processes and at the same time records, as symbolic action, Freud's own overcoming of the normative standard that he is setting in place. In this section of the chapter I describe Freud's double-writing on the overall level of his text, showing how he attempts to determine, figuratively, a peculiarly authoritative relation to the material he narrates and demonstrating also his designs for constituting his reader as a "Freudian" interpreter.

. . .

Consider first the book's epigraph, taken from Virgil's *Aeneid*: "Flectere si nequeo superos, Acheronta movebo"—"If I cannot bend the higher

---

[1] See Richard Ellmann's remarks on the general dissemination of Freud's vocabulary in "Freud and Literary Biography," *The American Scholar* (Autumn 1984): 465.

[2] For early reflections on the autobiographical content of *The Interpretation of Dreams* see Jones, *Life and Work of Freud*, 1:321–26, 356–64.

Peter Rudnytsky's valuable *Freud and Oedipus* also takes up the question of Freud's private relations to the text. See especially pp. 3–89. Also of interest is Didier Anzieu's *Freud's Self-Analysis*, trans. Peter Graham (London: Hogarth Press and the Institute of Psychoanalysis, 1986).

[3] See "Politics and Patricide in Freud's *Interpretation of Dreams*," in *Fin-De-Siècle Vienna, Politics and Culture* (New York: Random House, 1981), pp. 181–203; the quoted passage is from p. 183.

powers, I shall move the infernal regions."[4] The line appears in the *Aeneid*'s seventh book, when Hera, seeing Aeneas nearing his goal, cries out to hell's powers to aid in her revenge. What is probably the line's most prominent use in English literature occurs in a play that Freud, with his love for the Elizabethans, may have known, Webster's *The White Devil*. There Francisco de Medici is also calling for vengeance:

> Brachiano, I am now fit for thy encounter.
> Like the wild Irish, I'll ne'er think thee dead
> Till I can play at football with thy head.
> *Flectere si nequeo superos, Acheronta movebo.*[5]

Freud, too, dramatically aligns himself with the infernal powers, which are to him the powers of the unconscious, against his adversaries, of whom there are many. The text of *The Interpretation of Dreams* declares, by way of symbolic action, an ambivalent independence from the forces of cultural and ethical conservatism, scientific empiricism, and normative Judaism. But also, and most significantly for us, the *Traumdeutung* rebels against the priority of literature over Freud's new science of psychoanalysis.

This identification with the infernal powers of primary process continues covertly when Freud formulates his model for dream production:

> We may therefore suppose that dreams are given their shape in individual human beings by the operation of two psychical forces (or we may describe them as currents or systems); and that one of these forces constructs the wish which is expressed by the dream, while the other exercises a *censorship* upon this dream-wish and, by the use of that censorship, forcibly brings about a distortion in the expression of the wish. . . . It seems plausible to suppose that the privilege enjoyed by the second agency is that of permitting thoughts to enter consciousness. Nothing, it would seem, can reach consciousness from the first system without passing the second agency; and the second agency allows nothing to pass without exercising its rights and making such modifications as it thinks fit in the thought which is seeking admission to consciousness. (4:143–44, emphasis mine)

The dream-wish achieves its passage from the unconscious into the realm of representation through an encounter with the "censor," an authoritative agency and earlier version of the super-ego, which Freud does not officially distinguish as an independent region within the psyche until 1914. A confrontation ensues between the two "forces" and ends with a "compromise formation," or new representation.

[4] See Jean Starobinski's reflections on this line in *"Acheronta Movebo," Critical Inquiry* 13 (Winter 1987): 394–407.
[5] 4.2.135–38.

Freud is not unaware that his model for dream production, with its emphasis on the censor, is informed by the image of writing, in particular of writing carried out against resistance. In another passage, Freud uses the analogy of a "writer who has disagreeable truths to tell," to illustrate the methods of dream formation:

> If he presents [the truths] undisguised, the authorities will suppress his words. . . . A writer must beware of the censorship, and on its account he must soften and distort the expression of his opinion. According to the strength and sensitiveness of the censorship he finds himself compelled either merely to refrain from certain forms of attack, or to speak in allusions in place of direct references, or he must conceal his objectionable pronouncements beneath some apparently innocent disguise. . . . The stricter the censorship, the more far-reaching will be the disguise and the more ingenious too may be the means employed for putting the reader on the scent of the true meaning. (4:142)

Freud, of course, prides himself in this book on being a writer with the most disagreeable, if finally salutary, truths to tell. Chief among such truths is the one about the existence of an unconscious agency, the id or the it, in which powerful antisocial drives abide. That we are lived out by the forces of this impersonal agency can surely not be good news to anyone—except perhaps to Freud. By discovering the unconscious, and aligning himself with it, Freud, in symbolic terms at least, masters it. He calls up the infernal powers, as Hera does, and makes of them his agent, ally, and in a certain sense his principle of counterauthority, to be aimed at all of those who would "censor" (or resist) the truths of psychoanalysis. To write the unconscious is to avoid being written by it, perhaps to be the only writer in history not to submit blindly to the determining dynamics of the creative wish and the censoring opposition.

One might have expected Freud to figure the writer (and implicitly himself) solely as the censor, the one who must select what is of value from the onrush of uninhibited impulses. In fact, a more mature and established Freud probably would have. But by aligning himself with the powers of instinct, Freud declares his intention to overcome or outmaneuver any number of conventional "censors." To write, under the guise of a scientific treatise, a broadly speculative work that actually defies every genre classification, for instance, is quietly to undermine the "scientific" standards of his medical colleagues. So too, by masking his criticisms of Austrian political conservatism and anti-Semitism in the narratives of dreams, for which by his own theoretical account he can only be considered obliquely responsible, he cleverly evades some contemporary political censors.[6] Nor is it a minor achievement of Freud's to assault conventional sexual mores by pointing subtly to the absurd, pathetic dreams that repression, particularly of female sexuality, can provoke. All of these accomplishments could sustain lengthy commentary, but for now one might note the way that Freud's technique of double-writing helps him to arrive at a commanding authorial position.

By figuring his own act of writing as a mirror image for the way that dreams are "written," Freud begins to establish himself in the book as a plausible and effective antiauthority principle.[7] Yet Freud's alignment with the primary process is even more aggressive than I have indicated so far. His modification of the Romantic version of the unconscious, which he seems to receive largely from Schiller,[8] and which makes its appearance in England by way of Coleridge,[9] consists in asserting that the unconscious is a reproductive and a combinative, but in no case a creative, agency. That is, the unconscious draws on memory to form its images: it cannot, Freud says, give us anything that is new. Freud, in his future theorizing, makes the unconscious look very much like Coleridge's "fancy": "a mode of Memory emancipated from the order of time and space." For Coleridge's "secondary [that is, poetic] imagination" there is no equivalent in Freud's thought. The contrast may be put starkly: for Freud, its discoverer, the unconscious is a power that augments the writer's drive to "dissolve, diffuse and dissipate" all mere givens, while for his readers it is a repository of "materials ready made" through "the law of association" (Coleridge). By Freud's strategy of double-writing, the "discoverer" of the unconscious is the only one who will be able to claim it as a creative force.

Freud's description of the unconscious is a major stroke against the poetic imagination as the Romantics conceived of it. As George Steiner writes, "The trope of the unconscious, however we seek to locate its em-

[6] Two useful readings of Freud's relations to politics are Schorske's "Politics and Patricide" and William J. McGrath's *Freud's Discovery of Psychoanalysis: The Politics of Hysteria* (Ithaca, N.Y.: Cornell University Press, 1986).

[7] For the focus on Freudian "writing" I am of course indebted to Jacques Derrida, and particularly to "Freud and the Scene of Writing," which appears in *Writing and Difference*, trans. Alan Bass (Chicago: University of Chicago Press, 1978), pp. 196–231.

[8] Freud quotes Schiller on the workings of a "creative" unconscious in the early pages of the *Traumdeutung*. See 4:103.

[9] Coleridge's chief influences in his construction of the theory of secondary imagination were, as Thomas McFarland has shown, Schelling and the lesser-known Johann Nicolas Tetens. See his "The Origin and Significance of Coleridge's Theory of Secondary Imagination," in *New Perspectives on Coleridge and Wordsworth*, ed. Geoffrey Hartman (New York: Columbia University Press, 1972), pp. 195–246. See also Lancelot Law Whyte's *The Unconscious before Freud* (New York: Basic Books, 1960), especially pp. 107–52, which include citations from the Romantic period.

pirical validity, is a translation into a seemingly rational code of that which earlier vocabularies and thought systems referred to as the *daimon*, as the mantic breath of strangeness which speaks through the rhapsode, which guides the sculptor's hand."[10] It is possible that no single conceptual move in the modern period has been as influential in changing our conception of art as has Freud's redescription of the Romantic unconscious. Not only does Freud compel us to wonder if we have overvalued art, if it is based in regression or in obsessive fantasies. He also opens the way to any number of rational challenges to the power of the aesthetic. Structuralism and deconstruction, both of which posit what one might call a linguistic unconscious (in structuralism it is generative of literary forms, in deconstruction it undermines organic cohesion and authorial shaping), are difficult to conceive of without Freud. Both approaches lead the critic into contact with a level of determination of which the artist herself was supposedly unaware. They rely on Freud's view that the unconscious is susceptible to being known (or "read," to use the current term), has an order, or subverts order in a way that the rational mind can, given time, begin to apprehend. Freud's move against the poetic unconscious has repercussions not only for his own struggle against the priority of literature over psychoanalysis, but also for the way we apprehend art and the process of creation in the present.

But Freud is too shrewd to identify himself only with the unconscious and to leave it at that. At the same time that he aligns himself with the primary process to reinforce his position as a revolutionary, Freud also identifies with the censoring mechanism. He does so, I think, to attempt to shape the identity of his readers. In one of his first descriptions of the dream censor, Freud says that "the politeness which I practice every day is to a large extent dissimulation of this kind; *and when I interpret my dreams for my readers I am obliged to adopt similar distortions*" (4:142, my emphasis). Freud mentions his own habit of "censoring" his dreams repeatedly in the text. In fact, it is a privilege that he sometimes claims rather aggressively for himself. At the end of his first "specimen dream," the dream of Irma's injection, he writes that "considerations which arise in the case of every dream of my own restrain me from pursuing my interpretive work." And then he issues what is almost a dare: "If anyone should feel tempted to express a hasty condemnation of my reticence, I would advise him to make the experiment of being franker than I am" (4:121).

Yet it is in a footnote in the midst of his account of the dream about Irma that Freud is most intriguing. In reference to a perplexing image he notes that he

---

[10] *Real Presences* (Chicago: University of Chicago Press, 1989), p. 211.

had a feeling that the interpretation of this part of the dream was not carried far enough to make it possible to follow the whole of its concealed meaning. If I pursued my comparison between the three women, it would have taken me far afield.—There is at least one spot in every dream at which it is un-plumbable—a navel, as it were, that is its point of contact with the unknown. (4:111, n. 1)

I called this footnote intriguing: as soon as one reads it, one wants to know more. Where might the interpretation have gone? What is this dream *omphalos* and how can Freud, the scientist in search of origins, speak so calmly of a region called "the unknown"? Yet this intrigue, this drive to follow the image further, is a Freudian intrigue, a Freudian desire. For Freud is in the process of teaching us that what is most worth knowing about dreams (and in fact about much of life) is that which is most ingeniously concealed. To be provoked by these passages, in which Freud plays the part of the censor, is to take up a Freudian attitude, to adopt what Paul Ricoeur would call a "hermeneutics of suspicion." Time after time in this text Freud attempts to make over his readers in his image by telling them that he is censoring his dreams, after having given them the (Freudian) techniques for overcoming the work of the censor.

In the dream of Irma, for instance, one might find it hard not to read through Freud's account to see his dissatisfactions with his aging wife, his desire for Irma and her friend, and his overall impatience with the sexual mores that surround him. In Freud's anxiety "not to be responsible for the pains which she still had" (4:108–9), one could see Freud's fears about the future possibility of impregnating his patient. Freud does put himself at risk in this passage, but the gambit works when the reader attempts to become his double as an interpreter, and in so doing projects his own desires and anxieties onto the text.

But one does not just interpret Freud, one also interprets his interpretations. For another of Freud's methods is to proffer what still qualify as rather shocking explanations for the motives of human behavior, but also to extend to the reader the means for demystifying any interpretation that seems to possess a strong intention. Intentions, Freud teaches, are never what they appear to be; all motives are, at least to some degree, analyzable in terms of the unconscious. Thus Freud offers a number of threatening interpretations—interpretations that one might wish to resist—and then provides the resources for that resistance. The result is that we can be made over as Freudian readers in our efforts to defend against Freud.

Things become more interesting when Freud's "self-defense" functions at what might be called a second degree: if we take Freud seriously enough to interpret him or his readings with his own techniques, we must also interpret ourselves. Freud gets one to use his methods on him to begin with, but it would be unjust to stop there. The act of self-reading precipitated initially by the desire to defend against Freudian interpretations or to "understand" Freud himself is perhaps one of the ways that we come to conceive of ourselves normatively, as Freudian psyches. This self-reading is often accompanied by the sensation of penetrating depths, but it may in fact be the action by which those supposed "depths" of the psyche are brought into being. This "penetration" and these "depths" assume a quasireligious aura when they are experienced in what one might call a "descendental" act. The moment is no less a religious one by virtue of the reversal in which we value demystifying "depths" rather than conventional transcendent heights.

Nietzsche encourages one always to ask, "Who is the interpreter, and what power is he seeking to gain by his act of interpretation?" Freud's technique of inducing one to read him in his own terms plays upon the desire to take up an authoritative position without particular effort or risk. When we turn then to interpret ourselves, using Freud's terms, we pay the price for seeking an absolute interpretive power without having created a correspondingly fresh interpretive vocabulary. As Kenneth Burke says, Freud offers a comprehensive dictionary that renames and redefines every important phenomenon in life. You cannot refute a dictionary; you can only supply an alternative one that provides better orientations and more reliable cues for action.[11] To attempt to "refute" Freud with his established terms is to be bound in the Freudian lexicon.

The results of this failure to locate a new or an alternate terminology become evident, for example, in William Warner's closely argued and intelligent study, *Chance and the Text of Experience: Freud, Nietzsche and Shakespeare's "Hamlet."*[12] Warner attempts to contest the authority of Freud's "primal" scene by demonstrating the degree to which it is invested by dreams, fantasies, memories, and other events. The "scene" is actually a differential play, which has been consolidated in Freud's work in the interest of creating a commanding theory, one that offers definitive, comprehensive explanations. By showing how the various constituent aspects of the scene had to be distorted in the interest of theory, Warner convincingly deconstructs the theory's pretenses to totality. He thus rehabilitates the role of chance in Freud's text. Yet, at the end of his book, Warner puts forward a structural mapping in which the authors he considers are shown to discipline chance in identical ways. The theoretical mastery that he tried to dissolve thus returns in his own writing, in a way that seems to mirror the process he so ably located in Freud's text.[13] Like

---

[11] See "Freud and the Analysis of Poetry" in *Philosophy of Literary Form*, p. 272.

[12] (Ithaca, N.Y.: Cornell University Press, 1986).

[13] I quote Warner: "By rereading these three texts in relation to the life-writing of two people and one character, I have reconceived moments of imagined mastery as emerging as

Freud, Warner moves from difference to theory, conceding to what Frank Lentricchia, writing in the spirit of William James, has called "theory desire." Capitulation to theory desire, Lentricchia suggests, is always likely; one is perpetually inclined, for the sake of action or utterance, to stabilize one's terms.[14] If the field of analysis is a text as sophisticated as Freud's, an attempt to curtail its authority entirely from within (in this case by making use of a modified version of Freud's concept of "over-determination") is likely, as Burke predicts, to end up with a reiteration.

Again, one should stress the fact that Freud's authority is not merely the effect of a mode of writing that, as a deconstructive reader might have it, activates forces of determination inherent in the nature of language. I don't share the De Manian view that every effective mode of interpretation is fated to solidify into an inert theory, blind to everything it cannot encompass. Some vocabularies are, as I see it anyway, more flexible, capacious, and open to improvement than others. Freud's tropes have the capacity to rewrite us at least in part because they can enter into smooth commerce with various other discourses that consolidate power and imply that "everything is past and there is nothing new." Freud's normative terminology confers upon those who use it a sense of potency far greater than do the terminologies of, say, Hegel or Proust or Emerson, in that Freud teaches us to speak knowingly of what others have attempted, with all of the resources of their psyches, to conceal. Yet at the same time Freud's discourse makes us the mystified objects of the "insight" of others: our "deep selves" are as transparent to certain "educated" forms of scrutiny as they are inaccessible to us. It is difficult to conceive of an epistemology better adapted—as Foucault has often implied—to the creation of "subjects," to the control of populations, to the means and goals of surveillance. Normative psychoanalysis contributes perhaps as much as any other discourse to the existence of contemporary social forms that combine individualizing techniques and totalizing procedures. Yet Freud's work is more than merely normative.

I

I have a number of books to be read, among them
Oedipus Rex.
—Freud, at sixteen, to Emil Fluss

the effect of interpretations which have three distinct but related elements: a collaboration with an other, a turn into the labyrinths of language, and the perception of a decisive coincidence" (ibid., 302).

[14] See Lentricchia's *Ariel and the Police: Michel Foucault, William James, Wallace Stevens* (Madison: University of Wisconsin Press, 1988), pp. 124–27.

I invented psychoanalysis because it had no literature.
—Freud to Lou Andreas Salome

In the passages in which Freud attempts to fashion his readers and himself through the imagery of dream production, one question remains unaddressed. What is this dream navel, the unknown center of every dream? Perhaps it is not coincidental that the Delphic Oracle, who plays a complex role in Freud's account of *Oedipus Rex*, was stationed at the *omphalos* of the world. Freud moves to that unknown spot to bring what is dark to light and to formulate the Oedipal complex, which is at the center of every dream, as it is of every life. In doing so, Freud exercises again his double-writing, in which his own self-empowering Romantic terms manifest themselves to his readers as normative markers, signs of the severest limitation.

The six pages of *The Interpretation of Dreams* in which Freud brings forward for the first time the concept of the Oedipal complex may be the single most important passage of his career. Not only does it introduce the idea that would lie, with some modifications, at the core of psychoanalysis, but it allows Freud to rerepresent himself and his new science, conferring upon both, by way of symbolic action, an appropriately authoritative status. In this section, which arrives under the innocuous title of "Specimen Dreams," Freud formulates a persuasive myth of normative human development and, simultaneously, a fresh way of conceiving his own enterprise and its place in Western culture.

In my discussion of the Oedipal passage, I argue that Freud in some ways resembles those figures that Harold Bloom has called "strong poets," writers who make their entry into the tradition by way of creative rewriting of their predecessors.[15] In a similar vein, Richard Rorty speaks of the poet of genius as one "who can say of the relevant portion of the past, 'Thus I will it,' because she has found a way to describe the past which the past never knew, and thereby found a self to be which her precursors never knew was possible."[16] Bloom has contributed greatly to our understanding of poetic creation, but we need to modify his thinking a good deal in order to get an accurate sense of Freud's self-creating text.

In *The Anxiety of Influence* and elsewhere, Bloom imposes Freud's Oedipal model on almost every major post-Miltonic poet in English. What the present reading argues is that Freud's terms for symbolic regeneration are best used to describe him and only him. In other words, Freud's generative terminology is as singular as that of any of the major English or

[15] Bloom's best-known treatment of this subject is *The Anxiety of Influence* (New York: Oxford University Press, 1973).

[16] *Contingency, Irony, and Solidarity*, p. 29.

American Romantic writers, each of whom seems compelled to offer one or more stories about what originality is while trying, simultaneously, to exemplify that "originality" in the text. However, the capacity of Freud's terms to function as a part of a social mythology, which helps to naturalize contingent, historical conditions, enlarges the temptation to generalize those terms, a temptation to which Bloom's unwillingness to consider social issues in his readings of the poets has probably made him unduly susceptible. Bloom, in a manner that he himself describes frequently, has comprehensively literalized Freud's figurative terminology and in so doing has sacrificed the sense of the individual process by which Romantic poets dramatize their self-regenerations. Although Bloom has done invaluable work in pointing to the critical moments of genesis, achieved through dialectical encounter, that pervade the works of the Romantics, he has distorted those moments by assimilating them too readily to Freud's own (contingent) vocabulary. To put it simply, Bloom's Freudian theory of poetic genesis may be true rather exclusively of Freud. But this strays somewhat ahead of ourselves. We need to begin by considering Freud's text.

Freud's introduction of the Oedipal complex takes the form not of a report on clinical findings, nor even of an analysis of specimen dreams, but rather of a piece of literary criticism, a reading of *Oedipus Rex* and *Hamlet*.[17] Priority is the issue here, and Freud's opening gambit is to qualify Sophocles's claim to originality by pointing to the play's source in a legend. That legend, in turn, is only comprehensible by way of psychoanalysis: its "profound and universal power to move can only be understood," Freud writes, "if the hypothesis I have put forward in regard to the psychology of children has an equally universal validity" (4:261). Thus Freud tentatively locates himself with the legend, before the play.

His next step is to summarize the play. As is true of many literary critics, Freud's interpretive designs are most visible when he is rendering what seems to him to be an innocent, descriptive account. His synopsis of *Oedipus Rex* is curious for two reasons: its excessive stress on the part played by the Delphic Oracle in the drama, and the absence of any mention of the figure who is conceivably the play's second most important one, Teiresias. In a three-page account of *Oedipus*, Freud refers to the oracle seven times. The oracle warns Laius that his son will murder him; Oedipus appeals to the oracle to learn the truth about his origins; the Thebans send to the oracle to discover the cause of their plight; Oedipus recalls the oracle's pronouncement and is distressed, and so on. None of

---

[17] For a deconstructive reading of Freud's critical act see Cynthia Chase's "Oedipal Textuality: Reading Freud's Reading of *Oedipus*," in *Diacritics* (Spring 1979): 54–68.

these references is mistaken, nor do they become particularly noticeable
until Freud completes his account of the play with a dramatic flourish:

> The action of the play consists in nothing other than the process of revealing,
> with cunning delays and ever-mounting excitement—a process that can be
> likened to the work of pyscho-analysis—that Oedipus himself is the mur-
> derer of Laïus, but further that he is the son of the murdered man and of
> Jocasta. Appalled at the abomination which he has unwittingly perpetrated,
> Oedipus blinds himself and forsakes his home. *The oracle has been fulfilled.*
> (4:261–2, emphasis mine)

In the passage of analysis that follows, "the oracle" becomes Freud's image for the Oedipal burden that we all bear: Oedipus's "destiny moves us
only because it might have been ours—because the oracle laid the same
curse upon us before our birth as upon him" (4:262).[18] This "oracle"
resides within us, Freud suggests, as "a voice . . . ready to recognize the
compelling force of destiny in the *Oedipus*" (4:262), and the presence of
this sympathetic voice is what accounts for the play's impact.

The legendary oracle, whose motto was "Know thyself," habitually
spoke in riddles, and the corresponding "voice within us" must also be
interpreted or unriddled. This inner voice is also manifest in dreams: "It
is the fate of all of us, perhaps, to direct our first sexual impulse towards
our mother and our first hatred and our first murderous wish against our
father. Our dreams convince us that that is so. King Oedipus, who slew
his father Laïus and married his mother Jocasta, merely shows us the ful-
filment of our own childhood wishes" (4:262). The voice within us all,
the voice of fate and destiny, whose counterpart in *Oedipus Rex* is the
oracle, is also present in our dreams. And that voice has been interpreted
correctly, in the wake of more than two thousand years of erroneous approaches to the problem, by only one interpreter, the author of the
Traumdeutung. Freud has no inclination to historicize his discovery or to
limit its application to his own milieu, that of white, Western, middle-
class culture. He has come upon an eternal truth, accessible to all and
found by no one before him. A dream has always been the disguised fulfillment of a repressed wish, susceptible to interpretation by the psychoanalytic method. Freud has found the oracle and contrived a faultless key
to all of its riddles.

Dreams are Freud's specific domain, and so to posit a dream as the
origin of the legend that in turn originated Sophocles's play is not without
consequences:

[18] As he later writes, "Fate and the oracle were no more than materializations of an internal necessity" (20:63).

There is an unmistakable indication in the text of Sophocles' tragedy itself that the legend of Oedipus sprang from some primaeval dream-material which had as its content the distressing disturbance of a child's relation to his parents owing to the first stirrings of sexuality. At a point when Oedipus, though he is not yet enlightened, has begun to feel troubled by his recollection of the oracle, Jocasta consoles him by referring to a dream which many people dream, though, as she thinks, it has no meaning:

> Many a man ere now in dreams hath lain
> With her who bare him. He hath least annoy
> Who with such omens troubleth not his mind.

To-day, just as then, many men dream of having sexual relations with their mothers. (4:263–64)

The play, then, is rooted in a legend that derives in turn from a common dream. As the interpreter who has, for the first time in human history, rightly read the universal dream that provides the deepest layer of motivation in Sophocles's play, Freud can, in a certain imaginative sense, cast himself and his text as being prior to *Oedipus Rex*.

Freud is there, looking steadily into the origins to which the play itself and its author are apparently blind. To unlock the tragedy, to know it better than it knows itself, has been the aim of Freud's reading, and there is rhetorical evidence that he feels the force of his success. After Freud clinches his argument, placing dreams rightly read—Freudian dreams, in short—at the roots of the play, an odd change in diction occurs. Where Freud's synopsis of the play had been for the most part rather dry and cautious, he begins now to submit *Oedipus Rex* to the rhetoric of psychoanalysis. He speaks of "the fulfillment of childhood wishes," "detaching our sexual impulses from our mothers," and "the primaeval wishes of our childhood," as though the play had been put into its place as a case-study, capable, upon judicious analysis, of illustrating the truths of the new science. Freud's rhetoric signifies his confidence in his reading: he has taken a classical work whose theme is proud blindness and its undoing, and he has found its own point of blindness and shown it the light. (Jocasta's speech to Oedipus in which she affirms that many men have dreamt of lying with their mothers indicates that the play knows its true origins in much the way a neurotic "knows" his illness's cause, but thinks "it has no meaning.") To uncover the play's authentic origins may not be to banish it from the canon, but surely it is to modify its kingly place. No genuine aristocrat, *Oedipus Rex* begins in the commonest dreams of common men: its true lineage is humble.

Thus, one might go so far as to say that when in his description of the play Freud evokes Oedipus's ignorance of his own identity and origins, he is also speaking of the play's tendency to mistake itself as being a "tragedy of destiny," rather than "the disguised fulfillment of a repressed wish":

> Oedipus Rex is what is known as a tragedy of destiny. Its tragic effect is said to lie in the contrast between the supreme will of the gods and the vain attempts of mankind to escape the evil that threatens them. The lesson which, it is said, the deeply moved spectator should learn from the tragedy is submission to the divine will and realization of his own impotence. (4:262)

Who claims this to be the moral of *Oedipus Rex* Freud does not directly say. Yet he seems to be thinking of the chorus, that other voice in the drama that commends piety and submission in the face of the gods' unalterable will. Later, though, Freud is more to the point on where the erroneous reading of the events of the play actually originates:

> And just as [Oedipal] dreams, when dreamt by adults, are accompanied by feelings of repulsion, so too the legend must include horror and self-punishment. Its further modification originates once again in a misconceived secondary revision of the material, which has sought to exploit it for theological purposes. (4:264)

The "misconceived secondary revision" that Freud maligns can, as the classicist Bernard Knox argues, only be the literary act by which Sophocles translates the legend into a drama, working in much the way the censoring mechanism works upon a dream-wish.[19]

The "destiny theme" is thus a piece of Sophoclean distortion, defacing the dream at the center of *Oedipus Rex*, whose real motivating wishes are parricide and incest. The play is distanced from its own truth by the blindness of its author, which Freud corrects by locating the drama's modes of self-mystification. When Freud speaks of how "the poet, as he unravels the past, brings to light the guilt of Oedipus . . . , at the same time compelling us to recognize our own inner minds" (4:263), it is quite questionable whether he means Sophocles, whose own sense of the play seems to have been that it was a tragedy of destiny. For is it not Freud who is authentically "compelling us to recognize our own inner minds, in which those . . . impulses, though suppressed, are still to be found" (4:263)? If Sophocles himself compelled the "recognition" there would be no need for Freud's analysis of the play. Sophocles answered the riddle of the legend of Oedipus by calling it a tragedy of destiny, and he mounted to literary fame. But in Freud's reading, Sophocles's Oedipal blindness is re-

---

[19] See *Sophocles: The Three Theban Plays*, with an introduction and notes by Bernard Knox (New York: Penguin, 1982), pp. 132–33.

vealed, and the play and its author must succumb to the force of demystifying intelligence, as Freud teaches the play its own repressed truth.

Or does he? As I observed earlier, the second peculiarity in Freud's reading of *Oedipus Rex* is his elimination of Teiresias. Most of what the blind seer contributes to the play Freud assimilates to the actions of the oracle. And yet Teiresias, whose role in the unfolding of the play is implicitly compared by Freud to the part played by the doctor in psychoanalysis, may embody an awareness, in some ways comparable to Freud's, about the play's more universal applications. Sophocles's Teiresias is a figure of total, reductive knowledge that has been purchased by utter loss of power, to borrow terms from Wordsworth. His blind helplessness may be an emblem of the fact that earthly potency, like Oedipus's, depends upon a measure of self-mystification, or what Freud in later works calls "narcissistic self-regard," the source of all of our sustaining illusions. To be stripped of every fiction, to place oneself, through knowledge, beyond wishes and desires, is to become what Teiresias is, a figure of death-in-life. Now if Oedipus defines self-delusion in its most extreme form, and Teiresias stands as a figure of total self-disenchantment, then all of the rest of humanity must fall somewhere in between them. That Oedipus becomes Teiresias's wretched double after being disabused indicates the play's sense of their dark bond, despite the original disparity.

By representing the two figures as opposite extremes of total knowledge and total power and then emphasizing the fearful continuities between the two, thus presenting them as the extremes of a scale on which we might all measure ourselves, Sophocles seems close to anticipating some aspects of Freud's reading. The sense that Freud seems to attribute to Sophocles that *Oedipus Rex* is a tragedy of destiny hinges in part on the uniqueness of Oedipus's plight, on his status, that is, as a conventional "tragic hero." In the Aristotelian account, Oedipus is a victim in part because he is greater than common men and aspires to be yet more. Tragedy's lightning, in this view, always strikes the highest tree in the field. But if the dialectic of knowledge and power I have pointed to is at work, then the play carries an awareness that the figures of Oedipus and Teiresias chart between them a universal human destiny.

If Sophocles does not "know," as Freud does, that it is every child's wish to do away with his father and possess his mother, then he may somehow "know" that these desires adequately figure universal human desire in its most extreme form. So Freud's perception of the centrality of the Oedipal wish might not be quite so new a "discovery" as he would like to think. It may actually be something of a literalization, or naturalization, of Sophocles's myth.

Thus, one may want to consider the possibility that by eliminating the seer from his account, Freud removes the figure whose presence can provide some of the same insight into the play's action that he himself wishes to claim. On this view, Sophocles's play can answer whatever riddles Freud can pose, and we see that Freud may need to blind *Oedipus Rex* in order to shed his own bracing light upon it.

II

> The discerning will read, in his Plato or Shakespeare, only that least part,—only the authentic utterances of the oracle;—all the rest he rejects, were it never so many times Plato's and Shakespeare's.
> —Emerson, "The American Scholar"

> It is possible, therefore, that a work of art of this kind needs interpretation, and that until I have accomplished that interpretation I cannot come to know why I have been so powerfully affected. I even venture to hope that the effect of the work will undergo no diminution after we have succeeded in thus analyzing it.
> —Freud, "The Moses of Michelangelo"

It takes an effort of imagination to recapture the analogical leap by which Freud connected *Oedipus Rex* and *Hamlet*, so accustomed are we now to think of them together in connection with the Oedipal complex. *The Interpretation of Dreams*, though, may be the first occasion on which the works were coupled for critical or analytic purposes,[20] which might induce one to pose Kenneth Burke's pragmatic question: What is the writer trying to do for himself by way of symbolic action by yoking *Hamlet* and *Oedipus* in the way that he does?

The discussion of *Hamlet* is only half the length of that of *Oedipus*, and it was, in the first edition of the *Traumdeutung*, a footnote to the reading of Sophocles's play. In 1914, Freud's second *annus mirabilis*, the year in which he introduced the "narcissistic ego," the material on *Hamlet* was raised into the text proper. Freud's concern continues to be genealogical. Having shown that *Oedipus Rex* is blind to its identity and to its origins, Freud begins by addressing the ancestry of what is commonly taken to be one of the most original works of literature. Freud's first observation about *Hamlet* is that the play "has its roots in the same soil as

[20] The classical development on this theme is of course Ernest Jones's *Hamlet and Oedipus* (New York: Norton, 1949).

Oedipus Rex" (4:264). From there Freud goes on to place Shakespeare's play within a condensed genealogy of culture:

> Another of the great creations of tragic poetry, Shakespeare's *Hamlet*, has its roots in the same soil as *Oedipus Rex*. But the changed treatment of the same material reveals the whole difference in the mental life of these two widely separated epochs of civilization: the secular advance of repression in the emotional life of mankind. In the *Oedipus* the child's wishful phantasy that underlies it is brought into the open and realized as it would be in a dream. In *Hamlet* it remains repressed. (4:264)

By assimilating *Hamlet* to the Oedipal plot, Freud demonstrates that the play is, like *Oedipus Rex*, out of touch with its own true motives and beginnings. The line of descent from dream to legend to *Oedipus Rex* extends now to *Hamlet*, which reveals itself as the old desire displaced one degree further, and nothing so new as we had thought.

Freud's image of culture as the "Grand March of Secular Repression," a four-phase progress from the original dream to Shakespeare's inspired dream-work, implicitly poses the question of his own place in the line of descent. Given its power to demystify *Oedipus Rex* and *Hamlet*, the *Traumdeutung* might also claim a position in the cultural order that Freud swiftly evokes. Having already positioned himself in a symbolic sense at the beginnings of culture by being the first truly to unriddle the primal dream, Freud seems now to place himself at the end of the line, as the critical fulfillment of the process. Freud's later fascination with the issue of who "really" wrote Shakespeare's work may be a rather literal residue of this early demystifying urge.[21]

If the two plays have reflected the history of an ever-tightening repression, Freud's dream-book might be understood as the culmination that, by critical analysis, qualifies "the secular advance of repression," and does so to the general benefit of mankind. Thus *The Interpretation of Dreams* may represent a moment of enlightenment, the triumph of scientific insight over literary obfuscation in a benevolent restoration of the repressed. In a manner of speaking, Freud's text becomes the descendant of the two great literary works, though it is not overly constrained by filial piety. Having modified the genealogies of the two works in question, Freud implicitly modifies his own: he is beginning and end, origin and fulfillment.

III

Freud, in the passage I have just discussed, is symbolically displacing the figures of paternal authority, Sophocles and Shakespeare, and at the same

---

[21] See *Standard Edition*, 20:63–64, n. 1.

time claiming a peculiarly liberated form of descent from them. He fulfills their essential genius, but without being constrained by their delusions. Correspondingly, he is the possessor, and the only possessor, of what he will later describe as the source of literature and of culture in general, the primal (Oedipal) dream: he owns the origin, the source, one might even say the matrix, of human civilization. For if there is a significant place for femininity in Freud's Oedipal myth, it is only at the source, or oracle; in constructing his own genealogy, in which he plays the part of the enlightened descendant of Sophocles and Shakespeare, Freud erases the role of the woman. He is the culmination of an all-male line: no female presence qualifies or calls into doubt the purity of his symbolic lineage. And femininity, as a reading of "On Narcissism" reveals, stands always as a force that threatens the stability of the factual, scientific "basis" of psychoanalysis.[22] But the fact to note at present is that the Oedipus complex, whatever else it may be, manifests itself in the text of *The Interpretation of Dreams* as an allegory of Freudian reading and writing, a myth about the genesis of Freud's text in which the powers of the new science declare themselves against prior cultural forms, and particularly against literary forms.

However, by way of that technique I called Freudian double-writing, a narrative myth that serves the purpose of accounting (in a highly Romantic fashion) for Freud's auto-genesis also manifests itself to us, Freud's readers, as the embodiment of a universal and normative truth. To use Richard Rorty's terms, Freud's "effort to achieve self-creation by the recognition of contingency," by telling a new story about himself, works in its normative form as an "effort to achieve universality by the transcendence of contingency."[23] The Oedipal narrative presents itself as both trope and theory, enabling myth and truth.

But suppose that Freud, having listened to his patients, having read widely, having scrutinized himself, can legitimately offer a "just representation of general nature" (Johnson). What if he is doing what Thomas Mann and Paul Ricoeur have each in his way suggested—refining literary and oneiric material until he reaches central human continuities?[24] One answer would be that if Freud indeed had found a binding truth about

[22] On the problematic positioning of femininity in psychoanalytic thought see Sarah Kofman, *The Enigma of Woman: Woman in Freud's Writings*, trans. Catherine Porter (Ithaca, N.Y.: Cornell University Press, 1985).

[23] *Contingency, Irony, and Solidarity*, p. 25.

[24] Both Mann and Ricoeur tend to see literary and psychoanalytic writing as continuous and potentially collaborative modes of thinking. See Thomas Mann's "Freud and the Future" in *Essays of Three Decades*, trans. H. T. Lowe-Porter (New York: Knopf, 1947), pp. 411–28, and Paul Ricoeur's *Freud and Philosophy: An Essay on Interpretation* (New Haven, Conn.: Yale University Press, 1970), especially his brilliant reading of the "symbol" in dreams and literature, pp. 514–24.

human nature, he would not be at the same time transgressing, even symbolically, the limits that that truth establishes. By possessing the oracle and surpassing the poets, Freud represents an act that his own normative formulations ought to prevent him from even conceiving. How can the Oedipal repression be a binding repression—the cornerstone of all civilization, as Freud calls it—if he can so effectively overcome it? Freud's textual practice suggests rather that the Oedipal complex is the negative term in a symbolic drama of private self-recreation, the fruit of which is a new discourse, a new terminological field.

But I am uneasy with this response: it seems to confine, unrealistically, the relation a poetic imagining must have to some empirical world. Perhaps Freud can be understood as celebrating the triumph of his (true) insight by way of a certain literary hyperbole. It is difficult to say. No reading like mine can ever "disprove" the universal validity of the Oedipal complex, in part because, as Karl Popper has shown, psychoanalysis is, in scientific terms, nonfalsifiable anyway.[25] I do think, though, that having seen how the formulation of the Oedipal passage works as a piece of Freudian "double-writing," how it figures Freud's supremacy and the necessarily secondary place of his readers and of the literary tradition, one ought further to doubt its value as a transcendent truth. This doubt will be augmented, I think, when at the close of this chapter I make some enquiries into the social role that the myth plays. But before progressing to those broader issues, I want to spend some time looking at the process by which Freud arrived at his formulation of the Oedipal myth. For in that process, I believe, one finds what may be most hopeful about Freud's first self-genesis.

IV

One's sense of Freud's desire to offer the world a text that would exert the sort of authority that Sophocles's and Shakespeare's have is intensified when one notices the parallel between Freud's description of the genesis of his own book and the motives he ascribes to Shakespeare for writing *Hamlet*. In the 1908 preface to the *Traumdeutung* Freud reflects that:

> [T]his book has a further subjective significance for me personally—a significance which I had only grasped after I had completed it. It was, I found, a portion of my own self-analysis, my reaction to my father's death—that is to say, to the most important event, the most poignant loss, of a man's life.

---

[25] See Karl Popper, *Conjectures and Refutations* (New York: Basic Books, 1962). For a critique of Popper see Adolf Grünbaum, *The Foundations of Psychoanalysis* (Berkeley and Los Angeles: University of California Press, 1984).

Having discovered that this was so, I felt unable to obliterate the traces of the experience. (4:xxvi)

Freud's revelation closely echoes the account in the 1900 text of the psychogenesis of the play Freud took to be Shakespeare's supreme masterpiece:

[I]t can of course only be the poet's own mind which confronts us in Hamlet. I observe in a book on Shakespeare by Georg Brandes (1896) a statement that *Hamlet* was written immediately after the death of Shakespeare's father (in 1601), that is, under the immediate impact of his bereavement and, as we may well assume, while his childhood feelings about his father had been freshly revived. (4:265)

Thus the spiritual occasion for the writing of *Hamlet* and of *The Interpretation of Dreams* was the same, and in saying so Freud asks us to compare the two works. He is revealing, perhaps, an aspiration to write a major work in the literary vein: if Shakespeare's mind confronts us in Hamlet, then conceivably the *Traumdeutung* is the imaginative expression of its own creator.

Yet obviously more is at stake here. Freud is also implying that both he and Shakespeare were liberated by the deaths of their fathers to achieve their works. Nature suddenly modified Freud's relations to the personal past, and in turn Freud modified his relations to the cultural past. Similarly Shakespeare transformed the Oedipal dream, legend, and play in the writing of *Hamlet*. Perhaps the death of Jacob Freud and the temporary suspension of identity for Sigmund, no longer son and not yet the fully developed paternal figure whom we tend to remember, was related, at least in Freud's mind, to the possibility of a symbolic self-creation. It allowed Freud, in Burke's phrase, to undergo those "symbolic passes" that would "endow him with a new identity."

Nietzsche is melodramatic but astute when in *The Birth of Tragedy* he speculates on what it is that allows Oedipus to overthrow the Sphinx:

If we examine Oedipus, the solver of riddles and liberator of his mother . . . , we may conclude that wherever sooth-saying and magical powers have broken the spell of present and future, the rigid law of individuation, the magic circle of nature, extreme unnaturalness—in this case incest—is the necessary antecedent; for how should man force nature to yield up her secrets but by successfully resisting her, that is to say, by unnatural acts? This is the recognition I find expressed in the terrible triad of Oedipean fates: the same man who solved the riddle of nature (the ambiguous Sphinx) must also, as murderer of his father and husband of his mother, break the consecrated tables of the natural order. It is as though the myth whispered to us that wisdom, and especially Dionysiac wisdom, is an unnatural crime, and that whoever, in pride of knowledge, hurls nature into the abyss of destruction, must himself experience nature's disintegration.[26]

Is it possible to conceive of Freud in these terms? He does confront the legend of Oedipus and give to that enigma a new answer: it is *Everyman's* secret desire to do away with his father and embrace his mother: "Our dreams convince us that that is so." Where was the transgression that enabled Freud's reply?

Recall that Freud introduces his remarks on *Hamlet* with what seems to be a casual figure of speech: the play "has its roots [*wurzelt*] in the same soil as *Oedipus Rex*" (4:264). All of our roots are there, he might have added, in the soil of the Oedipus complex. Interestingly, in a letter to Wilhelm Fliess just after his father's death, Freud evokes his grief in a sentence-length paragraph: "I now feel quite uprooted" [*entwurzeltes*].[27] To be uprooted is to be naked, vulnerable, exposed, but also to take up a new position, unburied and unblinded, in a fresh relation to experience. The image occurs again in the section of *Wilhelm Meister* to which Freud refers in his passage on the Oedipal complex. There Freud finds the view, which he attributes to Goethe, that "Hamlet represents the type of man whose power of direct action is paralyzed by an excessive development of his intellect" (4:265). Wilhelm Meister diagnoses Hamlet as follows:

> To me it is clear that Shakespeare meant, in the present case, to represent the effects of a great action laid upon a soul unfit for the performance of it. In this view the whole play seems to me to be composed. There is an oak-tree [*Eichbaum*] planted in a costly jar, which should have borne only pleasant flowers [*Blumen*] in its bosom; the roots [*Wurzeln*] expand, the jar is shivered.[28]

Freud's own version of "habitual self" is comparably shivered by the event of his father's death, and yet he is determined to respond to the cataclysm, not as Goethe's Hamlet does, but by using it as an opportunity for transforming achievement.

What went on during the self-analysis? The letters to Fliess indicate that it was full of suffering, depression, and from time to time the most intense intellectual satisfaction. One might begin to understand it by looking at a "nice dream" Freud reported to Fliess that took place around the time of Jacob's funeral:

---

[26] Friedrich Nietzsche, *The Birth of Tragedy and The Genealogy of Morals*, trans. Francis Golffing (Garden City, N.J.: Doubleday, 1956), p. 61.

[27] *The Complete Letters of Sigmund Freud to Wilhelm Fliess, 1887–1904*, trans. and ed. Jeffrey Moussaieff Masson (Cambridge, Mass.: The Belknap Press of Harvard University Press, 1985), p. 202. Subsequent references are cited in the body of the text as *Letters*.

[28] *Wilhelm Meister's Apprenticeship*, trans. Thomas Carlyle, 2 vols. (Boston: S. E. Cassino, 1884), 1:223.

I was in a place where I read a sign:

> You are requested
> to close the eyes.[29]

I immediately recognized the location as the barbershop I visit every day. On the day of the funeral I was kept waiting and therefore arrived a little late at the house of mourning. At that time my family was displeased with me because I had arranged for the funeral to be quiet and simple, which they later agreed was quite justified. They were also somewhat offended by my lateness. The sentence on the sign has a double meaning: one should do one's duty to the dead (an apology as though I had not done it and were in need of leniency), and the actual duty itself. The dream thus stems from the inclination to self-reproach that regularly sets in among the survivors. (*Letters*, p. 202)

Literally, Freud is being instructed in the dream to close the eyes of his deceased father. Yet the process of introspection that will end in the creation of the Oedipal complex has probably already begun, and it is that process, I think, to which Freud is being admonished, by father, family, and tradition, to close his own eyes.[30] "Like Oedipus," Freud writes in the wake of his father's death, "we live in ignorance of these wishes . . . and after their revelation we may all of us well seek to close our eyes to the scenes of our childhood" (4:263).[31]

Freud, on the contrary, cherishes his painful state, retains his uprootedness, and keeps his eyes open. Four months after Jacob's death, Freud, who was in life a pious son, is compelled to admit to Fliess that Jacob, like the fathers of so many of his hysterical patients, had molested his children in their infancy. Though Freud had himself escaped (could the Romantic myth of a favored childhood be more negatively imagined?), Jacob is responsible for the hysteria of Freud's brother and of several younger sisters.

The self-analysis continues, and Freud begins to feel intimations that the seduction theory is wrong. In a letter to Fliess dated September 21, 1897, Freud recants the theory and is again left with no framework for explaining the origins of the neuroses. "Now I have no idea of where I stand," he writes, "because I have not succeeded in gaining a theoretical

---

[29] The German sentence reads, "Es wird gebeten die Augen zuzudrücken."

[30] See the similar comment of Marthe Robert on this dream in her book *From Oedipus to Moses—Freud's Jewish Identity*, trans. Ralph Manheim (London: Routledge and Kegan Paul, 1977), pp. 90–92.

[31] Strachey's translation coheres too well with my case. The German actually reads "und nach deren Enthüllung möchten wir wohl alle den Blick abwenden [literally: turn our glance away from] von den Szenen unserer Kindheit."

understanding of repression and its interplay of forces" (*Letters*, p. 265). But, considering the event, Freud is cheerful:

> The expectation of eternal fame was so beautiful, as was that of certain wealth, complete independence, travels, and lifting the children above the severe worries that robbed me of my youth. Everything depended upon whether or not hysteria would come out right. Now I can once again remain quiet and modest, go on worrying and saving. (*Letters*, p. 266)

He also goes on with his self-scrutiny and its record, the dream-book, which "stands entirely secure."

Now Freud begins to approach the formulation of the Oedipal complex. He "sees" that what his patients have reported to him as seductions by their parents have actually been projections of their own childhood desires onto their first love-objects. Yet, more intimately, Freud recognizes such desires as having been and still being his own. On October 3, 1897, Freud writes to his friend about his own initiation into desire and aggressivity: "Later (between two and two and a half years) my libido toward *matrem* was awakened, namely, on the occasion of a journey with her from Leipzig to Vienna, during which we must have spent the night together and there must have been an opportunity of seeing her *nudam*" (*Letters*, p. 268). Earlier in the same letter Freud speaks elliptically about his father's role: "I can only indicate that the old man plays no active part in my case, but that no doubt I drew an inference by analogy from myself onto him." Freud suggests here, I think, that indeed his father had never molested him or any of his brothers and sisters; rather, Freud had projected his own aggressive wishes against his father onto him.

In another letter to Fliess, written a few weeks later, Freud formulates the situation more concisely: "A single idea of general value dawned on me. I have found, in my own case too, [the phenomenon of being] in love with my mother and jealous of my father." And here comes a momentous turning, for the sentence continues, "and I now consider it a universal event in early childhood" (*Letters*, p. 272). The turning is momentous, of course, in that Freud has generalized his own condition. He can now say, taking up a familiar rhetoric, that "everyone . . . was once a *budding* [*im Keime*] Oedipus in fantasy and each recoils in horror from the dream fulfillment" in Sophocles's play (*Letters*, p. 272, emphasis mine). The trope that originally went with Freud's private situation now has a general applicability. Freud has left that space of indeterminacy or uprootedness, which is aptly described by Keats as "being in uncertainties, mysteries, doubts," and he has come to "repose," to proceed appropriately to Samuel Johnson, "upon the stability of truth."

During that year between the death of his father and the October 27 letter to Fliess, Freud is lost, suspended in a space of pure risk and speculation that he once described, in its negative form, as a "curious state of mind which one's consciousness cannot apprehend: twilight thoughts, a veil over one's mind, scarcely a ray of light here and there."[32] Freud, as he probed his own past, must have been tormented for some periods of time by the notion that the desires of Oedipus were peculiarly his. Having the courage to keep his eyes open to this, against the wishes of every form of authority and tradition, sustained Freud in a midspace of pure possibility. Freud's Nietzschean transgression would then involve all of the dark versions of family origins he entertained in the liminal space: liminality might, in this case, mean holding one's myths of origin in suspension and elaborating freely on the questions of "what and whither, when and how" (Wordsworth).

This is the Freud that I, at least, find most admirable, the one who sacrifices continuities and conventional affiliations and engages in a process of free elaboration, of spontaneous name-giving. Though Freud will eventually seek a form of interpretive closure by generalizing the Oedipal complex ("I now consider it a universal event in early childhood"), what is impressive is the length of time for which he holds off that closure and continues to read his situation, arriving as he does so at fresh tropes. Where does Freud derive the force to engage in this symbolic drama? The question is obviously a complex one, but Freud's text gives a useful hint for speculation. Freud indicates that both he and Shakespeare were put in a position to write their masterpieces ("Insight such as this falls to one's lot but once in a lifetime," said Freud of the *Traumdeutung*) by way of their fathers' deaths. That is, they set out from the position in which Hamlet found himself.

One of the effects of Hamlet's grief would seem to be a sense of dislocation: his speech surprises us in part because of the velocity with which he shifts perspectives. Thus Frank Kermode speaks of the mind of Hamlet in terms of "its affective power, its 'negative capability' or failure to assert any of the possible ethical or metaphysical positions it creates."[33] Hamlet's situation is vertiginous and it entails great suffering, but it may also be a source of eloquence. His brilliant language, then, might come not only from natural endowments but from the shifting points of view, the almost Nietzschean perspectivism, that loss enforces upon him. ("The world is interpretable . . . , it has no meaning behind it, but countless meanings.—'Perspectivism.' ")[34] Hamlet's grief permits him, in fact compels him, to take up ever-new positions in regard to himself and his situ-

---

[32] Jones, *Life and Work of Freud*, 1:325.

[33] See his introduction to the play in *The Riverside Shakespeare*, ed. G. Blakemore Evans (Boston: Houghton Mifflin, 1974), p. 1136.

[34] See *The Will To Power*, trans. Walter Kaufmann and R. J. Hollingdale (New York: Random House, 1968), p. 267.

ation. One might even make the case that Hamlet's delays are motivated, in some measure, by a desire to sustain his eloquence and his newly acquired vision. Killing Claudius would, perhaps, change Hamlet's relation to language and perception; he would lose his inventive energy.

Freud's letters to Fliess indicate that he may have found himself in a comparable state of dislocation after his father's death. (Recall Freud's line, "I now feel quite uprooted.") Although Freud's response is not a dramatic perspectivism like Hamlet's, grief does seem to give him intensified access to his inventive powers. Freud's response is like Hamlet's, in other words, in that, for some time, he reads and interprets, rather than attempting to solve his dilemma. Freud does give in at a certain point and mythologizes his condition, and thus presumably he decreases his "Oedipal burden." (Hamlet's fate suggests that the unwillingness to seek some kind of closure may lead to self-ruin, as speculation takes him further and further from normative, communal standards, rendering him more alien and dangerous, a more likely "scapegoat.") Thus Freud is a figure who, behaving somewhat in Hamlet's mode, sacrifices the comforts that continuity with the existing powers can bring and elaborates, at some cost to himself, a contingent story about his own origins and identity, one that would undermine socially accredited narratives of personal genesis. To do as Freud does in that year, it seems to me, is implicitly to challenge bureaucratized modes of representing the self, at least temporarily.

V

What ought to have come through in this account so far is the paradoxical nature of Freud's achievement: his discourse of self-genesis appears in one sense to be extremely idiosyncratic, contingent, and Romantic, yet at the same time, owing to existing social relations, it is susceptible to being generalized, or bureaucratized. One thing we might surmise from our scrutiny of Freud up to this point is that although there may be as many effective myths of authorial self-genesis as there are Romantic writers of achievement, most of these Romantic myths do not have the possibilities for filiation with social discourses that Freud's does. (Obviously the practice of analytic therapy is a crucial relay in Freud's passage into a social text, a matter I address more fully in the third chapter.) To transfer Freud's normative terminology onto other writers is to be used by Freud to cut off what I take to be one of the most potentially radical aspects of Romantic writing, its power to challenge and displace ideologically confirmed narratives about the self. Harold Bloom's sense of "lateness," to which he is fortunately inconsistently attached, is, I think, a precipitate of the Freudian reduction that he imposes—there can indeed be little discernibly "new" in the West if one assimilates attempts at invention to a preformulated terminology. But the impact of Freud's text is social as well as aesthetic, and in the section that follows I offer some observations (which because of the subject's breadth can hardly be comprehensive) on the ways that the Oedipal passage works within culture as an effective myth—works, in short, to naturalize the historical (to borrow terms from Roland Barthes) and to contribute to the creation of docile and uniform subjects.[35]

For the Oedipal complex to possess the cultural authority that it does, it must qualify as something more than a concentrated figure for private achievement. The Oedipal complex works and *is*, as Emerson might say, and one must approach the riddle of its prestige. Why does this narrative about desire and aggression still hold such a commanding place? Why do we need it?

To begin an answer it will help to pose a more fundamental question. Exactly what form of authority does the Oedipal narrative possess? Freud's creation of a new terminology for the self, which is for him a great breakthrough, enters culture as a trope of the severest limitation in its generalized, normative formulation as the Oedipal complex. This is what may be the major example of Freudian double-writing, through which Freud's personal terms of power exert a constraint on our own texts and lives. To put it in the most reduced form, the Oedipal complex as a theory insists that a moment of primal repression exerts a hold that is only slightly alterable on the destiny of everyone. J. H. van den Berg evokes this situation when he observes that "the theory of repression—and it is well to remember this—is closely related to the thesis that there is a sense in everything, which in turn implies that everything is past and there is nothing new."[36] If every event that matters in life and art bears the marks of the Oedipal complex, then the kind of self-renewal that Freud represents in *his* Oedipal passage is for us inaccessible. To put it in Emerson's language, we must pay tribute to the fact, and become "men of sense," because our futures are continuous with an unalterable past.

Freud is no blunt determinist, of course. For those few capable of sublimation there are some possibilities: the still-soft voice of reason, the life of culture, and analytical therapy can gradually effect change. Yet the ethical life that Freud's Oedipal formulation seems finally to call for is the one described by Northrop Frye in his account of the *eiron* figure in drama:

What is recommended is conventional life at its best: a clairvoyant knowledge of human nature in oneself and others, an avoidance of all illusion and

[35] For a more sanguine view of the mythical properties of Freud's text see Shoshana Felman, *Jacques Lacan and the Adventure of Insight*, especially pp. 152–59.
[36] *Changing Nature of Man*, p. 176.

compulsive behavior, a reliance on observation and timing rather than on aggressiveness. This is wisdom, the tried and tested way of life, which does not question the logic of social convention, but merely follows the procedures which in fact do serve to maintain one's balance from one day to the next. The *eiron* . . . takes an attitude of flexible pragmatism; he assumes that society will, if given any chance, behave more or less like Caliban's Setebos in Browning's poem, and he conducts himself accordingly. On all doubtful points of behavior convention is his deepest conviction. And however good or bad expertly conventional behavior may be thought to be, it is certainly the most difficult of all forms of behavior to satirize, just as anyone with a new theory of behavior, even if saint or prophet, is the easiest of all people to ridicule as a crank.[37]

Such "conventional behavior" takes full account of life's facts; indeed it can serve well enough to conceal the prophetic identity of oneself or of one's text. Freud is akin to the Romantics in his urge to generate fresh vocabularies and to refigure himself, but as a theorist of change he is sternly neoclassical, endorsing the ethos of imitation. In every act of sublimation, which is Freud's recommended mode for productive change, the subject makes the Oedipal concession once again. Instinctive drives are converted to the uses of culture in sublimation, just as the original desires energize the super-ego in the Oedipal resolution. The ethos of sublimation demands that one sacrifice the creative impulse to the uses of civilization, imitating the great and good who have come before. Freud, it is worth repeating, achieves something quite the opposite in his text, at least for himself. The formulation of the Oedipal complex calls into doubt precisely the kind of sudden change that Freud symbolizes for himself and his work.[38]

Freud's narrative stands where it does because it manifests itself as inevitable; it offers so compelling a force of tropes that its reader is induced to take them as literal truth. That is, she will have recourse to Freud's terms "spontaneously," using them in attempts to solve—rather than as Freud does, to interpret—the dilemma at hand. How does a modern myth become inevitable? First, it must work comprehensively; it must provide a compelling narrative account of the origins of a variety of painfully baffling instances in individual and cultural life.

The Oedipal myth, first of all, gives an account of how authority is internalized by the human subject. The super-ego, according to Freud, is

[37] Northrop Frye, *Anatomy of Criticism* (Princeton, N.J.: Princeton University Press, 1957), p. 226.

[38] For a critique of the Oedipal myth that is more radical in its goals than mine see Gilles Deleuze and Felix Guattari, *Anti-Oedipus*, trans. Robert Hurley, Mark Seem, and Helen R. Lane (New York: Viking Press, 1977).

the precipitate of the father's vocal threat (which I discuss in the next chapter) against the male child's desire for the mother. The child has the harsh choice of giving up either his first love object or his most precious bodily organ.[39] The child, Freud grimly says, chooses the former, though not without ambivalence. The narrative is, initially at least, rather difficult to accommodate. When one communicates it to students for the first time, without the benefit of the revisionist interpretation that allows one to see "the phallus" as merely a trope for male power, the students tend to be shocked and incredulous. But pragmatically we all know how hard it is to exert authority, and how much one tends to resist the influx of another's power. How then could something like an internal agency of authority—call it conscience or call it the super-ego—have gotten started except through an event comparable in its violence to the castration threat? When one poses this problem to students and asks them to come up with a plausible countermyth, they become no less incredulous, but they do become legitimately frustrated. For many it is the first direct experience of being contained within Freud's imagination.

The Oedipal myth also gives an account of another genuinely disturbing instance in life: it explains why eros and aggression seem, at least to many people, to be inseparable. Freud called this phenomenon primal ambivalence; his reflections on the subject are extremely rich, but they might be summarized somewhat as follows.[40] Freud tells us that our first drive is the drive to possess the mother, and that it is withdrawn due to the threat of paternal violence. If all desire from then on repeats the desire to possess the mother, then it will be sharply inflected with the violent threat that brought the primal desire to a close. We experience the repercussions of this early "contamination" (as Freud would call it) when we find ourselves unable to sustain a love relationship that does not, at almost every point, involve the dynamics of authority and domination. This has perhaps become a commonplace by now. What is less palatable is another phenomenon for which the myth begins to account. It gives us suggestive clues as to why, in practice, many relationships that are outwardly based on authority, such as those between supervisor and worker, teacher and student, doctor and patient, jailer and jailed, carry with them an erotic aura. With the exception of one idealized instance, the relationship between a mother and her mature son, love is for Freud always "love of authority," and the Oedipal complex originates this sad perplexity.

---

[39] The account of the "female" version of the Oedipal complex is less violent—she is disparaged for not possessing a penis, which guarantees, in turn, her inability to possess her mother—but it is no less shocking.

[40] For a fuller (and differently focused) treatment of this issue see Rieff's *Mind of the Moralist*, pp. 158–61.

Freud insists that wherever we throw our searching net, we will find Venus and Ares tightly embracing.

The Oedipal myth also anchors one of Freud's central axioms, that full satisfaction in erotic life (which to Freud is our most essential life) is humanly inaccessible. The kind of experience one would need to wither into such a truth is not pleasant to contemplate. But Freud believed that every quest fueled by the drives—and he did not admit to there being other sorts of quests—was bound to fail. Philip Rieff's observations on Freud's view of erotic "satisfaction" seem to me to be both accurate and profound:

> Freud did more than notice, with the Romantic novelists, that "something in the nature of the sexual instinct itself is unfavorable to the achievement of absolute gratification." He offered an answer: this "something" in the nature of the instinct that is unfavorable is its early attachment to the parents. The reason that "the value the mind sets on erotic need instantly sinks as soon as satisfaction becomes readily attainable" is that later loves are only surrogates for the original one. Though the child's desires for the parents are frustrated by the incest taboo, the sexual instinct remains related to its first object. The force of these original passions explains for Freud the individual's restiveness within monogamy, as it also accounts for the fatigue of promiscuity, whereby "the original object" is "represented by an endless series of substitutive objects none of which, however, brings full satisfaction." Far from being a champion of unbridled sensuality, Freud acutely understood the intimate connection between libertine and ascetic behavior. Both are excesses, derived from an imperfect emancipation from childhood's insatiable love of authority-figures. . . . If from Freud we may infer that monogamy is not a very satisfactory arrangement, the results of his science may also be taken to show that man is a naturally faithful creature: the most inconstant sexual athlete is in motivation still a toddler, searching for the original maternal object.[41]

Freud is right about the impossibility of human satisfaction if and only if erotic desire is genuinely the ruling paradigm (or the origin) for all other human desires. The Romantics sometimes ascribed that preeminence to the visionary urge, and they might have found in the speculative extravagances of Freud some evidence for the contention. Nevertheless, to the extent that we experience in our own lives the truth of Freud's normative pronouncements on desire, we must recognize in the myth of the Oedipal complex an account for the origins of that sorrow that is hard to better.

These are but a few of the explanatory reaches of the Oedipal complex. It addresses other questions as well: why women and men experience the demands of authority so differently; why women may feel that their failures derive from deep inadequacy; why men may feel that theirs are the

---

[41] Ibid., p. 166.

product of an internalized force that is always already limiting them; why civilization, our prime guarantor of comfort, provokes such relentless unease. It would not be entirely a mistake to see the rest of Freud's career as a process of developing the implications of this one metaphor of desire and loss. Thus the Oedipal myth earns its "inevitability" by being comprehensive. It is an economical narrative, but it is capable of explaining a great range and diversity of phenomena.

Still, as much as I admire the genius of the Oedipal myth, I find it quite troubling in its social effects. These effects are many, but I want to close this chapter by drawing on Foucault to consider two that are of particular contemporary note. The first involves the way that Freudian thinking contributes to the prevailing conception of power as an exclusively negative or repressive force. Power has been theorized throughout most of the Western tradition as being a force that denies, a conception that Freud's theory of repression works to underwrite. So, too, power has generally been construed as emanating from monolithic origins: the state, the court, the law, the father, the bourgeoisie, the super-ego. The results of this particular understanding have been many, but most significant among them may be a tendency to allegorical simplification in normative thought: one may become power's opposite, purely innocent, purely just; one may overthrow power by confronting negative and repressive with "liberating" force; one may appropriate power and no longer be its subject. In short, full liberation is at least theoretically possible. If restraint is conceived of as a blocking agency, then that agency might be lifted.[42] Within Freud's thought, then, there lies what I take to be a nostalgia for a state of being that is innocent of power.

Foucault's critique of power, which is itself, I think, significantly flawed, still provides a useful challenge to Freud and the tradition by arguing that power is never susceptible to clear allegorization, and never solely repressive.[43] To Foucault power is (note how the insight is transferred from Saussure's semiotics) never essential, always relational. Power is a force of creation that traverses every intersubjective relationship and that "produces things, . . . induces pleasure, forms knowledge, produces discourse. It needs to be considered as a productive network

[42] I am drawing here on the interview entitled "Truth and Power" in *The Foucault Reader*, ed. Paul Rabinow (New York: Pantheon Books, 1984), pp. 51–75. See also Foucault's *Discipline and Punish: The Birth of the Prison*, trans. Alan Sheridan (New York: Pantheon, 1977), especially pp. 23–31.

[43] Chief among these would be Foucault's refusal to make historical distinctions among various manifestations of power, such that power becomes an absolute, independent, perhaps even a transcendent, force in his thinking. See the critique Frank Lentricchia offers along these lines in *Ariel and the Police*, pp. 29–102.

which runs through the whole social body."[44] This vision of power as a creative and pervasive force calls into doubt Freud's ideologically more tractable version of power as either, on the one hand, founded upon the Oedipal resolution, largely unchangeable and thus a cause for despair or, on the other hand, as simply repressive and therefore, at least in an idealized sense, a force one might at some time completely evade—which offers a motive for simplistic hope. Both alternatives are likely to be politically debilitating. They do not allow for the kinds of complicated readings of a situation that can effectively orient action.

But there is, I think, a more serious social effect that might be justly associated with the cultural centrality of the Oedipus complex. Normative psychoanalysis has habitually presented itself as a discourse of liberation. The Oedipal myth ostensibly provides terms through which one might clarify, and by clarifying begin to alter, one's relations to loved objects and figures of authority. Difficulties arise not only because of Freud's monolithic concept of repression, but also because of the way the explanatory resources of the Oedipal myth are put to use. For even as the myth provides "illumination," each explanatory resource works as a matrix for a narrative that is both *individualizing* ("It's *my* Oedipal complex, the record of *my* peculiar experience") and *totalizing* ("It's *the* Oedipal complex, the one that Freud theorized"). By defying the taboo on speaking of incest, we engage in what seems to be a liberating exercise. But perhaps what we are chiefly doing is helping to consolidate the theoretical structure of the Oedipal complex, which determines the forms of our life stories and thus, in some measure, of our lives. The personalized version of the Oedipal narrative that each person engenders, or has engendered for him, helps render him more apparently stable, both to himself and to others. That is, it renders him more susceptible to domination, control, and limit.[45] He becomes what Freud himself never was, a Freudian subject.

It is thus tempting to oppose Freud's Romantic, "self-creating" drive to the kinds of accommodations that his normative terms represent. But that is a move that would need to be severely questioned. There was, as I see it, a great deal to admire in Freud's year-long stay in the regions of speculation, where he seems to have held all myths of identity in suspension and extemporized freely on his own nature. But that period ended not with a private vision of selfhood, fitted only to himself, but with the "realization" of a universal truth about all selves, a truth that has served the interests of the social norm.

---

[44] *Foucault Reader*, p. 61.

[45] On the power effects of the modern "discourse on sexuality" see Foucault's *The History of Sexuality*, vol. 1, *An Introduction*, trans. Robert Hurley (New York: Pantheon, 1978).

Freud is impressively inventive when he forges his own literary genealogy, making himself the ancestor and heir of Sophocles and Shakespeare,
and surely he is exhilarating, if a touch grandiose, in his drive to displace
literature with the new science of psychoanalysis. But one should remember that this self-canonizing gesture signifies as it does because it plays off
the normative terms that Freud is setting in place. Overcoming the paternal tradition and achieving sole possession of the oracle register as transcendent gestures in part because in formulating the Oedipal complex,
Freud is demonstrating to his readers that such triumphs are for all purposes humanly inaccessible. The Oedipal complex affirms that our fathers
make us who we are: we will never overcome their legacy. And it affirms
that we will never possess the love object we desire, the parent of the
opposite gender. In his own Oedipal passage Freud triumphs over both of
these limitations, at least imaginatively. But the reader is left characterized as the circumscribed subject of the Oedipal complex. Freud's Romantic gesture is thus inseparable from the limits his texts would impose
upon his readers. So tightly are the two strands, the normative and the
Romantic, intertwined that it is impossible, however desirable it would
be, to affirm Freud the Romantic overreacher and dismiss his law-giving
shadow.

The question we are left with, and which provides a great deal of the
impetus for the pages to come, is whether there can be a Romantic drive
for self-creation, in Freud or in anyone else, that does not work by denigrating the image of another. Does Romantic self-creation always involve
some form of scapegoating? Or does it provide what most of the Romantics seemed to hope for, inspiring possibilities for all women and men to
be active in the fashioning and refashioning of themselves?

We can go on to put this sort of question even to Freud's work, because
the image of selfhood provided in *The Interpretation of Dreams* is anything but final. Freud's vision of the narcissistic ego, first articulated in
1914, assimilates the Oedipal myth to the myth of Narcissus and arrives
at new terms not only for the "normal" human subject, for psychoanalytic patients, and for the analysts who will carry Freud's legacy into the
future, but for the founder himself.

Chapter Two

NEW THRESHOLDS: "ON NARCISSISM,
AN INTRODUCTION," 1914

THE NEXT major moment of transformation in Freud's work is far different from the drama of inception at the center of *The Interpretation of
Dreams*. The crisis of "On Narcissism" in 1914 is not that of a young,
rebellious spirit at ambivalent war with orthodoxy. Freud is now an authority in his own right, the founder and head of the psychoanalytic
movement. His effort in the 1914 text is to reconsolidate his power and
defend himself against the apostasy within his own ranks and latent
within his own writing. Yet even as he seeks to enforce normative continuity Freud is, imaginatively, at his most self-extemporizingly Romantic.
"On Narcissism" opens the major speculative phase of Freud's career, a
phase that does not culminate until "Analysis Terminable and Interminable." The difficulty of uncovering the dialectic of Freud's drives for continuity and for novelty in "On Narcissism" is formidable, for Freud is so
sophisticated here that he seems to anticipate almost any contemporary
interpretation that one might offer. This chapter approaches Freud, then,
by way of an intellect at least as large and subtle as his own. In Milton's
Paradise Lost, which Freud identified as his favorite poem, one finds the
terms to illuminate the literary designs of "On Narcissism."

I

On August 16, 1882, the twenty-six-year-old Sigmund Freud wrote a letter to his fiancée, Martha Bernays, in which he expressed his devotion to
the history and literature of England:

> I am taking up again the history of the island, the works of the men who were
> my real teachers—all of them English or Scotch, and I am recalling what is
> for me the most interesting historical period, the reign of the Puritans and
> Oliver Cromwell with its lofty monument of that time—*Paradise Lost*, where
> only recently, when I did not feel sure of your love, I found consolation and
> comfort.[1]

Freud's consolation probably came from one of his favorite passages in
the first book, in which Satan exhorts Beelzebub to rise up from the fiery

[1] Jones, *Life and Work of Freud*, 1:179.

lake and move with him to the shore: "Thither let us tend" (1:183), says
Satan,

> And reassembling our afflicted Powers,
> Consult how we may henceforth most offend
> Our Enemy, our own loss how repair,
> How overcome this dire Calamity,
> What reinforcement we may gain from Hope,
> If not what resolution from despair.
>
> (1.186–91)[2]

The lines may often have served as a spiritual rallying point for Freud,
who, like Satan and the poet who created him, often awakened his own
powers by invoking images of ruthless, potent adversaries. Freud even
considered using this Miltonic passage as the epigraph to *The Interpretation of Dreams* before settling on the famous lines from Virgil.[3]

The letter to Martha was probably written during that ten-year period
in which Freud read "nothing but English books."[4] Yet his involvement
with Milton's epic continued. Twenty-five years after the letter, when he
had published *The Interpretation of Dreams, The Psycho-pathology of
Everyday Life, Three Essays on Sexuality*, and a number of other manifestly psychoanalytical works, Freud received a letter from a Viennese
publisher, Hugo Heller, inviting him to submit a list of "ten good books."
Freud's good books included works by Twain, Macaulay, and Kipling,
but he added other categories to his response. "Nor did you even ask for
my 'favorite books,' " Freud wrote, "among which I should not have for-
gotten Milton's *Paradise Lost*."[5]

That Freud named John Milton among his "real teachers" and revered
Paradise Lost throughout his life will surprise only those who accept
Freud's reticence about naming "literary sources" as proof that literature
was of little consequence to the genesis of psychoanalysis. For most readers, though, the figurative action of Freud's text has been to some degree
absorbed by the claims psychoanalytical discourse makes for literal authority. The pages that follow attempt to awaken the literary elements of
the 1914 essay "On Narcissism, An Introduction"[6] by placing it beside a
moment in *Paradise Lost*: Eve's infatuation with her image in the pool, a

---

[2] Hughes, ed., *Milton: Complete Poems and Major Prose*. Here and henceforth references
to *Paradise Lost* will appear in the body of the text by book and line number.

[3] See Harold Bloom's *Agon*, p. 112.

[4] Jones, *Life and Work of Freud*, 1:21.

[5] Ibid., 3:422; also *Standard Edition*, 9:245–7.

[6] Richard Wollheim rightly takes the essay as the starting point for an account of the final
phase of Freud's work. See *Sigmund Freud*, pp. 201–52.

scene that occurs in book 4. Milton's text will, in effect, read Freud's and
bring the symbolic action of Freudian "self-creation" to the foreground.[7]
The chapter does not posit a detailed dynamic of influence between "On
Narcissism" and the "Narcissus" passage in *Paradise Lost*. (Freud's uneasiness about the literary in general, and about the poetic lineage of the
Narcissus topos in particular,[8] proves to be more determining than any
localized unease about Milton.) Rather, these pages outline some concurrences of symbolic action in the texts of Freud and Milton, which I take
to be of general significance in the Western tradition. Milton and Freud
are in remarkable (though hardly complete) accord in the ways that they
represent authority and its transmission, the achievement of authorial
voice, the workings—and dangers—of imagination, the structure of rebellion, the forms of erotic love, and a number of other subjects, all of
which I focus under the rubric of "self-creation." The complex play of the
normative and the Romantic in Freud's essay is here brought to light by
comparison to the tensions in *Paradise Lost* between Milton's urge to be
piously faithful and his desire to write an unprecedented work of literary
imagination, to "see and tell / Of things invisible to mortal sight."

In the following section I chart some of the immediate similarities between "On Narcissism" and Eve's scene at the pool. Establishing initial
coherencies clears the way for questionings of a more obstinate sort.

II

> For the world enjoys itself, and in itself all things that
> are. . . . The world itself can have no loves or any want
> (being content with itself) unless it be of discourse.
> —Francis Bacon, *De dignitate et augmentis scientarum*

---

[7] Cleanth Brooks, in an essay published in 1954, anticipates but does not develop this
approach. Brooks writes,

> The psychology of Eve is sound and convincing. To the student of Freud it may seem
> even preternaturally so; for Milton has made Eve recapitulate the whole process of the
> child's growing up and transferring the affections to the other sex. According to Freud,
> the child must transcend the mother image with which it has first associated warmth,
> nourishment, and affection, and center its affections elsewhere. In the case of the female
> child the task is more difficult, for it must transcend an image of its own sex.

See "Eve's Awakening," in *Essays in Honor of Walter Clyde Curry* (Nashville, Tenn.: Van-
derbilt University Press, 1954), p. 285.

[8] For a catalogue of literary incidents of the Narcissus topos in the Western tradition,
which run well past a thousand, see Louise Vinge, *The Narcissus Theme in Western Literature*, trans. Robert Dewsnap (Lund: Gleerups, 1967).

In the passage from Milton, Eve, with Satan listening in close by, recalls the circumstances of her nativity for Adam.[9] She tells him that her first impulse upon awakening had been to question her identity and origins:

> I first awak't, and found myself repos'd
> Under a shade on flow'rs, much wond'ring where
> And what I was, whence thither brought, and how.

(4.450–52)

In a certain sense, Eve receives two answers to her enquiries. The first response derives, apparently, from the natural world and presents her with visual emblems of her birth and identity:

> Not distant far from thence a murmuring sound
> Of waters issu'd from a Cave and spread
> Into a liquid Plain, then stood unmov'd
> Pure as th' expanse of Heav'n . . .

(4.453–56)

Eve seems to be seeing the pool born, delivered from the cave amid maternal murmurings. Her first sight, then, is potentially a fiction of her own genesis, a myth that is prior to language, culture, and the law.

The "Shape" that appears in the pool, offering Eve "answering looks / Of sympathy and love" (464–65), is a self-image invested with maternal tenderness.[10] Nature seems to respond to Eve's initial anxieties about origins and identity with intimations of a gentle self-generation: mother and self are combined in a composite image. Though this image of self-mothering appears to calm Eve somewhat, her interpretation of the scene will remain incomplete until she applies imaginative reason to it retrospectively, in an action analogous to Freud's *Nachträglichkeit*. Eve's description of the play between herself and the shape borrows a technique of verbal mirroring from the scene's matrix in pagan poetry, the Narcissus

[9] This scene has drawn progressively more attention from readers of *Paradise Lost*, and I am grateful to Louis L. Martz for emphasizing its importance to me. Notable recent commentary includes Cleanth Brooks, "Eve's Awakening"; Northrop Frye, "The Revelation to Eve," in *Paradise Lost: A Tercentenary Tribute*, ed. Balachandra Rajan (Toronto: University of Toronto Press, 1969), pp. 18–47; Arnold Stein, *The Art of Presence* (Berkeley and Los Angeles: University of California Press, 1977), pp. 93–97; Patricia Parker, "The Vision of Eve," in *Inescapable Romance* (Princeton, N.J.: Princeton University Press, 1979), pp. 114–23; Maureen Quilligan, *Milton's Spenser* (Ithaca, N.Y.: Cornell University Press, 1983), pp. 226–44; Diane Kelsey McColley, *Milton's Eve* (Urbana: University of Illinois Press, 1983), pp. 74–86; and Christine Froula, "When Eve Reads Milton: Undoing the Canonical Economy" (which anticipates a few points of my own approach), in *Canons*, ed. Robert von Hallberg (Chicago: University of Chicago Press, 1984), pp. 149–75.

[10] See William Kerrigan, *The Sacred Complex: On the Psychogenesis of "Paradise Lost"* (Cambridge, Mass.: Harvard University Press, 1983), p. 74.

sequence in Ovid's *Metamorphoses*. Thus the scene in which Eve encounters her reflection itself reflects, although with purifying distortions, a prior text:

> A Shape within the wat'ry gleam appear'd
> Bending to look on me, I started back,
> It started back, but pleas'd I soon return'd,
> Pleas'd it return'd as soon . . .
>
> (4.461–64)

It is as though Eve's narration absorbed Ovid's Echo, using verbal reflection to represent the visual doublings of her form in the water. In a passage that activates tensions between the seen and the spoken, repeated image and unique pronouncement, these lines occupy a richly ambiguous place.

Turning to Freud, one finds a representation of an early stage of life, comparable to what Eve experiences by the pool, defined as "primary narcissism," the developmental stage between autoeroticism and object love: "We are bound to suppose that a unity comparable to the ego cannot exist in the individual from the start; the ego has to be developed. The auto-erotic instincts, however, are there from the very first; so there must be something added to auto-eroticism—a new psychical action—in order to bring about narcissism" (14:76–77).

In the "auto-erotic stage" the infant takes sexual pleasure from discrete bodily parts, in "narcissism" he has developed an attraction to his entire body conceived for the first time as a totality. "Narcissism differs from autoeroticism," Richard Wollheim writes, "in that it involves a concept of the infant's own person or ego: the infant loves himself *as himself*."[11] Jacques Lacan's implicit reading of "On Narcissism," his essay on "The Mirror Stage," usefully locates the psychoanalytic Narcissus scene in a misapprehension in the realm of the Imaginary, before the intervention of the Symbolic.[12] Thus "primary narcissism," in the spirit of Eve's self-infatuation, is self-love prior to self-consciousness; it is self-love that, because it is confined within images (or the imaginary, as Lacan would have it), cannot name itself. By advancing the trope of the "stade du miroir" Lacan restores the poetic imagery of the Narcissus myth, which Freud's cooler term, "narcissism," attempts to absorb and transform. The next movement in Milton's passage offers fertile possibilities to continue re-mythologizing "On Narcissism."

Both originary states, Eve's desire for the "shape within the wat'ry

---

[11] Wollheim, *Sigmund Freud*, p. 126.
[12] "The Mirror Stage as Formative of the Function of the I," in *Écrits*, trans. Alan Sheridan (New York: W. W. Norton, 1977), pp. 1–7.

gleam" and Freud's "primary narcissism," undergo a significant disruption. In Milton's text a voice intervenes to draw Eve away from her reflection:

> there I had fixt
> Mine eyes till now, and pin'd with vain desire,
> Had not a voice thus warn'd me, What thou seest,
> What there thou seest fair Creature is thyself . . .
>
> (4.465–68)

The voice insinuates itself into the scene of mirrorings by framing a near repetition. But the interjected word "there" delicately begins to undo Eve's fascination with pure iteration. By introducing an element of temporal movement, repetition with difference, it brings Eve's desire under the limiting rule of time. The intrusion of the voice also summarily asserts the power of speech over image and of the invisible over the seen, relationships of some importance, I think, to the genesis of *Paradise Lost*. The voice protects Eve (although at a cost) from the shock of Narcissus's discovery: "iste ego sum."

This insertion of paternal, commanding voice has, for Milton, a textual genealogy. The voice's most conspicuous ancestor is the ironic intrusion by the narrator in Ovid's Narcissus story.[13] When Narcissus becomes captivated by his image, the narrator issues a warning: "O fondly foolish boy, why vainly seek to clasp a fleeting image? What you seek is nowhere; but turn yourself away, and the object of your love will be no more. That which you behold is but the shadow of a reflected form and has no substance of its own. With you it comes, with you it stays, and it will go with you—if you can go."[14] The narrator's admonitions cannot penetrate an event in the mythic past, but they serve to point up the part that being immune to the voice of the *auctor* plays in Narcissus's fate.

Two other versions of the myth Milton would have known occur in Spenser and Shakespeare. In book 3 of *The Faerie Queene* Britomart's nurse, Glauce, intervenes with a speech to convince Britomart that the image she has fallen in love with in the magical mirror is not her own, but that of another, Artegal. ("Nought like . . . that same wretched boy [who] / Was of himselfe the idle Paramoure" [3.2.45].) In *Twelfth Night* Viola pronounces the curse of Narcissus on Olivia: "Love make his heart of flint that you shall love, / And let your fervor . . . be / Plac'd in contempt"

---

[13] There are of course important analogies within the Christian tradition itself, particularly in the Book of Job. In Milton's own work it might be useful to compare Eve's scene with the passage in *Paradise Regained* (1.289) in which Christ, standing in his baptismal pool, hears the intervening voice of the Father, which confers upon the Son "Authority . . . from Heaven."

[14] Ovid, *Metamorphoses*, p. 155.

(2.1.286–88). Olivia passes beyond narcissistic attraction (a Freudian reading might hold), when she becomes deeply enough initiated into convention to sense that "Viola" echoes "Olivia" too closely. "Viola" is a narcissistic doubling, a woman, rather than the completely other, Sebastian. On the periphery is Malvolio, who never understands what his name means and persists, "sick of self-love" (1.5.90), "practicing behavior to his own shadow" (2.5.17). Eve does hear the voice and is reborn into self-consciousness. Implanted with the "umpire conscience" (3:195) and a social sense, she is suddenly aware of being an object for another. The voice promises Eve new reflections, though slightly displaced, "hee / Whose image thou art" (471–72) and "multitudes like thyself" (474).

Then the voice leads Eve to Adam, transferring the powers of language to the man (Eve is still silent). In their first encounter Eve and Adam reproduce the scene at the pool, with Eve being drawn back to her image— in what Freud might call "secondary narcissism"—and Adam taking the part of the intervening voice to exert his claims:

> what could I do,
> But follow straight, invisibly thus led?
> Till I espi'd thee, fair indeed and tall,
> Under a Platan, yet methought less fair,
> Less winning soft, less amiably mild,
> Than that smooth wat'ry image; back I turn'd,
> Thou following cri'd'st aloud, Return fair Eve,
> Whom fli'st thou? Whom thou fli'st, of him thou art . . .
>
> (4.475–82)

This structure of self-fascination, intervention of voice, and the subsequent transformation of the subject also dominates the form of Eve's narrative. In telling Adam the story, she seems to become again fascinated by repetition:

> I started back,
> It started back, but pleas'd I soon return'd,
> Pleas'd it return'd as soon . . .
>
> (4.462–64)

Suddenly Eve intervenes upon herself in the way the voice had, deploying the subtly potent word "there": "there I had fixt / Mine eyes till now, and pin'd with vain desire" (465–66). With similar effect Adam's first word to Eve, "return," echoes through her narration.[15] Eve's seeming capacity

---

[15] "Pleas'd I soon return'd, / Pleas'd it return'd" (463–64); "back I turn'd" (480). Notice also the linguistic troping of the visual image in the phrase "answering looks" (464), suggesting the ascendency of the verbal over the visual.

to recall the voice's pronouncements verbatim and her introductory remark, "That day I oft remember," combine to intensify one's sense of
how deeply Eve has been impressed by the events.

The voice has imposed another answer to Eve's "wond'ring where /
And what I was," which usurps the prior visual tropes of self-generation.
To replace the "wat'ry image" as a potential figure of identity, the voice
confers a name upon her, "Mother of human Race," which Adam translates as "Eve." Eve *is* her name now, not her image, and the voices that
name her become her symbolic progenitors, as the self-image in the pool
had been. It would not be so easy to call the image in the pool and the
voice comparable, though contending, tropes, if the voice were clearly
that of Eve's maker. But the voice is not so attributed in this passage, and
in fact it is never securely assigned. Eve is here reconstituted, if only temporarily, by an imposed system of discourse that appropriates her into its
laws.[16] Where the first, maternal scene of genesis had offered her the prospect of *being in herself,* she is now a *being for* or *being in relation to
others.*[17] This second birth into self-awareness presents itself, moreover,
as a Miltonic allegory for the transmission and internalization of authority. In this transmission the subject's desires undergo a reaiming: where
there was image there is voice, where there was self there is authoritative
other. The process is, for Milton, bound intimately to the transfer of language from a higher source, a transfer analogous, perhaps, to the one that
effects the composition of *Paradise Lost.*

This intervention of commanding voice has a distinctive parallel in the
text of Freud. "Narcissism," as Freud understands it, is no more permanent than "auto-eroticism." Primary narcissism gives way to the "castration complex": "in boys, anxiety about the penis—in girls envy for the
penis" (14:92). The "castration complex" occurs at the point in the

---

[16] Bryan Jay Wolf's reading of this scene in his fine book *Romantic Re-Vision* (Chicago:
University of Chicago Press, 1982), pp. 82–88, is more normative in spirit than my own:
"Eve's act of renunciation, whether of narcissistic self-image or pastoral plentitudes, is followed by the affirmation of an order in which the individual plays only a subordinate
part. . . . The model of maturation she presents is a paradigm of both the evolution of sublime poetics and of the self's movement outside itself to God through the power and guidance of grace" (p. 88).

[17] Again, Lacan may be helpful: "Qu'un nom, si confus soit-il, désigne une personne de-
terminée, c'est exactement en cela que consiste le passage à l'état humain. Si on doit définir
à quel moment l'homme devient humain, disons que c'est au moment où, si peu que ce soit,
il entre dans la relation symbolique." *Le Seminaire de Jacques Lacan* (Paris: Éditions Du
Seuil, 1975), 1:178. Fredric Jameson has translated this passage in his "Imaginary and Symbolic in Lacan," *Yale French Studies* 55–56 (1977): 338–95: "That a name, no matter how
confused, designates a particular person—this is precisely what the passage to the human
state consists in. If we must define that moment in which man [*sic*] becomes human, we
would say that it is at that instant when, as minimally as you like, he enters into a symbolic
relationship" (p. 362).

child's development when the fear of the father's power causes the child to internalize him as a figure of authority. "The phallus is an essential component of the child's self-image, so any threat to the phallus is a radical danger to this image."[18] The father's threat to the child dissolves her or his primary narcissism: it enforces a prohibition on the maternal object for both the boy and the girl, and initiates the girl's desire for the penis. (As Freud says later, "She rebels against [the] unwelcome state of affairs" [21:229].) The boy's feeling of vulnerability and the girl's perception of her inadequacy serve, in Freud's model, to undo the illusions of self-perfection they have so far sustained. The dissolution of primary narcissism and the subsequent internalization of authority result in the setting up of an agency in the unconscious that Freud names for the first time in "On Narcissism," the "ego-ideal." (The "ego-ideal" is the child's image of what she or he ought to be, after the child's claims to perfection have been denied by the judgments implicit in the father's threat of castration [for the boy], or in his refusal to supply a penis [for the girl]):

> This ideal ego is now the target of the self-love which was enjoyed in childhood by the actual ego. The subject's narcissism makes its appearance displaced on to this new ideal ego, which, like the infantile ego, finds itself possessed of every perfection that is of value. . . . What [the subject] projects before him as his ideal is the substitute for the lost narcissism of his childhood in which he was his own ideal. (14:94)

The intrusion that dissolves Eve's self-infatuation (with the same swiftness, though hardly the severity, with which the castration threat undoes primary narcissism) offers her a comparable ideal image of her future state as "Mother of human Race." It is significant that this "image" is conveyed to Eve through language, which is exactly how Freud's "ego-ideal" is made manifest to the subject. The "ego-ideal" is responsible for the ego's sense of being observed critically by an invisible agency, which makes its strictures known "by the medium of the voice" (14:96).[19] The extreme instance of this phenomenon is found in paranoics, yet their situation only extends and exaggerates the norm:

[18] J. Laplanche and J. B. Pontalis, *The Language of Psycho-analysis*, trans. Donald Nicholson-Smith (New York: W. W. Norton, 1973), p. 57.

[19] The precise relationship between the terms *ego-ideal* (Ichideal) and *super-ego* (Über-Ich, first introduced by Freud in the 1923 text *The Ego and the Id*) is not easy to determine. At some points, such as in *The Ego and the Id*, Freud uses the terms synonymously. In the *New Introductory Lectures* (1933) the ego ideal seems to be but one aspect of the super-ego, which embodies the three functions "of self-observation, of conscience and of the ideal." (See Laplanche and Pontalis, *Language of Psycho-analysis*, pp. 144–45.) Consistently, however, Freud associates the "super-ego" with voice and with "verbal residues." "It is as impossible for the super-ego as for the ego to disclaim its origin from things heard," Freud notes in *The Ego and the Id* (19:52).

Patients of this sort complain that all their thoughts are known and their
actions watched and supervised; they are informed of the functioning of this
agency by voices which characteristically speak to them in the third person. . . . This complaint is justified; it describes the truth. A power of this
kind, watching, discovering and criticizing all our intentions, does really exist. Indeed, it exists in every one of us in normal life. (14:95)

In the paranoic, the "evolution of conscience is reproduced regressively"
because of his urge "to liberate himself from . . . influences" (14:96).
Later in this chapter, I show how Eve's fall is related to a revolt against
an anterior version of the censorious voice Freud describes. By listening
to Satan she is hoping to replace the voice that captivates her at the pool
with another, one ostensibly more of her own devising.

.   .   .

A number of other immediate parallels bring Freud's essay and Milton's
Narcissus scene into contact with one another. The texts offer similar
paths of development by which the woman can supersede her initial self-
love. The voice at the pool cannily attempts to displace Eve's love for her
own image by promising her generations of offspring: "Multitudes like
thyself" (474). Freud offers a comparable path for "narcissistic" women:
"In the child which they bear, a part of their own body confronts them
like an extraneous object, to which, starting out from their narcissism,
they can then give complete object-love" (14:89–90). Yet Milton's text is
less concerned with this option for the undoing of Eve's self-love than
with a remedy of another kind that fully anticipates the Freudian category
of "sublimation."

A normative reading of Milton's passage might describe it as a heuristic
progress in which Eve learns the true uses of the word "fair." When the
voice addresses Eve as "fair creature," she seems to associate the term
with the attractiveness of the image in the water, and thus with herself.
This eroticized sense of the word comes out in Eve's description of her
first sight of Adam:

> I espi'd thee, fair indeed and tall,
> Under a Platan, yet methought less fair,
> Less winning soft, less amiably mild,
> Than that smooth wat'ry image . . .
>
> (4.477–80)

Eve turns back to her image, and Adam asserts the commanding voice
that has been transferred to him, calling "Return fair Eve." By "fair" the
male voices mean not only comely but (potentially) judicious, equitable.

In Eve's choice of Adam over her own image, a normative reading might maintain, her sense of the word "fair" undergoes a sort of Miltonic sublimation. The erotic content of the word is converted or sublimated to the uses of its "higher" ethical sense. The guarantor of the concept's power for Eve will be its investment with transformed erotic energy. Sublimation places eros in the service of culture or society—it depends upon "the capacity to exchange [an] originally sexual aim for another one, which is no longer sexual but which is psychically related to the first" (9:187). (Freud, of course, felt women to be far less capable of the process than men.) When Eve closes her account by professing that "wisdom . . . alone is truly fair," her commitment to the quotidian sublime seems assured. But Satan has a Freudian awareness of how precarious sublimation is and will make the ambiguities of "fair" (remember that he overhears Eve's account) a key to the temptation in book 9.

There is also significant agreement between Milton and Freud on the distinction between the early erotic orientations of women and men. Women, Freud observes, love principally in the "narcissistic way," and men in the "anaclitic," based on their early cathexis of the woman who feeds and tends them. As Laplanche points out, however, anaclitic attachment, no matter how Freud defines it, is invariably absorbed by the category of narcissism, "if not in every libidinal relation at least in every love relation."[20] So, too, Eve's self-love is inseparable from love of a mothering image; and Adam, who is supposed to love God subserviently and Eve condescendingly, seems prone to self-infatuation as well. Thus his words on seeing Eve: "Bone of my Bone, Flesh of my Flesh, my Self / Before me" (8.495–96). Self-love seems to be the dominant form of erotic commitment for both sexes in Milton and Freud, though both insist on its being characteristic of women.

Two other points of similarity bear remarking. Freud suggests that the "observing agency" might be involved with the genesis of the "time factor" (14:96, n. 1), which the intrusive voice, of course, introduces to Eve. In *Moses and Monotheism*, Freud associates the development of language, the invisibility of God, and the movement from matriarchy to a patriarchal order. These values, too, seem implicit in Eve's nativity scene.

Virginia Woolf gives the tendency to identify femininity with narcissism a satisfying twist in *A Room of One's Own*: "Women have served all these centuries as looking-glasses," she writes,

> possessing the magic and delicious power of reflecting the figure of man at twice its natural size. Without that power probably the earth would still be swamp and jungle. The glories of all our wars would be unknown. . . . Super-

---

[20] Jean Laplanche, *Life and Death in Psychoanalysis*, trans. Jeffrey Mehlman (Baltimore, Md.: The Johns Hopkins University Press, 1976), p. 77.

men and Fingers of Destiny would never have existed. The Czar and the Kaiser would never have worn their crowns or lost them. Whatever may be their use in civilized societies, mirrors are essential to all violent and heroic action.[21]

When Freud met Virginia Woolf in London in 1939, one is further gratified to learn, he brought her a gift of a narcissus plant.

Although the literary textures of "On Narcissism" are now apparent, not until we can see how Freud's figures are put into action will we have an authentic reading of the essay. The goal of such a reading is a fuller interpretation of Freud's tropes of "narcissism" and the "ego-ideal." Why, in 1914, did Freud feel compelled to posit a distinct agency of authority in the psyche, when up until that time the ego had been a sufficient figure for internal attempts to order and command the instincts? Why did a meditation on the particular topic of "narcissism" and engagement with the literary myth of Narcissus provoke the invention of a new center of authority, the "ego-ideal"? And how does Freud's fresh conception of the self stand in relation to the dialectic of the normative and the Romantic that informed the Oedipal passage in the *Traumdeutung*? If this Miltonic view of Freud is to be useful as a ground for criticism, it ought to help us see what the invention of the "ego-ideal" is doing for Freud, both theoretically and pragmatically. Thus in the section that follows I go back to *Paradise Lost* to interpret some of the broader meanings of self-love and self-mirroring in the poem and then observe what I take to be at least partial counterparts to Milton's symbolic action within the text of Freud.

III

But of this Tree we may not taste nor touch;
God so commanded, and left that Command
Sole Daughter of his voice . . .
Paradise Lost, 9.651–53

By listening to Eve's account to Adam, Satan learns all he needs to know to cause the Fall of Man. His "better teacher" is, in fact, the voice that intrudes on Eve, and that Milton criticism has usually not hesitated to call God's voice. Satan's technique is repetition: he replays the scene at the pool twice, once in Eve's dream and once at the climax of the poem, the temptation scene in book 9. Thus Satanic repetition sets out to undo Eve's appropriation by the voice, which was itself enforced by repetition. First comes the celestial voice, then Adam's voice, then Eve's own moment of

[21] (New York: Harcourt Brace, 1929), pp. 35–36.

self-restraint in her narrative. Satan's objective is to present Eve with the prospect of restoring for herself an earlier state of things dominated by repetitions of her own image. The temptation scene is Satan's foremost piece of dramatic revision.

In Eve's proleptic dream in book 4 Satan begins his action against the "warning voice." As the dreamer describes it,

> Methought
> Close at mine ear one call'd me forth to walk
> With gentle voice, I thought it thine; it said,
> Why sleep'st thou Eve?
>
> (5.35–38)

The voice Eve hears sounds like Adam's, which is in turn a descendant of the authoritative voice at the pool. Yet this time it invites her to look and be looked upon:

> Why sleep'st thou Eve? now is the pleasant time,
> The cool, the silent, save where silence yields
> To the night-warbling Bird, that now awake
> Tunes sweetest his love-labor'd song; now reigns
> Full Orb'd the Moon, and with more pleasing light
> Shadowy sets off the face of things; in vain,
> If none regard; Heav'n wakes with all his eyes,
> Whom to behold but thee, Nature's desire,
> In whose sight all things joy, with ravishment
> Attracted by thy beauty still to gaze.
>
> (5.38–47)

Now is the silent time, the dream voice whispers, "save where silence yields," not, as one would expect, to this new voice, but to "the night-warbling Bird," the counterpart, perhaps, of the "murmuring sound / Of waters" (4.453–54) in the first scene. The dream voice submerges its own presence in silence and in maternal, prelinguistic melodies. It is a voice before the birth of authoritative voice, hence "preposterous." What Satan begins here to offer Eve is the prospect of her own (lyric) voice as a permissive substitute for the prohibiting discourses of God, the epic poet par excellence, and of that unremitting essayist, Adam.

"Wonder not, sovran Mistress," Satan begins the temptation, "if perhaps / Thou canst, who are sole Wonder" (9.532–33). The verbal mirroring (Wonder / Wonder), a ploy Satan learns from Eve and the celestial voice, will make the temptation scene resound like an echo chamber. (William Empson makes a comparable point, claiming that Raphael prepares Eve for Satan's approach by promising the human pair that they might, in time, "wingd ascend / Ethereal, as wee . . ." In the dream, Satan promises that Eve will be "not to earth confin'd / But sometimes in the air, as wee . . ."[22]) Platonic wonder initiates philosophy, engaging an internal dialogue. Don't wonder, Satan says, subdue the second voice that brings self-consciousness or, rather, revise it into a verbal reflecting pool:

> Wonder not, sovran Mistress, if perhaps
> Thou canst, who are sole Wonder, much less arm
> Thy looks, the Heav'n of mildness, with disdain,
> Displeas'd that *I* approach thee *thus*, and gaze
> Insatiate, *I thus* single, nor have fear'd
> Thy *awful* brow, more *awful* thus retir'd.
> *Fairest* resemblance of thy Maker *fair*,
> Thee *all things* living gaze on, *all things* thine
> By gift, and thy Celestial Beauty adore
> With ravishment *beheld*, there best *beheld*
> Where universally admir'd . . .
>
> (9.532–42, emphases mine)

Satan understands fully the uneasiness of Eve's profession to Adam that "wisdom . . . alone is truly fair" (4.491), and he restores the erotic charge to the contested word by calling Eve "Fairest resemblance of thy Maker fair." The line also works to challenge the chain of authority seemingly secured in the fourth book. Adam, after all, is the one made in God's image: "Hee for God only, shee for God in him." Satan offers her Adam's place, transforming the hierarchically ordered succession of figures, God/Adam/Eve, into a reflection, Eve/God, God/Eve. Lars Engle writes with characteristic eloquence and insight on this subject:

> And since Satan shares Eve's sense of injury with respect to heavenly hierarchies, his advice can direct itself to her nature far more accurately than Raphael's did, and his hurt pride can understand part of her better even than Adam's love. He approaches her with subservience from below, as no articulate being has ever done before, and offers her a fantasy in which angels compensate her for Raphael's indifference to her presence.[23]

Eve is shocked and charmed to hear the serpent speak:

> What may this mean? Language of Man pronounc't
> By Tongue of Brute, and human sense exprest?
>
> (9.553–54)

The serpent's acquisition of "human voice" (9.561) from eating the fruit may lead Eve to hope for a comparable advance from her transgression:

---

[22] *Milton's God* (London: Chatto and Windus, 1965), pp. 147–50.

[23] See Engle's doctoral dissertation, "Character in Poetic Narrative: Action and Individual in Chaucer and Milton" (Yale University, 1983), pp. 188–89.

she wishes, perhaps, to possess her own voice, not God's, not Adam's. By calling God's prohibition of the fruit "that Command / Sole Daughter of his voice," Eve shows how voice and prohibition are bound with her conception of herself. Satan, for his part, is restoring to Eve a myth of self-origination in which she is no one's daughter but her own, and commands are unborn.

Eve's scene at the pool, as many critics have noticed, also directs us back to a description of an encounter in which Satan is fascinated by his own image. In book 2 Satan's impulse to rebel is represented as a self-mirroring creature with whom Satan falls in love before falling from heaven. Born out of Satan's forehead, Sin is herself "heav'nly fair" (2.757), and she tells Satan the story of her own generation somewhat as Eve tells Adam:

> Out of thy head I sprung: amazement seiz'd
> All th' Host of Heav'n; back they recoil'd afraid
> At first, and call'd me Sin, and for a Sign
> Portentous held me; but familiar grown,
> I pleas'd, and with attractive graces won
> The most averse, thee chiefly, who full oft
> Thyself in me thy perfect image viewing
> Becam'st enamor'd, and such joy thou took'st
> With me in secret, that my womb conceiv'd
> A growing burden.
>
> (2.758–67)

The issue of Satan's union with Sin is Death, a figure whose description as

> The other shape,
> If shape it might be call'd that shape had none
>
> (2.666–67)

seems to anticipate Eve's account of the "Shape within the wat'ry gleam." The corresponding word in Ovid is "umbra," which means both shadow and ghost, and darkly anticipates both of Milton's uses of "shape."

Why, one might ask, does Milton place Eve's infatuation with her image and her ambivalences about authoritative voice at the dramatic fulcrum of the Fall? And why does he make Satan's self-love and its incestuous consummation a primary figure for his rebellion? What accounts for the strong negative appeal for Milton of loving one's own image? More important for our purposes, how might a reading of Milton, guided by these questions, help illuminate that major commonplace of Freudian psychoanalysis, "narcissism"? Before turning to these problems, I want to look again at the text of "On Narcissism" and locate on its surfaces some Freudian reflections of Milton's extended uses of the trope of self-love.

· · ·

"On Narcissism" opens by considering a difficulty in clinical treatment. Freud has encountered a category of patients, "paraphrenics," who are inaccessible to the authority of the psychoanalyst and cannot be cured. The paraphrenic is untreatable because she cannot have a "transference," that is, she cannot invest the person of the analyst in therapy (or any other object outside herself) and is thus immune to treatment. The paraphrenic is repeating "primary narcissism," that point in earlier development that was supposedly dissolved by the intervention of parental voice. (One remembers the words of Ovid's Narcissus: "I'll die before I give you power over me.") The "narcissist," then, is one who, in attempting to reclaim an originary state (or for whatever other cause), is programmatically resistant to authority.

Freud goes on to find analogies for "narcissism" in the mental lives of children and of primitive people:

> In the latter we find characteristics which, if they occurred singly, might be put down to megalomania: an over-estimation of the power of their wishes and mental acts, the "omnipotence of thoughts," a belief in the thaumaturgic force of words, and a technique for dealing with the external world—"magic"—which appears to be a logical application of these grandiose premises. (14:75)

The issue of this belief in the "omnipotence of thought," of the preference for ideas over empirical fact, of egotism against respect for the principle of reality, comes up only a few pages later in "On Narcissism."

There Freud inveighs against one who refuses to accept his distinction between ego and object libido (a distinction Freud himself more or less surrendered in the 1920 text, *Beyond the Pleasure Principle*), accusing his adversary of a fondness for "speculative theory" (*spekulative Theorie*) at the expense of "empirical observation":

> It is true that notions such as that of an ego-libido, an energy of the ego-instincts, and so on, are neither particularly easy to grasp, nor sufficiently rich in content; a speculative theory [*spekulative Theorie*] of the relations in question would begin by seeking to obtain a sharply defined concept as its basis. But I am of opinion that that is just the difference between a speculative theory [*spekulative Theorie*] and a science erected on empirical interpretation. The latter will not envy [*neiden*] speculation [*Spekulation*] its privilege

of having a smooth [*glatten*], logically unassailable foundation, but will gladly content itself with nebulous, scarcely imaginable basic concepts, which it hopes to apprehend more clearly in the course of its development, or which it is even prepared to replace by others. For these ideas [*Ideen*] are not the foundation of science, upon which everything rests: that foundation is observation alone. They are not the bottom but the top of the whole structure, and they can be replaced and discarded without damaging it. (14:77)

The priority given to ideas, speculation, and theory aligns Freud's adversary with the type who characteristically overestimates the power of thoughts, attributing unrealistic capabilities to words and mental images. Nor would the classically educated interpreter, who found that dreams and parapraxes dissolve the boundaries among languages,[24] be unaware of the etymological commerce between "Spekulation" and the Latin word for mirror, *speculum*. The speculator sees what he wishes to see—sees, perhaps, his own image mirrored on the surface of phenomena.

The scientist's system is securely built (*gebaut*) and founded, and it does not need to "envy" (*neiden*) what is "smooth" (*glatt*). If these figures gesture only indirectly to an opposition between the sexes, the essay will not be long in dramatizing its polarities in exactly these terms. The speculator may have an "economic" motive as well. As the narcissist will not cathect erotic objects outside himself, so the speculator hopes to realize a windfall of results without investing in observation, in the empirical "objects" of investigation. The speculator and the narcissist demand profit without risk.

Freud's polemic in "On Narcissism" is directed specifically against Jung's monistic theory of libido and Adler's formulation of the masculine protest.[25] The defection of these two promising members of the first generation of psychoanalysts after Freud had provoked a crisis of continuity in the International Psychoanalytical Association.[26] Who, now that Jung, the "crown prince" designate,[27] had departed, would inherit the father's mantle and continue his work? Freud's anxiety is manifest in three figurative peregrinations, two in "On Narcissism" itself, one in the essay written between drafts of "On Narcissism," *On the History of the Psycho-analytic Movement*. The essay is less a history than a diatribe, fierce at times, against Jung and Adler. The two figures in "On Narcissism"

[24] George Steiner is good on this subject. See "A Remark on Language and Psychoanalysis" in *On Difficulty and Other Essays* (New York: Oxford University Press, 1978), pp. 48–60.

[25] Samuel Weber also sees the relations between Freud's polemic against the "speculators," Jung and Adler, and his formulation of the narcissistic ego. See *The Legend of Freud* (Minneapolis: University of Minnesota Press, 1982), pp. 3–31.

[26] See Jones *Life and Work of Freud*, 2:126–51.

[27] Ibid., 2:140.

come in the opening section and are deployed against Jung's assertion of a single libidinal type:

> The individual himself regards sexuality as one of his own ends; whereas from another point of view he is an appendage to his germ plasm, at whose disposal he puts his energies in return for a bonus of pleasure. He is the mortal vehicle of a (possibly) immortal substance—like the inheritor of an entailed property, who is only the temporary holder of an estate which survives him. (14:78)

Slightly later occurs a comparable passage:

> It may turn out that, most basically and on the longest view, sexual energy—libido—is only the product of a differentiation in the energy at work generally in the mind. But such an assertion has no relevance. It relates to matters which are so remote from the problems of our observation, and of which we have so little cognizance, that it is as idle to dispute it as to affirm it; this primal identity may well have as little to do with our analytic interests as the primal kinship of all the races of mankind has to do with the proof of kinship required in order to establish a legal right of inheritance. (14:79)

In *The History* Freud uses a related figure to illustrate the self-deceptions involved in Jung's desexualizing of the Oedipus complex:

> Suppose—to make use of a simile—that in a particular social group there lives a *parvenu*, who boasts of being descended from a noble family living in another place. It is pointed out to him, however, that his parents live somewhere in the neighbourhood, and that they are quite humble people. There is only one way of escape from his difficulty and he seizes on it. He can no longer repudiate his parents, but he asserts that they themselves are of noble lineage and have merely come down in the world; and he procures a family-tree from some obliging official source. (14:61)

At the center of each of these three passages is a figure with illusions about who he is and about his genuine place in a familial line of descent. There is the one who does not realize that his possession of the whole property, which so pleases him, obtains to serve higher social needs (keeping the estate from being distributed among a number of heirs and thus broken up); the parvenu who transparently attempts to repudiate his parents and fake his lineage; and the suggestion, in the second passage, of the fool who tries to establish legal kinship for the purpose of obtaining a legacy by claiming that all men are related because they descend from Eve and Adam. The figure overestimates his own importance and his own place. He does not understand that things will continue as they would have with or without his complicity. The law is the guarantor of continuity in these fables. The estate will be preserved intact; property will pass to the one who is legally deserving; and, presumably, the parvenu's bogus family tree will be quickly pulled up and the parents' humble lineage confirmed. In short, the law will intervene peremptorily on the one who has composed a self-aggrandizing myth of origins. The voice of the law will restore to the "narcissist," who has attempted to exert the power of imagination over the reality principle, his genuine progenitor, the work and person of Sigmund Freud.

It is easy enough, then, to identify the central figures in these brief allegories, speaking in one breath of Jung, Adler, women, narcissism, theoretical speculation, illusions of autochthony, the presumptuous litigant, and the parvenu—in short, of impulses one might associate with a Romantic drive—and in the next breath of Freud, masculinity, science, the reality principle, continuity, and the law of the norm. Accordingly, one will remember Freud's oft-repeated dictum: "The super-ego is the heir of the Oedipus Complex" and rephrase it slightly: "The super-ego is the heir to [Jung's] Oedipus Complex," or "The super-ego is the heir [instead of Jung] to the Oedipus Complex." Where continuity fails and "speculation" threatens science there has to be a strengthening of the law, a new severity. Seen from this perspective, the invention of the "ego-ideal" in 1914 appears to be a defensive move. Its deployment is against Jung's personal Oedipal wishes on Freud, Jung's enervated theory of the Oedipus complex, and Jung's abdication from the family of psychoanalysis. If Freud could not depend on Jung or on anyone else to continue his work, then he needed to make provisions on his own for the perpetuation of psychoanalysis after his death. What Freud did was to develop a new, more authoritative voice in which to present his vision and an image for that voice, the super-ego. The authority of the super-ego is, then, the authority that Freud aspired to have in culture. Accordingly, he will disseminate a super-ego's voice not only in his future texts, but also, as I show in the next chapter, in the therapeutic scene itself.

But surely it is too easy to say that the super-ego is the heir to the crisis of authority within the psychoanalytical ranks in 1912–1913, particularly if "crisis of authority" is understood in a restricted sense. There is more at stake here, beginning of course with Freud's own ambitions and particularly with his urge to engage in Romantic speculation. One might glance back for a moment at the fable of the parvenu and remember that the writer who called himself a conquistador was himself a newcomer who treasured his role as an outcast and a Jew in anti-Semitic Vienna, associating both of these things with his power to be original. One might also recall that no one has done more to fracture ideal conceptions of generational continuity than the inventor of the myth of the primal horde and the family romance. Nor is it irrelevant to recall that Freud's own intellectual career involved taking up "masters," like Brücke, Meynert, Fleischl, Charcot, Breuer, and Fliess, whose powers he overvalued and from whom he eventually broke or became estranged, sometimes because he would not stifle his own speculative urges. "On Narcissism," moreover, is arguably Freud's most speculative text to that point.

Freud's ambivalence over speculation is finally what is at stake here,[28] and the following pages show that Freud's invention of the "ego-ideal" functions both as a defense against his tendency to speculate and as an inspiration to do so. Speculation is a danger to Freud, I argue, to the extent that it implicates him in the literary: in textual terms the super-ego is the agency that intervenes on Freud's infatuated gaze into literary figuration (in the case of "On Narcissism" that means Ovid and Milton's texts) as it is embodied in the Western tradition and transforms those figures into the scientific discourse or law of psychoanalysis. The voice of the super-ego defends both Freud and his readers from the literary origins of psychoanalysis. It also defends Freud's own Romantic impulse by making it more difficult to detect and assaults the poetic drive in others in the name of the reality principle and the norm.

In Milton's text, too, one finds an ambivalence over self-love and the repeated image and a complex content and function for the "warning voice." I return now to these issues in *Paradise Lost* in order, finally, to reacquire a Miltonic position from which to extend this reading of "On Narcissism."

IV

> His mind seems to have united the sharpest contrasts. He was exact and sober in his physical and physiological researches, yet he did not shrink from the obscurities of mysticism, and built up cosmic speculations of astonishingly imaginative boldness.
> —Freud on Empedocles of Acragas, "Analysis Terminable and Interminable"

[28] A passage in Jones's *Life and Work of Freud* yields some further support:

Daring and unrestrained imagination always stirred Freud. It had captured him with Fliess years before, and to some extent with Jung. It was an integral part of his own nature to which he rarely gave full rein. . . . Still the sight of this unchecked imagination in others was something Freud could seldom resist, and the two men [Freud and Ferenczi] must have had enjoyable times together when there was no criticizing audience. When that happened there was always the risk of his native skeptical judgment yielding to the seduction of speculation. (2:158–59).

See also Philip Rieff in *Mind of the Moralist* (p. 26): "Though privately, in the letters to Fliess, he used the word 'speculative' pridefully, to convey his sense of his own theoretic daring, publicly he stood against speculation."

> The super-ego of an epoch of civilization has an origin similar to that of an individual. It is based on the impression left behind by the personalities of great leaders—men of overwhelming force of mind or men in whom one of the human impulsions has found its strongest and purest, and therefore often its most one-sided, expression. In many instances the analogy goes still further, in that during their lifetime these figures were—often enough, even if not always—mocked and maltreated by others and even dispatched in a cruel fashion. In the same way, indeed, the primal father did not attain divinity until long after he had met his death by violence.
>
> —Freud, *Civilization and Its Discontents*

Paradise Lost seems often to realize textually St. Augustine's description of God: a sphere whose circumference is nonexistent and whose center is everywhere. "Every word is to the purpose," as Richardson famously wrote, "there are no lazy intervals." Eve's nativity becomes a particularly important interpretive center, however, when we see its structural affinities with the invocation passage of the third book. John Guillory's reading of the invocation scene detects a crucial moment of suspension, or pure transition, between lines 37 and 38:

> Then feed on thoughts, that voluntary move
> Harmonious numbers . . .

Guillory comments:

> The status of "move" hovers momentarily as an intransitive before resolving itself as transitive with the unexpected object. Notice, however, that the subject has disappeared altogether (because the sentence is imperative), and Milton no longer needs to specify what mind is feeding upon what thoughts. Merely to have hesitated at this crossing—for a moment not to go across (intransire)—permits the influx of power that turns the invocation around.[29]

This moment of textual poise between "no longer" and "not yet" enacts syntactically a state of self-dispersal ("the subject has disappeared altogether") preliminary to the transference of divine authority to the poet. Guillory associates this transference with submission on the poet's part: Milton literally chooses his physical blindness and submits it as a sacrifi-

[29] *Poetic Authority: Spenser, Milton, and Literary History* (New York: Columbia University Press, 1983), p. 126.

cial offering to the Father, aware that He then may or may not be willing to extend poetic power as just compensation.

William Kerrigan, on whose book *The Prophetic Milton* Guillory relies, is attuned to the dialectical tension between submission and demand at work in the invocation's midspace:

Unwilling and unable to conceal himself, [Milton] permits his anguish free expression. The blind man has been denied the images of God in nature—denied the freshness of the turning seasons, the surpassing beauty of the human face. Though the blind man continues to worship the God of Light, requesting the compensatory vision of a holy prophet, he expresses a position beyond all compromise: without an inner light, blindness is utterly intolerable. We feel that even the refusal of God could not modify this necessary and radical condition. "So much the rather thou Celestial Light/Shine inward." Because of his daring integrity—man as well as man of God—we understand with irrefutable force that to serve is not indeed to be servile. He commands his tone, his humanity and his God.[30]

The fruitful dissension between Kerrigan and Guillory on the dynamics of power's transference in the invocation is already implicit in what remains the most formidable interpretation of Milton's passage, Wordsworth's scene of crossing at the Simplon Pass in book 6 of *The Prelude*, which I discuss in the next chapter.

For each of these readers the encounter of poetic and divine will is crucially antagonistic, involving conflict or the suppression of conflict and ending in a version of collaboration. The invocation's apostrophe to the light, prior to the poet's imaginative entry into the midspace, or *limen*, proves futile: "thou / Revisit'st not these eyes" (22–23). The resources of poetic rhetoric, acquired through the human dedication to art and craft of John Milton, are insufficient to effect his passage to authentic inspiration. Self-reliance and the painful withdrawal of the energies of the self from the world are not enough. By opening himself to an encounter with authoritative force, though, the poet is, in terms of symbolic action, reborn on the other side of the gap, authorized and augmented by superior power.

Eve's nativity scene in book 4 turns on a moment of suspension or staying in a region comparable to that middle space in which the invocation seems momentarily to hover. The instant of indeterminacy at the pool involves, of course, the silent echoing of looks, which Eve says she would never have resolved through her own powers: "there I had fixt / Mine eyes till now . . . / Had not a voice thus warn'd me . . ." The moment of poise in an uncertain middle space—here a "wat'ry gleam" rather than

[30] William Kerrigan, *The Prophetic Milton* (Charlottesville: University Press of Virginia, 1974), pp. 265–66. See also p. 154.

the invocation's "dim suffusion veil'd"—is also a moment of self-uncertainty: the subject has not "disappeared altogether," rather, it is inchoate, unconstituted. There is nothing dialectical, though, about the encounter with authority that follows. Eve's infatuation with her image and her uncertainties as to who or what she might be leave her vulnerable to being taken over by the voice that intercedes on her version of the threshold state. Rather than receiving an epic voice in a complex transfer, as the poet does, Eve is appropriated by a voice that speaks her—for it is in the rhetoric of this superior voice that she later relates her nativity to Adam.

What, one can now ask, is Milton doing for himself as a poet by restaging the invocation scene in Eve's sequence at the pool? What is it, exemplified by Eve and her attraction to her own image (comparable of course to Satan's attraction to his image, Sin), that needs to be so thoroughly disciplined, and why does the poem use the structure of the invocation scene to dramatize the process? Another way to pose the question might be this: what might Eve have realized for herself at the pool had not the voice so powerfully intervened?

·   ·   ·

When Job's creator asks him where he was when the earth rose from chaos, Job is humbled. He suddenly and very frighteningly knows a time when he was not as now. Eve's quest for origins seems open to a solution in terms, or rather in images, very much her own. The intervening voice, one might say, usurps from Eve access to the powerful fiction that the maternal self-image in the pool is her point of origin. Satan becomes a revolutionary in his own right by rejecting the pure Word of God, the Son, who God claims was Satan's creator.[31] By giving birth to his "own self-image," Sin, Satan figuratively (and parodically) fathers himself, and then he fathers a figure for his kingdom ("a universe of death") and his works. Sin and Death are Satan's response to God's decree that his Word, the Son, had created Satan and the rest of the angels. We "know none before us," Satan tells Abdiel,

> self-begot, self rais'd
> By our own quick'ning power . . .
>
> (5.860–61)

To both Satan and Eve images of self-creation present themselves as radical alternatives to the heavenly Word.

This contest between figures of representation, the image-making power or imagination versus the divine Word or inspiration,[32] is ex-

---

[31] See Kerrigan, *Sacred Complex*, p. 169, for fine commentary on this.

[32] A more historical account would also consider Puritan strictures against graven images here.

pressed, somewhat conventionally, in Adam's diagnosis of Eve's dream in book 5. "Imaginations" are composed of "aery shapes," and in dreams, when the rule of reason (Logos, speech) is in abeyance,

> Fancy wakes
> To imitate her; but misjoining shapes,
> Wild work produces oft . . .

> (5.110–12)

Imagination's business is with imitations (reflections) and with deceitful shapes—the "shape within the wat'ry gleam" that mesmerizes Eve, and that "other shape / If shape it might be call'd that shape had none" that Satan fathers from his self-image. These are the shapes of error in *Paradise Lost*, emblems of the power to frame fictions of self-generation and the power to create ex nihilo, which Milton denies even to God in *De Doctrina*. Proffering his blindness as a fit sacrifice for poetic inspiration in the invocation, Milton turns away symbolically from the image and the image-making power. This too is part of the price for divine inspiration.[33]

By petitioning for inspiration as a transference of power, Milton accepts a position in an authoritative chain linked by resemblance, but a resemblance that always recalls (as a condition of its power) its difference from, and submissiveness to, that which rules it. The Son "expresses" the Father (3.140; 6.720; 10.66–67) and stands as the Father's "image" in something like the way the poet of the invocation aspires to stand. One might speak of an ethics of signification in *Paradise Lost*, since all of blessed creation refers back to an ultimate signified, God. The Son, for instance, is a representation of God, but emphatically not a mirror image: "in him all his Father shone / Substantially express'd" (3.139–40). Rebellion in the poem is self-referential, autotelic: Derrida's critique of the theological residues in conventional theories of signification might have begun in a reading of Milton. The admission of secondariness and createdness that Milton offers in the book 3 invocation is explicitly at odds with a sensibility like Eve's that threatens to find in her image not only a beloved object, but her own beginnings. When Adam piously and a little bumptiously responds to Raphael's question about human origins by saying,

> For Man to tell how human Life began
> Is hard; for who himself beginning knew?

> (8.250–51)

---

[33] My distinction between "Imagination and Inspiration" derives from Owen Barfield's essay of that title in *Interpretation*, ed. Hopper and Miller, pp. 54–76.

Eve might well have interjected her (imaginary) knowledge of women's origins.

This contest between, to phrase it bluntly, imagination and inspiration, image and voice, self-generation and createdness—or, to look ahead to Freud somewhat, between the urge to speculate Romantically and the urge to give laws, enforce the norm—would be of little consequence without a strong authorial ambivalence. Though Milton seems on one level to repudiate Eve's self-love, on another she may be, as Hazlitt said, "the idol of the poet's imagination." The poet who submits in the invocation and who apparently disciplines Eve at the pool is also fiercely committed to priority: "Things unattempted yet in Prose or Rhyme" (1.16). The unattempted is the principal temptation of the poet who, in the first book, "with no middle flight intends to soar" (14), and who does soar in the flight of Satan across Chaos (itself perhaps a sort of demonic crossing scene) and in Eve's dream-flight. Marvell feared that Milton's imaginative strength would "ruin . . . / The sacred truths," and Kerrigan's contemporary assessment is equally hard to discount: "if the poet claims higher inspiration than Moses, it seems distressingly easy to conclude (let rude ears be absent) that the epic intends to be a document superior to a portion of Holy Scripture."[34] Milton's urgency to "see and tell / Of things invisible to mortal sight" betrays a desire to see for himself—to stay upon the image rather than bearing the Word—as Keats may have been aware when he opened Milton's line to his own uses in the "Ode to Psyche": "I see, and sing, by my own eyes inspired."

The critic most acutely tuned to the temptation of the unattempted in Milton was of course Samuel Johnson, who himself fought a great rearguard action against the luxuries of Romantic imagination: "He had accustomed his imagination to unrestrained indulgence. . . . He sometimes descends to the elegant, but his element is the great. . . . Milton's delight was to sport in the wide regions of possibility; reality was a scene too narrow for his mind.[35] For Milton "the wide regions of possibility" were a vacuum tempting his impious urge to create ex nihilo, an urge exemplified in different stages by Satan and by Eve, and by the poet of *Paradise Lost* himself, a member of the Devil's party, perhaps, who speaks in God's voice.

Aware of what is at stake when Eve stays upon her image, one appreciates the complex act of celestial ventriloquism in the "warning voice" that draws her away. The voice remains unattributed in Eve's narration,

[34] *Prophetic Milton*, p. 129. See also p. 264, and *Sacred Complex*, p. 157. On the reader's response to the prophetic stance, see Quilligan in *Milton's Spenser*, pp. 153ff.

[35] *Lives of the English Poets*, ed. George Birkbeck Hill (London: Clarendon Press, 1905), 1:177–78.

its identity seemingly suspended until book 8, when Adam recalls his first
sight of Eve:

> On she came,
> Led by her Heav'nly Maker, though unseen,
> And guided by his voice . . .
>
> (484–86)

So it would seem that the voice is God's (the word *God* itself goes back
to a root meaning "calling" and "being called"). Previously, though, in
the fourth book, the narrator has told us that a

> genial Angel to our Sire
> Brought her in naked beauty . . .
>
> (712–13)

This mild inconsistency invites us further to consider the voice's genealogy, and to recall the way Milton opens book 4:

> O for that warning voice, which he who saw
> Th' Apocalypse, heard cry in Heav'n aloud
>
> (1–2)

The plea for a "warning voice" associates the narrator with St. John and
the prophetic tradition, as well as with the voice that "warn'd" Eve. That
the voice at the pool remains for some time unattributed, and is then am-
biguously assigned, suggests its overdetermined status. The voice seems
to be at once God's, an angel's, that of the prophetic tradition, and, finally, that of the narrator of *Paradise Lost*. What one encounters at the
pool is, I think, an image of Miltonic voice in its most authoritative form.
I thus follow Leslie Brisman in his description of Milton's two voices.

> In "Lycidas" the distinction is between an orthodox or authoritative voice
> and a milder one associated with pastoral, with poetry. The "Lycidas" dis-
> tinction may be said to stand for that encounter throughout Milton's po-
> etry. . . . Within Milton's own lines there are moments that represent a
> higher voice, and moments that seem more a human response to such a
> voice.[36]

The lineage of Milton's image of voice (the fruit, one might presume,
of the invocation to book 3) is still incomplete. The "warning voice" also
defines itself by overpowering the voice with which Ovid's narrator intervenes to taunt Narcissus: "O fondly foolish boy, why vainly seek to clasp
a fleeting image?"[37] Where one of Milton's principal pagan sources is

---

[36] *Romantic Origins* (Ithaca, N.Y.: Cornell University Press, 1978), p. 29.
[37] Ovid, *Metamorphoses*, p. 155.

brisk and unpleasant, perhaps nastily parodying the line of garrulous advisors that begins with Nestor, Milton is gently but forcefully righteous. Milton's need to rewrite his pagan predecessors has been a longstanding commonplace in the criticism of *Paradise Lost*,[38] and one might say that the warning voice absorbs and translates the voice of pagan poetry in much the way that it appropriates Eve herself. It would also be possible to approach Eve's scene slightly differently and uncover an allegory for Miltonic rewriting in which the subordination of Eve's self-love to heavenly Logos dramatizes Milton's own fascination with pagan poetry and its subsequent absorption into *Paradise Lost*.

We are now in a position to say something about the image of authoritative voice that Milton devises in book 4. First, we have seen that the drama of the voice's intervention allegorizes Milton's relation to his poetic antecedents: he usurps Ovid's voice and banishes his name from the text—a point to which I return later. Milton's prophetic aspirations seem also to be invested in the voice, allowing one to read its impact upon Eve as an emblem for the authority Milton aspires to have with his readers and with posterity. In the warning voice's identification with God, established in the preceding book, one sees Milton's aspirations for authority at their most developed.

The poet's principal adversary, however, because it calls forth the full force of ambivalence, is the image-making power, which now has three names: Eve/Satan/Ovid (as a synecdoche for the constellation of pagan poets), or only one name, John Milton. Another characterization is available though: recall Freud's description of the narcissist as the one associated with speculation, animism, the thaumaturgic powers of words, femininity, and myths of self-generation. She is, in short, beyond the reach of psychoanalytical authority. The fiction of the "narcissist" provides Freud with a compound figure of adversary and accomplice as necessary to the text of psychoanalysis as the composite fiction of Eve/Satan/Ovid is to the genesis of *Paradise Lost*.

I want now to use this characterization of Milton's "warning voice" to approach Freud's trope of the "super-ego," beginning, as the reader might expect, by observing some relations between the "warning voice" and the voice that narrates "On Narcissism."

. . .

"On Narcissism" commences by turning against (unnaming) its textual predecessors: the literary exerts a pressure on Freud comparable to, yet

---

[38] Frank Kermode describes this process with characteristic acuity in his essay "Adam Unparadised" in *The Living Milton*, ed. Kermode (London: Routledge and Kegan Paul, 1967).

stronger than, that of pagan writing on Milton. In fact Freud's resistance begins in his title. The editors of *The Standard Edition* note Freud's use of *Narzissmus* "against the possibly more correct '*Narzissismus*,' " which Freud defended "on the ground of euphony" (14:73, n. 1). Our reading of Freud's essay might understand his choice as an attempt to distance his discourse by the length of one syllable from the name "Narcissus" and the myth.[39] Moreover, in writings before and after "On Narcissism" Freud acknowledged the Narcissus myth as the source for the term *Narzissmus*, yet the 1914 essay's opening move is to deny the literary: "The term narcissism is derived from clinical description and was chosen by Paul Näcke in 1899 to denote the attitude of a person who treats his own body in the same way in which the body of a sexual object is ordinarily treated" (14:73). "Narcissism," Freud is saying, was born in the year psychoanalysis was born, 1899, when Freud completed the manuscript of *The Interpretation of Dreams*. For "Paul Näcke" one is tempted to read "not Ovid," "not Milton," "not any of the hundreds of writers who have made use of the Narcissus myth." (In a similar way, "G. T. Fechner," who in *Beyond the Pleasure Principle* is said to have anticipated Freud's views of "pleasure/unpleasure," stands—fairly shakily—for "not Schopenhauer.") In 1920, however, Freud admitted he had made an error in attributing the term *Narzissmus*: it had been Havelock Ellis's invention.[40]

The ambitious writer's absorption or suppression of her literary progenitors has become a tenet of contemporary criticism. Here, though, both writers have spawned antagonists whose failures are emphatically associated with their desires to fictionalize their origins rather than accept createdness. The "warning voice" in Milton and the narrative voice of "On Narcissism," by unnaming their textual genealogy, appear to posit for themselves that which they attempt to demystify in others, fictive claims to originality. With his opening stroke in "On Narcissism," Freud tries to achieve for himself exactly what he criticizes Jung and all Romantic overreachers for attempting.

The unnaming of origins by the "warning voice" and Freud's narrative voice opens a space for comparable acts of naming in the texts. The "warning voice," as we have seen, attempts to dominate the woman and all she represents by giving her a name. The voice calls her "Mother of human Race," which Adam translates as Eve ("not Narcissus"). Freud's banishing of literary origins allows him to redefine and redeploy the term *narcissism* for his own uses. In the course of the essay Freud takes possession of the word, expanding its application from the particular "perver-

---

[39] I am grateful to J. Daniel Kinney for this point.

[40] 7:218, n. 3. Ellis tried to arbitrate the controversy in his 1928 essay "The Conception of Narcissism," which begins by considering the myth. The essay was published in *Studies in the Psychology of Sex*, 4 vols. (New York: Random House, 1937), 2:347–75.

sion" described by Näcke into the name for a universal and normative stage in human development, as well as associating it with a general personality type. Freud also invests the term with a fresh polemical content by covertly identifying "narcissism" with the presumptions of his adversaries. The narrative voice of "On Narcissism," as we have seen, attempts to discipline the "speculators," submitting them to a normative standard of evaluation, much as the "warning voice" disciplines Eve. At the same time, "On Narcissism" is Freud's most speculative and Romantic text to that point, and the voice that attempts to curb Jung extemporizes on its own an Ovidian, inconstant ego and an entire new agency in the psyche.

Pragmatically, then, Freud's narrating voice in "On Narcissism" acts in many ways analogously not only to the voice that intrudes upon Eve but also to the agency that is first named in this essay, the "ego-ideal." The narrative voice seeks to curtail the self-love of others, staunch speculation, enforce continuity in analytical doctrine, name its antagonists, unname its predecessors, and establish authority. In writing "On Narcissism," one might speculate, Freud is in the act of creating a trope, the "ego-ideal" or super-ego, that will characterize his own voice and writings in their most authoritative form. After 1914 the "ego-ideal"/super-ego is Freud's covert image of voice and his primary fiction of authority and defense. This authoritative voice will serve to disguise Freud's own urge to Romantic speculation and his relation to prior literary texts by revising literary figurations such as the intervening voice into "scientific" and normative terms like "ego-ideal." In *Moses and Monotheism* Freud summarizes, and fully anticipates, this response to his essay: "In its implications the distortion of a text resembles a murder: the difficulty is not in perpetrating the deed, but in getting rid of its traces. . . . Accordingly, in many instances of textual distortion, we may nevertheless count on finding what has been suppressed and disavowed hidden away somewhere else, though changed and torn from its context. Only it will not always be easy to recognize it" (23:43).

As Freud's career progresses through the middle period of "On Narcissism" through *Beyond the Pleasure Principle, Civilization and Its Discontents,* and *Moses and Monotheism,* his conception of the super-ego changes. It becomes harsher, more punitive; larger portions of the agency are located in the unconscious. Eventually the super-ego will be associated with the trope of the Death Drive. All the while, Freud's style is becoming more condensed, ironic, and severe. Imaginatively, though, Freud flies higher and further.

As an agent in the genesis of Freud's own text, the super-ego may function in part as an internal adversary against which Freud must contend in order to work at his most authentically literary. The extraordinarily speculative *Moses and Monotheism* (1939) seems often to resolve itself into a

contest between Freud the speculator and a voice that intervenes, sometimes fiercely, to challenge speculation. "Once again I am prepared to find
myself blamed" (23:41), the refrain runs. At his most literary Freud seems
compelled to summon the spirit of science, the super-ego, to do battle.
Indeed, Freud's imaginative victories over inhibiting force could not be
better expressed than by Milton's Serpent when he extolls the powers to
be gained from a transgression of which others are constitutionally inca-
pable:

> Round the Tree
> All other Beasts that saw, with like desire
> Longing and envying stood, but could not reach.
> Amid the Tree now got, where plenty hung
> Tempting so nigh, to pluck and eat my fill
> I spar'd not, for such pleasure till that hour
> At Feed or Fountain never had I found.
> Sated at length, ere long I might perceive
> Strange alteration in me, to degree
> Of Reason in my inward Powers, and Speech
> Wanted not long, though to this shape retain'd.
> Thenceforth to Speculations high or deep
> I turn'd my thoughts, and with capacious mind
> Consider'd all things visible in Heav'n,
> Or Earth, or Middle
>   (9.591–605)

Yet, surpassing Satan by far, Freud has become the guardian of the tree
from which he plucked his own visionary powers.

                              .   .   .

In this chapter I have chronicled the intricacies of Freud's act of self-creation in "On Narcissism"; I have shown how Freud represents human
limitations with a normative model for the self and, simultaneously, rein-
vents himself symbolically in ways that defy the very limits that he is setting out. Having divided the world into those who love narcissistically, in
the feminine manner, and those whose relation to the object is "anaclitic," or masculine, Freud proceeds to appropriate for himself qualities
from both types. He is poet and scientist (one might even say woman and
man) at the same time, though he works to displace and disguise the former identity. Thus in the act of setting up a pair of binding normative
categories by which to define all others, Freud also symbolically transcends those categories.

This double-sided action naturally reminds one of the comparable dynamic at work in the Oedipal passage. But I want to close this chapter by reflecting briefly on the distance that separates Freud's 1914 version of the self from the one that he propounded in the dream book and by doing so indicate the larger trajectory of Freud's thinking on the nature of the self. What then are the major distinctions between the narcissistic and the Oedipal egos?

The extraordinary synthetic power of Freud's mind was surely evident in his feat of yoking together *Hamlet* and *Oedipus Rex* to illustrate the dynamics of the Oedipal complex—and also, of course, to undermine the priority of the literary imagination. Yet an even more impressive act of association underlies the composition of "On Narcissism." To propound his 1914 version of the self, Freud had to divine the fact that the myths of Narcissus and of Oedipus could merge with one another, and that such a merger would be conducive to his authority and his Romantic ambitions alike.

Freud adopted the Oedipal myth when he was a striving, ambitious, and relatively young man. And of course the myth naturalizes generational strife, naturalizes rebellion. If you believe in the validity of the Oedipal myth, then you believe that fathers and sons must always be, in some measure, at odds. The antagonistic stance that Freud assumes all through the dream book and, in particular, the aggression he aims against the fathers of the literary tradition, are, given the nature of the male Oedipal self, all but inevitable. All men must behave so—though naturally none of us will rebel as successfully as Freud does.

In the *Traumdeutung* the story of the Oedipal conflict is told from the child's point of view. There is no mention there about how the father brings the Oedipal stage to a close with the castration threat. The resolution of the complex seems, rather curiously, to rest upon the child: Freud speaks of our having "succeeded, in so far as we have not become psychoneurotics, in detaching our sexual impulses from our mothers and in forgetting our jealousy of our fathers" (4:262). He has nothing to say in this section about the particular mode of the father's triumph. Later in the dream book Freud mentions the part that a threat of castration played in a particular dream (5:619), but the "castration threat" proper doesn't receive its extended theoretical formulation until the 1905 volume, *Three Essays on the Theory of Sexuality*. In *The Interpretation of Dreams*, Freud's focus is on the rebellious wish and on the son.

In the 1914 text, matters are different. One rather basic way to describe the myth of the narcissistic ego is as a revision of the story of the Oedipal ego, which shifts the focus away from the child and onto the father, a father who is cast in a comparatively benevolent way. But Freud's normative brilliance lies in his not having to change his view of the self in any dramatically obvious manner. The shift, in fact, is quite subtle. Both myths have the same overall form: they deal with a subject, with his un-requited desire, with an authoritative intrusion, and with loss. After writing "On Narcissism," Freud can go on talking about the Oedipal complex. But the Narcissus story, as Freud tells it, sublimates his myth of Oedipus, mutes its violence, emphasizing the father's power to save the child from self-suffusion and to mediate his entry into culture. For Freud to have maintained his Oedipal version of the self, in which generational strife is understood as being natural, would have been to encourage rebels like Jung and Adler. The Narcissus story is the Oedipal myth told from the point of view of the father, the father of psychoanalysis.

The rewriting of Oedipus as Narcissus affirms Freud's authority in the psychoanalytic establishment and, perhaps, aids in defending his own texts against the kinds of readings that he aimed at Shakespeare and Sophocles. It establishes the necessity for his own commanding voice. But the introduction of the narcissistic ego has a bearing on the practice of analytic therapy as well; and accordingly the next two chapters look at the therapeutic and practical consequences of Freud's new version of the self. They focus on the ways that the creation of the narcissistic ego, which was for Freud a Romantic triumph, works to enforce norms, to fix laws of human nature and human development. In the pages to come I locate Romantic drives in Emerson and in Wordsworth to contrast with and to illuminate Freud's therapeutic designs. The question, ultimately, is whether these two major Romantics can provide inspiration for resistance to what is most delimiting in Freud and in our contemporary "culture of psychoanalysis."

Chapter Three

THERAPEUTIC EXCHANGES:
PAPERS ON PSYCHOANALYTIC TECHNIQUE,
1911–1915

THE MASTERING ambition that I associated with Milton's image of voice is clearly perceptible in some of the key moments of dramatic encounter in *Paradise Lost*. By turning in this chapter to the Freudian drama of the therapeutic exchange and reading its relation to the scene of Narcissus as Milton and Freud delineate it, one begins to see the dynamics of Freudian authority in action. In the second part of the chapter, I approach Freud's therapeutic scene by comparing it to Wordsworth's preeminent scene of self-creation, the crossing of the Simplon Pass in *The Prelude*. The issue at hand is the power of Wordsworth's Romantic text to offer an authentic alternative to the ideologies of the norm that invest the therapeutic exchange.

But I also turn the focus around somewhat. Having asked what the poets have to teach us about Freud, I now enquire into what Freud, in the form in which this book has begun to reconceive him, can tell us about the Romantic faith in regeneration and rebirth. Can Wordsworth's sublime defend itself against Freudian demystification? Does Wordsworth give us a mode of Romantic recreation that does not depend on demeaning others? What are the costs of a sublime poetry that, as Keats suggested, makes the poet an isolate, one who "stands alone"?

I

> The disciple must break the glass, or better the mirror, the reflection, his infinite speculation on the master. And start to speak.
> —Jacques Derrida, "Cogito and the History of Madness"

The conception, writing, and rewriting of "On Narcissism" coincided with another key project of Freud's. Between 1911 and 1915 Freud published a series of six essays on psychoanalytic technique. These papers, which were meant for working analysts and emphatically not for patients

or prospective patients, mark a major shift in the practice of psychotherapy. In the early stages of psychoanalysis (around the turn of the century)
Freud, then working in collaboration with Breuer, had used hypnosis to
restore the patient's memory of the early traumatic event. The goal was
"abreaction," the discharge of the energy that invested the repressed moment, and compelled the patient to repeat the trauma in displaced, symp-
tomatic form. Having found hypnosis to be unreliable over the long run,
Freud went on to employ "free-association" as a method for circumvent-
ing the patient's resistance. He writes that "the situations which had given
rise to the formation of the symptom and the other situations which lay
behind the moment at which the illness broke out retained their place as
the focus of interest; but the element of abreaction receded into the background and seemed to be replaced by the expenditure of work which the
patient had to make in being obliged to overcome his criticism of his free
associations" (12:147).

The six papers on technique record the transition to a third and for all
purposes final mode of treatment, one which is focused on the relations
between the therapist and the patient or, more exactly, on the desires and
hostilities that the patient "transfers" to the person of the physician. Thus
around the time of the introduction of the narcissistic ego, and of Freud's
self-rewriting as a figure of enhanced authority, one encounters a new
version of therapeutic procedure, one in which the role of the analyst is
unquestionably heightened. I want, then, to pose the question of the relations between these two developments, Freud's rewriting of Oedipus
into Narcissus, and his revision of therapeutic practice.

But first one needs to ask a more elementary question: what exactly
does Freud mean by transference? What role does the word play in his
reflections on therapy? The critical term in any Freudian account of transference is "repetition": as James Strachey succinctly characterizes the
phenomenon, it is "the process of 'transferring' on to a contemporary
object feelings which originally applied, and still unconsciously apply, to
an infantile object" (5:562, n. 2). In therapy, Freud maintains, the analysand invariably transfers investments from past object relations (usually
with the mother and father) on to "the person of the physician":

> What are transferences? They are new editions or facsimiles of the im-
> pulses and phantasies which are aroused and made conscious during the
> progress of the analysis; but they have this peculiarity, which is characteristic
> for their species, that they replace some earlier person by the person of the
> physician. To put it another way: a whole series of psychological experiences
> are revived, not as belonging to the past, but as applying to the person of the
> physician at the present moment. Some of these transferences have a content
> which differs from that of their model in no respect whatever except for the

substitution. These then—to keep to the same metaphor—are merely new impressions or reprints. Others are more ingeniously constructed; their content has been subjected to a modifying influence—to *sublimation*, as I call it—and they may even become conscious, by cleverly taking advantage of some real peculiarity in the physician's person or circumstances and attaching themselves to that. These, then, will no longer be new impressions, but revised editions. (7:116)

Freud's use of textual terms—new editions, facsimiles, new impressions, reprints, and revised editions—in this early reflection on transference identifies the psyche's bondage to the past with an inability to create original texts. At the same time, the passage puts the analyst in the place of the bibliographer, who can achieve a determinate view of the text's status by way of a certain sort of reading. But is the trope of reading as a bibliographer true to the intricacies encountered in the "text" of the psyche? Isn't the analyst closer to the fallible critic? And doesn't the presence of this passage in a text, which is an "original" act of authorship and authority, overstress the distinctions between the patient bound to his facsimiles and the writer-analyst, whose ability to compose and publish places him, in at least one sense, outside the scene of textual repetition that he describes? Yet the existence of essays that generalize the therapeutic procedure, giving it something of a structural mapping, suggests that a certain repetition may be enforced upon the analyst. The question is then whether either the patient or the Freudian therapist after Freud will be able to work to the point where she can compose something that would qualify as a "primary" text.

. . .

Freud tells us that although the patient's love (and/or hate) for the therapist reproduces the form of prior attachments, the patient is generally not aware that he is acting in the service of a compulsion to repeat. What he sees in the image of the therapist, according to classical theory, is a reflection from his own interior life. "He . . . link[s] the doctor up with one of the imagos [or a composite imago] of the people by whom he was accustomed to be treated with affection" (12:139–40). Yet the analysand takes the doctor to be a new presence, and his early enthusiasm depends largely on that impression of novelty.

The patient comes to the analyst in a state of confused anxiety and with a "need for love [that] is not entirely satisfied by reality" (12:100). He encounters an image that he himself generates and that he erroneously supposes to be capable of returning his love. The image is a composite, partly the analyst, partly the patient's first loved objects, and partly—

because those objects are "narcissistically" generated—the patient himself. Freud's last word on the genesis of the object comes in *An Outline of Psychoanalysis*, where he writes that "there is no doubt that, to begin with, the child does not distinguish between the breast and its own body; when the breast has to be separated from the body and shifted to the '*outside*' because the child so often finds it absent, it carries with it as an '*object*' a part of the original narcissistic libidinal cathexis. This first object is later completed into the person of the child's mother" (23:188). Every object, from this point of view, is thus a narcissistically generated one. This is a matter on which Freud becomes quite specific in the final and most important paper on technique, "Observations on Transference Love." Calling upon himself in that essay to draw a distinction between transference love and the love met in actual experience, Freud says,

> It is true that the love consists of new editions of old traits and that it repeats infantile reactions. But this is the essential character of every state of being in love. There is no such state which does not reproduce infantile prototypes. It is precisely from this infantile determination that it receives its compulsive character, verging as it does on the pathological. Transference-love has perhaps a degree less of freedom than the love which appears in ordinary life and is called normal; it displays its dependence on the infantile pattern more clearly and is less adaptable and capable of modification; but that is all, and not what is essential. (12:168)

From a humanistic point of view, the notion that there is little to choose between the feelings a suffering patient has for a physician who represents the possibility of a cure, and those of one lover for another outside the liminal zone of therapy is surely an unacceptable one. What matters more at present is that Freud is not himself consistently attached to the idea of there being an equation between pathology and love.

His more dialectical reflections on the subject deal with what he describes as the two principal currents in erotic life, the tender and the sensual. The difficulty facing the human subject is in uniting these currents in relation to a single object, for this is a resolution that both society and the drives work consistently to undermine. And yet in any number of texts, such as "On Narcissism," *Group Psychology*, and the papers on therapeutic technique, Freud abandons his dialectic for a more or less monistic version of eros, a version that, if I am right, he absorbs largely from the literary tradition. The myth of object love as being, in the last analysis, displaced self-love is, needless to say, highly conducive to literary fiction making; the narcissistic lover is forever in conflict, forever producing and being encompassed within dramas. One is hard pressed to find a happy marriage in Shakespeare's work, and the famous first lines of *Anna Karenina* indicate the resistance happy families pose to the literary imagination. So I would suggest that in some measure Freud's less developed reflections on erotic life may derive from having rather unself-consciously employed a literary trope for the human subject, the narcissistic ego. Freud is in this sense, perhaps, made use of by literary convention. But the myth of the narcissistic ego is also one that works particularly well to underwrite a certain sort of therapeutic relation between analyst and patient.

The analyst's commitment to erotic restraint with his patient ("analysis must be carried out in a state of frustrations" [23:231]) is an attempt to preserve his status as pure reflection, or, to use Milton's words for the form that mesmerizes Eve, "Shape within the . . . gleam." The therapist proffers only the "evenly suspended attention" of a reflecting surface: "The doctor should be opaque to his patients and, like a mirror, should show them nothing but what is shown to him" (12:118). "Answering looks / Of sympathy and love" are the beginnings of the "strong transference." So too should the doctor make his own unconscious a perfect mirror of the patient's: "He must adjust himself to the patient as a telephone receiver is adjusted to the transmitting microphone. Just as the receiver converts back into soundwaves the electric oscillations in the telephone line which were set up by sound waves, so the doctor's unconscious is able, from the derivatives of the unconscious which are communicated to him, to reconstruct that unconscious" (12:115–16).

How does the therapist manage to maintain this level of detachment throughout the analysis, particularly when the patient is always trying to induce him to return her affections and thus "to drag him down from the analytic level" (12:170)? Clearly he has the resources of his character and of the institutional values of psychoanalysis to draw upon, but he may be augmented in another way, too. Consider the rhetoric Freud uses to describe the psychoanalytic drama: the therapist is first purged and purified by the long ascetic discipline of analytic training; he then enters into a contest with a force that Freud invariably personifies, *the* Resistance, an adept Archimago that makes use of every possible mirage and deflection to block access to the patient's past; note also how, particularly in the last paper on transference love, the patient is cast as a female, presumed beautiful, who is in thrall to the nefarious mage, waiting to be delivered. Then there are the figures of speech to which Freud is prone: he speaks of calling up spirits from the deep, of refusing to slay his antagonist in absentia or in effigy, of struggling with the resistance in something like an archetypal trial by combat. Of course, one might describe the project of almost all of the major English Romantics as involving the "purification" of traditional forms of Romance. But this process is a highly self-conscious one: Wordsworth's Nature both is and is not the goddess Natura of classical myth. A certain archaic inheritance persists, a condition not only inescapable but, at least for Wordsworth, desirable. It sometimes seems that Freud's ambition to develop a completely cleansed discourse leaves him all the more open to being appropriated by literary conventions: he does not wish to see them in his text. Here the effect may be that the therapist trained under the auspices of Freud's essays will develop a partially mystified sense of self, one incompatible with Freud's own severe reflections on the nature of subjectivity. But it also puts the therapists in the dangerous position of being quest knights unequipped with the armor of self-awareness: Freud's Romance of therapy may initially strengthen the practitioner, but in the end it is likely to constitute a danger.

For his part, the patient is compelled only to be honest. Thus Freud addresses a hypothetical analysand:

> You will notice that as you relate things various thoughts will occur to you which you would like to put aside on the ground of certain criticisms and objections. You will be tempted to say to yourself that this or that is irrelevant here, or is quite unimportant, or nonsensical, so that there is no need to say it. You must never give in to these criticisms, but must say it in spite of them—indeed, you must say it precisely *because* you feel an aversion to doing so. (12:134–35).

The patient is instructed to suspend the voice of critical self-consciousness, which Freud attributes to the super-ego. "Wonder not," Satan begins his temptation, which returns Eve from the domination of Logos to the primal image. The patient suppresses self-criticism, the capacity for wonder; as Philip Rieff observes, he gives up "reflection" for "observation." In the terms of this enquiry, the patient surrenders one version of reflection for another in a return to the "mirror stage."[1] The patient

> has to learn above all . . . that mental activities such as thinking something over or concentrating the attention solve none of the riddles of a neurosis. . . . One must be especially unyielding about obedience to that rule with patients who practice the art of sheering off into intellectual discussion during their treatment, who speculate a great deal . . . (12:119)

In the patient, speculative excess is a sign of paranoia, the disease that places one beyond analytical authority. The doctor's speculative liberties are unbounded, however, because she is not obsessively attached to her ideas. The power to dismiss a "speculation" at will is proof of its healthy

---

[1] As Freud puts it, "Act as though, for instance, you were a traveller sitting next to the window of a railway carriage and describing to someone inside the carriage the changing views which you see outside" (12:135). The objective is to preserve an uninterrupted flow, as close to prelinguistic experience as possible.

character, and Freud indicates that analysts ought to test themselves by this standard.

Remember that in classical psychoanalysis the patient cannot see the doctor: "I hold to the plan of getting the patient to lie on a sofa while I sit behind him out of his sight. . . . I cannot put up with being stared at by other people for eight hours a day (or more)" (12:133–34). Thus the image of the analyst to which the patient becomes enthralled ("with vain desire") is of the patient's own creation. More important, it is pure voice that descends upon the patient when the doctor breaks the analytical silence. Freud shares with (and perhaps derives from) Eve's maker the aversion to being looked upon. And the patient, comparably to Eve, who is probably kneeling at the pool, is supine. As Rieff indicates, "Posture has been an essential strategy of all spiritual exercises. To be prone (even face up) also suggests submission, a postural analogue to the demand that the patient become intellectually 'completely passive.' "[2] The patient is, theoretically, caught in a state of dependent, unrequited love for a projected image he fails to recognize: he is susceptible now to the intervention of voice, to Freudian authority.

The initial appearance of this potentially transforming authority comes with what Freud calls the "first communication":[3] prior to this, one may assume, utterances by the doctor have consisted of questions and remarks meant to bring on the transference. Included in these may be the analyst's echoic gambit. The patient makes an observation such as, "It wasn't my mother in that dream," and the doctor returns soothingly, "It wasn't your mother."[4] Only in retrospect, after the "first communication," may the patient detect the slight ironic distortion in what appeared to be a flattering verbal reflection. The analyst also engages in a rather surprising technique of refocusing the patient's gaze when it appears to fade or wander. Freud writes that "if a patient's free associations fail the stoppage can invariably be removed by an assurance that he is being dominated at the moment by an association which is concerned with the doctor himself or with something connected with him. As soon as this explanation is given, the stoppage is removed" (12:101). Notice that Freud does not say that the patient *is* thinking of the analyst, only that it is useful to tell him so: it is as though Eve's pool possessed a seductive voice as well.

For the "first communication" to be effective, Freud observes, the transference must be under way. It is unrequited love for an unattainable object that breaks down defenses and allows for authoritative intervention, except in the cases of those women, upon whom Freud remarks,

---

[2] *Mind of the Moralist*, p. 85.

[3] 12:144.

[4] For a discussion of the rather modest value Freud places on the patient's denial of the doctor's constructions see "On Negation" (19:235–39).

who will not take "no" for an answer when they offer the therapist their love. Like Narcissus, they cannot hear the commanding voice. They pursue the impossible object but do not always "pine," and sometimes they get what they want. But the average patient "makes use of the instruction in so far as he is induced to do so by the transference; and it is for this reason that our first communication should be withheld until a strong transference has been established" (12:144).

Freud characterized the transference as a midspace or *limen*: "an intermediate region between illness and real life through which the transition from one to the other is made" (12:154). The patient is compelled to promise "not to take any important decisions affecting his life during the time of his treatment—for instance, not to choose any profession or definitive love-object—but to postpone all such plans until after his recovery" (12:153). In a similar vein Ferenczi, whose 1909 paper on the transference precipitated Freud's own series of essays on method, speaks of a liminal "bridge" between the habits and appearance of the physician and his transference identity.[5] Perhaps more illuminating here is the work of Victor Turner on Ndembo initiation rituals.[6] Turner represents these rites of passage as involving movement through a midspace in which the initiate's social, familial, and personal identities are suspended, and he assumes a state characterized as "pure possibility." Watched over by a priest or guide, the initiate enters a mode of instructive illusion in which the mysterious inner forces of society and self become manifest, often through the voices and images of ancestors. On the other side of the threshold the initiate takes his place in the social hierarchy, fully integrated in and reconciled to the world as it is. One wonders if Freud, with his interest in ethnographic writing, might not have read of similar ceremonies and seen the application to his own therapeutic ritual. Regardless, the therapeutic midspace does bear a certain likeness to the originary liminal zone in which Eve finds herself and also, of course, to the state of narcissistic self-enclosure that Freud associates with the developmental stage from which the Oedipal intrusion wrests the subject.

Are we in the presence of an archetypal figure here? We have encountered a structure that seems to be implicated in scenes of poetic inspiration, in Freud's narrative of the narcissistic ego's development, in the psychoanalytic transference, and in tribal initiation rites. My own inclination is skeptical. The structure is too elementary, and for the purposes of illustration I have perhaps downplayed too many differences. But if the approach lacks elegance, it also begins to yield critical access to Freud's

---

[5] See "Introjection and Transference" in *First Contributions to Psycho-analysis*, trans. Ernest Jones (London: Hogarth Press, 1952), pp. 34–93.

[6] See "Betwixt and Between: The Liminal Period in Rites de Passage" in *The Forest of Symbols* (Ithaca, N.Y.: Cornell University Press, 1967), pp. 93–111.

work. R. P. Blackmur seems to have the right sense of how to proceed in these matters:

> We ought scrupulously to risk the use of any concept that seems propitious or helpful in getting over gaps. Only the use should be consciously provisional, speculative, and dramatic. The end-virtue of humility comes only after a long train of humiliations; and the chief labor of humbling is the constant, resourceful restoration of ignorance.[7]

We have barely begun to read Freud; these first thick strokes must serve as background to the more detailed perceptions that can follow.

Let us return to the subject of the "first communication." Its function, as Freud sees it, is to begin to dissolve the transference by "giving the resistance a name" (12:155). The analyst, or rather his disembodied voice, intervenes on the scene of repetition and instructs the patient on how the "new" strong feelings for him fulfill "old" patterns, and how the beloved image by which the patient is enthralled is of his own devising: or, in the words of Milton's celestial presence, "What thou seest, / What there thou seest . . . is thyself." Perhaps the most shocking thing about the technique of Freudian "communication" is revealed in what appears to be a casual bit of advice Freud extends to analysts. "Even in the later stages of analysis," he writes, "one must be careful not to give a patient the solution of a symptom or the translation of a wish until he is already so close to it that he has only one short step more to make in order to get hold of the explanation for himself" (12:140).[8] In other words, the analyst ought to intervene upon the patient to usurp his instant of self-awareness. That point of intrusion is certainly an aggressive one, and Freud is shrewd if not a little cruel in his insistence that the analyst use this (and seemingly every) opportunity to claim authority over the patient.

One is tempted to extend the comparison between Milton and Freud and to see the intervening voice in therapy as doing something akin to what the celestial voice does, that is, inducing the woman to enter normative erotic life. Freud speaks of using therapy to restore to the female patient a freer command over her instincts by releasing them from infantile fixations, but pragmatically this may mean using analytical authority to lead her into loving in a heterosexual, monogamous manner, in that her relations to her husband will echo those she developed with the analyst. (So Eve's relations with Adam were, at least initially, a repetition of her relations with the celestial voice.) Psychoanalysis, from the perspective of a feminist critique, consolidates its social authority by first con-

---

[7] *Language as Gesture: Essays in Poetry* (Westport, Conn.: Greenwood Press, 1977), pp. 373–74.

[8] Freud affirms this strategy of heading off the patient's own insight in his last major consideration of therapeutic technique. See *An Outline of Psycho-analysis*, 23:178.

structing a mythical image of woman as a threatening force, then proffering the means to contain the crisis. Lévi-Strauss's view that civilization is in some sense dependent upon the bonds established by the exchange of women is relevant here, as is Karl Kraus's acid remark that psychoanalysis inflicts the disease that it then achieves its status by being able to cure.

Perhaps this puts matters too strongly. Overall Freud is not explicit about the dialectics of exchange in the psychoanalytic midspace. Is the patient's encounter with authoritative voice more like Milton's in the invocation or Eve's at the pool? The extent to which the patient is reconstituted by the analytical discourse involves too many factors, and, as Freud acknowledged in his later work, even the most apparently successful analysis is never wholly resolved. Yet, I would still suggest that the best literary companion piece to the 1937 *summa* "Analysis Terminable and Interminable," which describes the inevitable return of a negative transference, is Eve's temptation scene in book 9. There one might see, as from the patient's point of view, what the stakes are in a contention with an internalized authoritative discourse. In "Analysis Terminable and Interminable" Freud describes the resistances that prevent healing change from finally taking place in psychoanalysis. "We often have the impression that with the wish for a penis and the masculine protest we have penetrated through all the psychological strata and have reached bedrock" (23:252). I am inclined here to suggest that we substitute "wish for a voice" for penis envy and the desire not to have one's voice assimilated too readily to a norm of any sort for "masculine protest." In the modern poet's urgency to "find" his or her own voice, even if it is marginal or obscure, one may see a comparable desire not to be a dutiful daughter or son to any commanding word.

It is no doubt clear by now that the drama of the transference, as Freud represents it in the 1911–1915 papers on technique, reproduces the dynamics of the formation of the "ego-ideal"/super-ego described in "On Narcissism." For the second time in the patient's life, a commanding voice intervenes on a state of self-infatuated error, this time to revise the reigning structures of desire and authority. Freud held the perception, now commonly associated with Hannah Arendt, that authority, defined as a force that impels obedience without threat or coercion, was no longer present in the modern world.[9] He believed that the disappearance of the classical mode of authority, and the Roman commitment to being tied back (*re-ligare*) to the past, did not signify ultimate human liberation. Rather the human subject was thus deprived of those mediating figures of cultural achievement whose example and influence might gradually ma-

[9] See "What Is Authority?" in *Between Past and Future, Six Exercises in Political Thought* (Cleveland, Ohio: World Publishing Co., 1963), pp. 91–141.

ture the super-ego. The result was that the super-ego simply remained as it was in childhood, punitive and archaic. The loss of creditable social authority rendered the psyche authoritarian, as *Civilization and Its Discontents* implies. And if this is truly the case, the social and private intervention of Freud's own voice, humane, shrewd, and tolerant, may seem to stand as a creditable alternative. To ask for more is to be reminded of Freud's observation that in matters of psychological health the better is frequently the enemy of the good. Moreover, Freud appears to have struggled, at least at times, to keep his urge for posthumous cultural power in check. In his late work *An Outline of Psychoanalysis*, for example, Freud seems to recognize that the aim of analysis is less to strengthen the ego than to modify the super-ego, and he calls upon the analysts of the future to restrain their powers of re-creation.

Yet, accurate and useful as Freud's reflections on authority may be, the consonance between the representation of the dynamics of the transference and of the super-ego's formation strikes me as legitimately disturbing. Formal theorizing of the "transference" begins in 1909 with Ferenczi's paper, preceding "On Narcissism" by five years. It is as though the figure by which the self is to be represented throughout the rest of Freud's work, a self-figuration that is still very much with us, derives in part from the image of the patient under analysis. The "narcissistic ego" is, perhaps, a trope for the self as patient. Thus considered it attempts to confer upon the self prior to analysis a form that will make it susceptible to the physician's power within therapy and to the power of Freud's therapeutic text. To put it more strongly, to the extent that we unconsciously make use of the figure of the "narcissistic ego" and Freud's tripartite topography, we are depicting ourselves as patients in need of the cure of Freudian authority.

Nor should one forget the genealogy of the voice that breaks the therapeutic silence. Such a voice will be composite, somewhat in the manner of Milton's "warning voice" which synthesizes a variety of prior discourses. Yet the most notable voice implicit in the analyst's own utterance is the one that intervened on the self-admiring gazes of the first generation of analysts. This voice has descended through all of the following generations, and into Western culture generally; it is the voice of the one analyst who both during his lifetime and largely since has remained unanalyzed, Sigmund Freud.

II

But surely it is true that we all possess—or are possessed by—some interior version of authority. Challenging Freud's super-ego as a myth, and a rather self-serving one, does not deny the existence of some comparable agency: I only suggest that one might figure it differently, for surely only figuration can represent it. One might consider, at least provisionally, the countermyth offered by Michel Foucault.

It is well known that Jacques Derrida's key term for epistemological hubris is "the metaphysics of presence," which refers to the Western refusal to examine the metaphorical maneuver by which knowledge is equated with a clear and authoritative vision of the thing "known." Foucault's emblem for the same power play is material and historical; it emphasizes the repressive effects on those who become the objects of disinterested knowledge. The key emblem in what I take to be Foucault's most important book, *Discipline and Punish*, is of course Bentham's panopticon, the ingenious mechanism that allows a corrections official in a modern, "humane" prison to keep simultaneous watch over a great number of prisoners in their individual cells without himself being seen. The confined man is always susceptible to scrutiny, but he does not know when the observing station is being manned, does not know when he is actually being looked upon. And this not knowing has powerful effects:

> He who is subjected to a field of visibility, and who knows it, assumes responsibility for the constraints of power; he makes them play spontaneously upon himself; he inscribes in himself the power relation in which he simultaneously plays both roles; he becomes the principle of his own subjection. By this very fact, the external power may throw off its physical weight; it tends to the non-corporal; and, the more it approaches this limit, the more constant, profound and permanent are its effects: it is a perpetual victory that avoids any physical confrontation and which is always decided in advance.[10]

It would be an error to read this passage as relevant exclusively to the state of penology in nineteenth-century England. Rather, Bentham's panopticon provides Foucault with a figure for the workings of a society that is dedicated to controlling its population by ever more effective means of surveillance. Foucault means to suggest that the development of a comprehensive inner life for the subject, of a "universe within," which is said to be the crucial quality of modern life, is a product of material conditions. Romantic subjectivity is not, to Foucault, the invention of Rousseau or Wordsworth, but rather the result of ever more sophisticated means of compelling social discipline, of which the panopticon may serve as an emblem. Foucault writes about the treatment of criminals, the insane, and the physically ill because to him their lot is representative of the modern situation. In the way that they have been forced to internalize a whole array of social prohibitions, we are supposed to find an exagger-

[10] *Discipline and Punish*, pp. 202–3.

ated but illuminating image of the ways that we middle-class readers have been constituted as human subjects.

One might think of Foucault's vision of the panopticon as a counter-myth, posed against Freud's story about how authority is internalized by the human subject. For Freud, because all humans experience the Oedipal complex, all have super-egos; it is for him a universal, natural, and ines-capable fact, part of human destiny. And it is this "naturalized," ahistor-ical idea about the origins of internal authority that Foucault's vision of the panopticon implicitly challenges. For Foucault, our being watched, punished, and disciplined from within is a cultural phenomenon, the ma-terial result of living in societies that have developed the art of silent sur-veillance to a horrible degree. Like Foucault's incarcerated man, we in-scribe within ourselves the power relation in which we play roles of both the observer and the observed, and thus become the principles of our own subjection. But if this subjection is determined by culture and is a mani-festation of actual power, then it is one we might revise, or divert. Fou-cault is, at least implicitly, asking us to displace Platonic, Christian, and Freudian allegories about the origins of internal authority and to embrace his own in the hope that it will better orient us for political action. If Foucault's allegory does not get work done—if it turns out that the form interior authority takes is more realistically and usefully conceived of as inevitable—then we ought to forget about this aspect of Foucault.

For his own part, Jacques Lacan reveals himself to be (as he claims) Freud's true disciple, by uninhibitedly endorsing the dynamic of authority and submission that we have uncovered in Freud's texts on therapeutic technique. It is Lacan's conviction that the purpose of analysis is to break down the *moi*, the narcissistic construct that is precipitated in the mirror stage. In the *stade du miroir* the child is compelled to identify himself with the bodily totality he apprehends in the mirror, even though his actual experience of his body is fragmented and incoherent. The subject's life-long attempt to coincide with the totality represented by his image results in the creation of a pervasive false-consciousness. (Lacan uses the phe-nomenological term for what Freud would simply call an aggravated case of secondary narcissism.) Lacanian therapy aims to undo the false self, or the *moi*, until the subject "ends up by recognizing that this being has never been anything more than his construct in the Imaginary and that this construct disappoints all his certitudes."[11] This critical sense of iden-tity as a defensive fabrication is at the core of Lacan's rejection of ego-psychology, and of his pronouncement that the ego is finally a paranoid structure.

[11] *Speech and Language in Psychoanalysis*, trans. Anthony Wilden (Baltimore, Md.: The Johns Hopkins University Press, 1968), p. 11.

The source of the *moi*'s dilemma is the unfulfillable wish to coincide perfectly with its primary love-objects. The subject's symptoms derive from this impossible need for unqualified possession. To be cured, the subject must accept the truth of secondariness and recognize that no object can be more than a substitute for the originals, which are themselves inevitably constructed, over time, as substitutes. To learn that, in Freud's words, there is "something in the nature of the sexual instinct itself [that] is unfavorable to the achievement of absolute gratification," is to be on the way to replacing need with desire. For Lacan the heuristic means for initiating the patient into a knowledge of secondariness is the process of gradually restoring him to the rule of the signifier. By reinitiating the patient into the symbolic order of language, which is made necessary by absence to begin with, the Lacanian analyst converts the analysand to a pervasive ethos of mediation. Having been restored to "the Symbolic," the patient can renounce the hunger for full possession and accept secondariness in all things.

Like Freud, Lacan believes that neurosis derives from the patient's failure fully to resolve his or her Oedipal crisis. Part of Lacan's not inconsiderable achievement lies in his uncovering of the linguistic dimension of the Oedipus. He recognizes that the super-ego originates with the father's voiced prohibition (the Name of the Father), and that authority henceforth will make itself manifest though the interior voice. Thus in the well-resolved Oedipal complex the prohibitive word comes to stand between the child and his or her object, and that mediacy of the object henceforth becomes determinate; it becomes a constitutive part of every relation to "the Other." The neurotic, for Lacan, is one who did not make that transition successfully, and thus in therapy he is submitted once again to the Oedipal rite; the analyst, in the place of the father, reinitiates him into the realm of the Symbolic. I have argued that this is more or less the situation in Freud's therapeutic practice as well, but unlike Freud, Lacan is quite overt about the dynamics of the exchange.

Though Lacan is taken by some to be an archetypal postmodern thinker, he is nonetheless entirely unembarrassed about the theological aspects of the analyst's *Logos*: "In order to liberate the subject's Word," he writes, "we introduce him into the Language of his desire, that is, into the primary Language in which, beyond what he tells us of himself, he is already talking to us unbeknownst to him."[12] Nor is he any more apologetic about the coercive powers of what he calls the full word of the analyst, which replaces the *parole vide* of the subject: "For in its symbolizing function the Word is moving towards nothing less than a transformation of the subject to whom it is addressed by means of the link which it estab-

___
[12] Ibid., p. 57.

lishes with the one who emits it—in other words, by introducing an effect of the signifier."[13] Later in the same essay he writes that "analysis can have for its goal only the advent of a true Word and the bringing to realization of his history by the subject in his relation to a future."[14]

Derrida is quite right to see that although Lacan's theory of "desire" as endlessly metonymic seems to be in accord with the ethos of *différance*, Lacan counterbalances his radicalism by positing the analyst's word as a transcendental signifier. Lacan's word aspires to the condition of the Logos, in the old-fashioned biblical sense. As Derrida puts it, "Speech, here, is not full of something beyond itself which would be its object: but this is why all the more and all the better, it is full of itself, of its presence, its essence. This presence . . . requires irreplaceable properness, inalienable singularity, living authenticity."[15] Anthony Wilden is thus not wrong to reduce things as far as to say that for Lacan the subject can only be cured when he finally makes "the symbolic identification with the father—that is to say, he must take over the function of the father through the normalization of the Oedipus complex. This is an identification with a father who is neither Imaginary nor real: what Lacan calls the Symbolic father, the figure of the Law."[16] To be saved we must accommodate ourselves to the status quo as it is embodied in the current ruling discourses and as it is summarized in the literal, authoritative language of the father or of the analyst, the purveyor of truth.[17]

Yet Lacan's position is broadly significant in our time, particularly in the polemical distinctions it draws between "the Imaginary" and "the Symbolic." Freud himself associated the progress of civilization with the development of abstract language, belief in an invisible God, and a concomitant turning away from the image. A common strain in much of the advanced criticism of the past three decades has been a concerted effort to continue the work of the Enlightenment (to which the normative Freud contributed) and to eradicate the superstitions associated with visual or "unmediated" perception and, accordingly, with the visionary imagination. Derrida's endorsement of writing over speech can be seen as another step toward demystification, comparable to the one Nietzsche claimed Socrates took when he championed dialectic over Dionysian dream-vision. Now it is Socrates with his commitment to transparent speech who

---

[13] Ibid., p. 60.

[14] Ibid., p. 65.

[15] *Post Card*, p. 472.

[16] Lacan, *Speech and Language*, p. 165.

[17] Fredric Jameson issues a comparable but far more developed critique of Lacan in his essay "Imaginary and Symbolic in Lacan." See especially p. 373. Yet Jameson sees possibilities for a doctrine of resistance in Lacan based on, among other things, his commitment to alienation as a precondition for genuine insight.

must be consigned to superstition, along with that entire long footnote to his work, the Western metaphysical tradition. Such a tendency to more severe abstraction leads literary critics to speak of tropes, revisionary ratios, discourse, and other comparably normative entities when once they addressed the representation of reality and prophetic vision. This gradual demystification is in harmony with the needs of an increasingly secular society, which demands a life beyond illusion—which may be synonymous, as Nietzsche's portrait of "the Last Man" implies, with a life beyond risk.

III

I want now to bring together Freud's drama of therapeutic "self-creation" and what is conceivably William Wordsworth's major scene of poetic self-genesis. At issue is the power of Wordsworth's Romantic claims for the self to provide a plausible challenge to the normative vision of the narcissistic self that Freud puts forward in his 1914 essay. But to understand what is at stake in Wordsworth's scene at the Simplon Pass one must, it seems to me, turn first to a scene in *The Prelude* in which Wordsworth arrives at a version of the myth of Narcissus that is brilliantly at odds with the story as both Milton and Freud tell it. I believe that for Wordsworth, as for Freud and Milton, the Narcissus myth is an absolutely crucial one. Wordsworth's retelling of the myth in the "Boy of Winander" segment is at the center of *The Prelude*'s Romantic design.[18]

"The Winander Boy" story dramatizes what is inititally at least an idealized version of poetic initiation, comparable to the one that is evoked at the outset of Keats's *Fall of Hyperion*. There the poet proclaimed what was more a wish than a tested truth for him, that the poetic gift was natural and might devolve upon him with as little exertion as it took to win a mother's love:

> Since every man whose soul is not a clod
> Hath visions, and would speak, if he had lov'd,
> And been well nurtured in his mother tongue.[19]

The Winander Boy is well nurtured at his own point of poetic origins by having his "mimic hootings" returned to him by the owls at twilight. The poet in youth is he, not to whom all things speak as Ruskin had it,[20] but

---

[18] All references to *The Prelude* are to the 1850 version as printed in *The Prelude 1799, 1805, 1850*, ed. Jonathan Wordsworth, M. H. Abrams, and Stephen Gill (New York: Norton, 1979). Hereafter citations appear in the body of the text.

[19] *The Fall of Hyperion*, in *The Complete Poems of John Keats*, ed. Jack Stillinger (Cambridge, Mass.: Harvard University Press, 1982), ll. 13–15.

[20] The better-known use of this formulation is Paul Valéry's.

to whom some things, the right ones for his moment of development, answer:

> —many a time
> At evening, when the earliest stars began
> To move along the edges of the hills,
> Rising or setting, would he stand alone
> Beneath the trees or by the glimmering lake,
> And there, with fingers interwoven, both hands
> Pressed closely palm to palm, and to his mouth
> Uplifted, he, as through an instrument,
> Blew mimic hootings to the silent owls,
> That they might answer him; and they would shout
> Across the watery vale, and shout again,
> Responsive to his call, with quivering peals,
> And long halloos and screams, and echoes loud,
> Redoubled and redoubled, concourse wild
> Of jocund din . . .

(5.365–79)

The owls sound at the border of evening and day across a "watery vale," a particularly gentle liminal zone. The currency of exchange is a dialect of Nature's mother tongue, which locates the boy between the solipsism that would be implied by mere echo and the accommodations and confinements inherent in human discourse. The boy conducts a wild symphony, "echoes loud, / Redoubled and redoubled," seemingly raising the prospect of visual reflection offered by the "glimmering lake" into a principle of acoustical composition. The implication, so early in the episode, may be that this kind of echoing symbiosis lies always at the interior of authentic poetic utterance, and that the poet never needs to leave Nature or break a serene continuity.

This scene of aural reflection preserves the reciprocity Wordsworth finds between Nature and his childhood self, particularly in the early books of *The Prelude*. The child's being is then, in certain ways, indistinguishable from the "one life" of Nature, and from the mother's presence: the "one dear Presence . . . / . . . which irradiates and exalts / Objects through widest intercourse of sense" (2.238–40). The vocal continuity the boy establishes across the vale promises that, in Stevens's words, the mother's face may preside as the purpose and, one can add, the origin of the poem. From Wordsworth's point of view, the boy is in an ideal position in regard to origins. He summons the owls' cries, but Nature calls with its own voice as it has for ages and in answer to a cry that it has taught the boy. He enters Nature smoothly without disrupting it, initiating without having to provoke the sharp break associated with origination.

Thus far we have read enough instances of this topos to anticipate the authoritative intrusion that transforms the scene. The wounding that characteristically breaches the closed economy of Narcissus arrives in Wordsworth's episode as a sudden silence. (J. Hillis Miller's description of this moment as one purely of suspension and indeterminacy ignores the literary history of the scene and Wordsworth's active rewriting of the received myth. To me the suspension signifies in the context of the other versions of the Narcissus story, signifies by contrast to the authoritative voices in Ovid, Milton, and Freud.)[21] The owls cease to return the boy's calls, and he is left in suspension, left hanging:

> when a lengthened pause
> Of silence came and baffled his best skill,
> Then sometimes, in that silence while he hung
> Listening, a gentle shock of mild surprise
> Has carried far into his heart . . .
>
> (5.379–83)

To "hang" is for Wordsworth to enter a threshold state, with all of the possibilities and risks that open out when those borders of selfhood, which work both as preserving defenses and as limitations that block poetic change, suddenly dissolve. Heidegger evokes this state effectively, I think, in the essay "What Is Metaphysics?":

> We 'hover' in anxiety. More precisely, anxiety leaves us hanging because it induces the slipping away of beings as a whole. This implies that we ourselves—we men who are in being—in the midst of beings slip away from ourselves. At bottom therefore it is not as though 'you' or 'I' feel ill at ease; rather it is this way for some 'one.' In the altogether unsettling experience of this hovering where there is nothing to hold onto, pure *Da-sein* is all that is still there.[22]

What is lost in Heideggerian anxiety is the defensive carapace of the "they-self," what one might call "character" or "personal identity." For Wordsworth this return to Being, "the one life within us and abroad," is most easily achieved in childhood, before the boundaries of the self become fixed. Then to enter liminality is invariably to see further into the life of things: "Oh, when I have hung / Above the raven's nest, by knots of grass" (1.330–31), he recollects:

---

[21] See *The Linguistic Moment—From Wordsworth to Stevens* (Princeton, N.J.: Princeton University Press, 1985), p. 76.

[22] Martin Heidegger, *Basic Writings*, ed. David Farrell Krell (New York: Harper and Row, 1977), p. 103.

> With what strange utterance did the loud dry wind
> Blow through my ear! the sky seemed not a sky
> Of earth—and with what motion moved the clouds!
>
> (1.337–39)

Without harsh perplexity, the boy feels the very strangeness of being, but also its tranquil, nurturing presence.

Yet in time the prison house begins to close. In the first "spot of time" (12.208–87) the boy is separated from his "guide," a servant of his father, and enters a taboo space, where a murderer had been executed:

> I led my horse, and, stumbling on, at length
> Came to a bottom, where in former times
> A murderer had been hung in iron chains.
> The gibbet-mast had mouldered down, the bones
> And iron case were gone; but on the turf,
> Hard by, soon after that fell deed was wrought,
> Some unknown hand had carved the murderer's name.
> The monumental letters were inscribed
> In times long past; but still, from year to year,
> By superstition of the neighborhood,
> The grass is cleared away, and to that hour
> The characters were fresh and visible:
> A casual glance had shown them, and I fled.
>
> (12.234–46)

Here the poet, looking backward, suffers intimations of the risks involved in the threshold state. To suspend defense and limitation (signified by separation from the paternal guide) is to transgress against the law: the punishment for liminal hanging is, imaginatively, to be hanged. In this scene the rule of the literal, which is the rule of paternity, priority, custom, convention, and the law, asserts itself against the poet's urge to trespass.[23] Discourse in its most normative guise suddenly manifests itself, with an appropriately literal insistence, to thwart the drives of a poet who would reinvent the word.

Yet the kind of accommodation to which Wordsworth as a poet of the beautiful eventually travels is only ambivalently or secondarily present in the Winander Boy passage. There the poet impressively rewrites the Narcissus myth, a myth that, as we have seen, tends in its conventional form to affirm normative if not authoritarian values. When the silence intervenes on the boy, it does not separate him from his former plenitude but

---

[23] See Thomas Weiskel's remarks on this scene in *The Romantic Sublime: Studies in the Structure and Psychology of Transcendence* (Baltimore, Md.: The Johns Hopkins University Press, 1976), pp. 177–78.

takes him deeper into poetic origins, into a self-consciousness not verbal
but aural and visual:

> when a lengthened pause
> Of silence came and baffled his best skill,
> Then sometimes, in that silence while he hung
> Listening, a gentle shock of mild surprise
> Had carried far into his heart the *voice*
> *Of mountain torrents*; or the visible scene
> Would enter unawares into his mind,
> With all its solemn imagery, its rocks,
> Its woods, and that uncertain heaven, received
> Into the bosom of the steady lake.
>
> (5.379–88, emphasis mine)

A voice, yes, but not a usurping logos; rather it is the "sound of waters,"
which in the great ode signals regeneration, the impending presence of the
poet's childhood spirit. "Or," and the equivalency between the two
phrases is a fine touch, the boy reproduces the scene internally, "un-
awares"—without loss or pain. There is also the rich indeterminacy of
the last two lines: does the watery reflection enter into his mind, or is his
mind itself the "bosom of the steady lake" that reproduces the scene?
Notice, too, how "bosom" preserves that maternal aura even to the far
side of what appears to be a crossing. Wordsworth has, it seems, evaded
the problems of poetic authority and of the already written: the voice of
the torrent resolves into the placid reflecting surface into which Eve and
Narcissus gazed. The crisis vanishes, but then reappears.

"Had I met these lines running wild in the desert of Arabia," Coleridge
said of the last two in this passage, "I should have instantly screamed out
'Wordsworth!' " Coleridge's remark displays more than a sensitivity to
his friend's singular rhetorical style. One senses in the passage a tension
about the boy's identity, his name. Who was he? A pre-1805 draft was
directly autobiographical: "And when it chanced / That pauses of deep
silence mocked *my* skill," and so on. Then, with revision, identity is generalized: he is "this Boy." He never has a name in that he never encounters
the order of discourse. "To name, to give names," says Derrida, "is the
gesture of the arche-writing: arche-violence, loss of the proper, of absolute proximity, of self-presence."[24] So the boy is never constituted, appropriated, fixed—but he is never quite human either. His fate seems close to
that of Narcissus:

---

[24] See Jacques Derrida, *Of Grammatology*, trans. Gayatri Spivak (Baltimore, Md.: The
Johns Hopkins University Press, 1974), p. 112.

> This Boy was taken from his mates, and died
> In childhood, ere he was full twelve years old.
>
> (5.389–90)

This boy, who was and was not Wordsworth, dies when the poet encounters the antipathies and promises of discourse. The gap between the internalization of the "steady lake" and the word of the boy's death is the gap between the experiencing child and the articulate poet, who composes the boy an epitaph that never names him properly. It is as though Narcissus's wounding has been transferred out of story of the boy's experience by the lake only to appear in the form of his early death. To name the boy would be to foreclose the possibility that the text of *The Prelude* is informed essentially by this scene of prelinguistic reciprocity. (Recall the impulse to discipline by naming the other found in Milton and Freud.) Holding the name in suspension implies, accordingly, that this idealized scene of crossing is the model of inspiration for Wordsworth's poem and that he will, at some point, make the word so much his own that he can remain true to the image of poetic self-genesis that the Winander Boy episode offers.

For Paul de Man an ethic of renunciation, which he takes to be Wordsworth's characteristic gesture, dominates the Winander Boy sequence. In it de Man finds "the transformation of an echo language into a language of the imagination by way of the mediation of a poetic understanding of mutability." For him Wordsworth's liminal state is one of "consenting submission" in which "consciousness admits mortality."[25] Yet in this case, Wordsworth seems more subtle than his critic. The poet both demystifies his idealized fiction of origins by admitting that the boy never crossed over into a fully human identity and uses the aspirations for poetic autogenesis implicit in the boy's story to invest the critical scene of self-creation at Gondo Gorge. Wordsworth's capacity both to demystify and to sustain his crossing of Narcissus (and to do so in brilliant verse) would perhaps qualify, at least in his own mind, as "Knowledge not purchased by the loss of power."

In the "Winander Boy" sequence Wordsworth divines the centrality of

[25] See "Wordsworth and Hölderlin" in *The Rhetoric of Romanticism* (New York: Columbia University Press, 1984), pp. 47–65. The quotations are from pp. 54–55.

Two other important deconstructive readings of the passage are Frances Ferguson's in *Wordsworth: Language as Counter-Spirit* (New Haven, Conn.: Yale University Press, 1977), pp. 242–50; and Andrzej Warminski's "Missed Crossing: Wordsworth's Apocalypses," *Modern Language Notes* 99 (December 1984): 983–1006. Both of these excellent treatments suffer from an unwillingness to read the "crossing" figure diachronically; an account that focuses on rewriting, on repetition with difference, cannot demote the presence of the poetic will as easily as these do.

the Narcissus myth in the Western tradition and its normative designs as well. When the myth is rehearsed by Ovid and Milton and Freud, it affirms the need of the self to submit to some single and ultimate authority and emphasizes the dangers in being "self-begotten and self-raised." Wordsworth, it would seem, comprehends this moral, but he is not ready to acquiesce to it. He depicts himself as someone who will ultimately not submit to the cultural imperative embodied in the traditional narrative. But here he attempts not so much to overcome the Narcissus myth as to circumvent it. He evades the full consequences of the conventional scene of Narcissus in that he is not usurped by an authoritative voice. But by including the boy's death in his account Wordsworth expresses his unwillingness, at least at this point in the poem, to declare that he has completely overcome the normative strictures that invest the myth. His key image for that overcoming is the Simplon Pass sequence.

. . .

The Simplon Pass episode separates into three segments. In the first, Wordsworth and his companion learn to their dismay that they have unknowingly crossed the Alps without having encountered any epiphanic experience. The second segment is the famous hymn to Imagination, and the third is Wordsworth's passage through Gondo Gorge. I begin by considering this third segment, which was composed in 1799, five years prior to the other two:

> Downwards we hurried fast,
> And, with the half-shaped road which we had missed,
> Entered a narrow chasm. The brook and road
> Were fellow-travellers in this gloomy strait,
> And with them did we journey several hours
> At a slow pace. The immeasurable height
> Of woods decaying, never to be decayed,
> The stationary blasts of waterfalls,
> And in the narrow rent at every turn
> Winds thwarting winds, bewildered and forlorn,
> The torrents shooting from the clear blue sky,
> The rocks that muttered close upon our ears,
> Black drizzling crags that spake by the way-side
> As if a voice were in them, the sick sight
> And giddy prospect of the raving stream,
> The unfettered clouds and region of the Heavens,
> Tumult and peace, the darkness and the light—

(6.619–35)

A great deal turns upon this final dash, which I come back to after looking at the passage. To my knowledge no one has pointed out that Wordsworth's description of the "chasm" descends from a classical literary topos, the depiction of Chaos. The vision of the originary elements at strife enters the tradition with Hesiod in the "Theogeny" (line 116) and occurs in, among others, Ovid, Augustine, Boccaccio, Guillaume du Bartas, Spenser, and perhaps of most consequence for Wordsworth, Milton. In *Paradise Lost* Milton describes Satan's entrance into Chaos:

> Into this wild Abyss,
> The Womb of nature and perhaps her Grave,
> Of neither Sea, nor Shore, nor Air, nor Fire,
> But all these in their pregnant causes mixt
> Confus'dly, and which thus must ever fight,
> Unless th' Almighty Maker them ordain
> His dark materials to create more Worlds.
>
> (2.910–16)

From Milton and the tradition Wordsworth appropriates the vision of primal strife: "Winds thwarting winds, bewildered and forlorn"; "The unfettered clouds and region of the Heavens, / Tumult and peace, the darkness and the light." Milton's Chaos, an "abyss" to Wordsworth's "chasm," is a wild amalgam, "neither Sea, nor Shore, nor Air, nor Fire," and true to the topos Wordsworth does get all of the primal elements into action. What seems singular in Wordsworth, and of particular interest in this enquiry, is the articulate landscape: muttering rocks, "crags that spake by the wayside," "the raving stream." The image is Dantesque, but Milton's Chaos anticipates it too:

> At length a universal hubbub wild
> Of stunning sounds and voices all confus'd
> Borne through the hollow dark assaults his ear
> With loudest vehemence . . .
>
> (2.951–5)

Conventionally, in both Christian and classical authors, Chaos is the inchoate rebellious matter that the presiding deity shapes into organic life, and so it is for Wordsworth.

Suddenly, at the dash, Wordsworth's vision turns around, as with the might of waters:

> The unfettered clouds and region of the Heavens,
> Tumult and peace, the darkness and the light—
> Were all like workings of one mind, the features
> Of the same face, blossoms upon one tree;

>   Characters of the great Apocalypse,
>   The types and symbols of Eternity,
>   Of first, and last, and midst, and without end.

>   (6.634–40)

The poem moves vertiginously from a depiction of first matter at inter-
necine war into a vision of last things in which all time—"first, and last,
and midst, and without end"—is resolved to a still point. The poem
passes in an instant from Chaos to Apocalypse, from the Bible's first
pages to its last, comparing indirectly but unmistakably the creation of
The Prelude to creation in the Bible.

The cacophony of voices in the first part of the passage—muttering
rocks, speaking crags, a raving stream—is suddenly compressed into a
pellucid text, the "Characters of the great Apocalypse." This turning,
which dramatizes the acquisition of an exalted poetic language, is comparable in form, I think, to Milton's great moment of crossing in book 3:
"Then feed on thoughts, that voluntary move / Harmonious numbers."
But how does Wordsworth do it? He gives us only the dash, refusing, it
seems, to represent the middle phase of his crossing. In imaginative terms,
he has forcefully entered the realms of existing discourse. Then he has
seemingly commanded this linguistic Chaos into the symbolic order of an
Apocalypse. The evasion of a threatening discourse we found in the "Boy
of Winander" scene seems at least momentarily overcome in the passage
through the gorge. Yet this potentially vast midspace, all that comes between Chaos and Apocalypse, is compressed into a dash.

Of course I am straining the question here: I mean to offer the hypothesis that the paean to Imagination composed in 1804 and placed prior to
the gorge sequence in the text is a proleptic image of the middle term in
the crossing.[26] It stands, I think, as Wordsworth's retrospective effort to
articulate a moment originally ineffable, to evoke the poetic power that
turns Chaos to Apocalypse:

>   Imagination—here the Power so called
>   Through sad incompetence of human speech,
>   That awful Power rose from the mind's abyss
>   Like an unfathered vapour that enwraps,
>   At once, some lonely traveller. I was lost;

[26] For a different approach, attuned to Wordsworth's displacement of political hopes onto
the scene, see M. H. Abrams's *Natural Supernaturalism: Tradition and Revolution in Romantic Literature* (New York: Norton, 1971), pp. 451–53. See also "English Romanticism:
The Spirit of the Age" in *The Correspondent Breeze: Essays on English Romanticism* (New
York: Norton, 1984), pp. 44–75, especially pp. 62–67.

For a more recent "historical" reading of the imagination passage see Alan Liu's "Wordsworth: The History in 'Imagination' " in *English Literary History* 51 (Fall 1984): 505–48.

Halted without an effort to break through;
But to my conscious soul I now can say—
'I recognize thy glory': in such strength
Of usurpation, when the light of sense
Goes out, but with a flash that has revealed
the invisible world, doth greatness make abode. . . .

(6.592–602)

Notice how certain phenomenal details of Wordsworth's entry into the gorge appear to reoccur in this passage in transmuted form, as if by transference. The "rising" of the "awful power" seems anticipated by the shooting torrents and fierce running stream, the "unfathered vapour" by the "winds thwarting winds" and "unfettered clouds," the "mind's abyss" by the "narrow chasm" of the gorge itself, and the "lonely traveller" by the "fellow travellers in this gloomy strait." More deeply, the scene of poetic passage or crossing itself is figured as taking place within the physical crossing of the gorge in which the poet also seems momentarily "lost."

The flash that reveals the invisible world, transforming Chaos to Apocalypse, unfolds beneath an "unfathered vapour" at the instant that "the light of sense goes out." Here Wordsworth guarantees that he is giving us the very type of sublime creation by paraphrasing Longinus, who writes of how "a well-timed stroke of sublimity scatters everything before it like a thunderbolt, and in a flash reveals the full power of the speaker."[27] "I was lost," Wordsworth says, and indeed the "I" is lost in this midspace: the self disappears altogether, somewhat in the manner of Milton's crossing. Missing from Wordsworth's description of the gorge and the Apocalyptic alphabet that follows is the slightest trace of Wordsworthian self-consciousness,[28] which, if one follows Milton and Freud, is not the cogito observing its own process but the internalized voice of the other—of tradition, law, limit, custom imposing its authority.[29] The wild proliferation of voices that assails Wordsworth when he enters the gorge signifies, in

[27] Aristotle, Horace, Longinus: Classical Literary Criticism, trans. T. R. Dorsch (New York: Penguin, 1965), p. 100.

[28] The point is Thomas Weiskel's in The Romantic Sublime, p. 199.

[29] My reading of this scene is in many ways at odds with what is probably the most influential "constructive" approach, that of Geoffrey Hartman in Wordsworth's Poetry 1787–1814 (New Haven, Conn.: Yale University Press, 1964), pp. 36–69. Our primary disagreement might center on his conception of imagination as "consciousness of self raised to apocalyptic pitch" (p. 17). My reading tends to accept the deconstruction of self-consciousness arrived at by our readings of Milton and Freud.

Weiskel's view of Wordsworthian imagination as "a saving resistance to the passage from image to symbol," although attractive in its implied sympathy for the visionary, seems to me to fail to account for the symbolic action of the Gorge sequence, in which imagination is more than a "defensive" faculty.

this reading, a foregrounding of vocal prohibitions. The effort of imagination, then, is to move through self-consciousness, through authorized and constitutive discourse, into a utopia of harmonious and unanimous signification, which resolves time and difference in a point of perpetual revelation. It is as though the perfect presence and present of Narcissus were recaptured on the far side of the intervening signifier in an achieved vision of the poet's own word beatified. From another point of view, the "I" disappears in the midspace in order to be reconceived and reborn in a fiction of origins that places the self prior to language and renders the very being of language contingent upon the will of the poet. Language waits upon man: the poet is the creator God who draws order from the abyss.

This reading might be tempered somewhat by the fruitful ambiguity that surrounds the word "usurpation" in the passage. Certainly it brings us in touch with the Satanic current in the crossing: the vision of Chaos on which I take Wordsworth to rely is Satan's in book 2, and the epithet "unfathered vapour" will recall the lines to Abdiel: "We know no time when we were not as now; / Know none before us, self-begot, self-rais'd / By our own quick'ning power" (5.859–61). Yet the Satanic urge for self-creation seems interfused with a more properly pious rhetoric. Wordsworth's evocation of "a flash that has revealed / The invisible world" is not far from Augustine's very representative depiction of Christian inspiration: "for a moment like a blinding light, a lightning flash through heavy darkness." This instant of physical blindness as prelude to spiritual insight draws one to the sacred invocation in book 3 and to Milton's offer of his blindness in exchange for prophetic power. The concurrence of blessed and demonic strands leaves us with at best a vital indeterminacy when we ask if the poet is here taken over by his imagination, usurped upon, or if he wills an assault on order and priority.

No matter what the answer to this difficulty, the stakes here remain high, and it will not take a resolutely deconstructive reader to resist the passage, or at least the reading I have offered. What is to Wordsworth an enabling fiction of self-genesis and of the "originality" of *The Prelude* may burden us with its presumption and displaced theology. To demystify the passage, one need only return to the text of "On Narcissism" and note the parallel between Wordsworth's Chaos of dark voices and Freud's description of the paranoiac's tendency to bring the internalized voices of the super-ego to consciousness in order to liberate himself from authority. This reading of the "Gondo Gorge" is bound to an undemonstrable tenet: that there is a "borderline condition" (and in this phrase the rhetorics of poetry and clinical diagnosis fortuitously meet) that is nonregressive. We might feel more confident in making this assertion when we recall what was at stake for Freud in his characterization of "narcissists" and "para-phrenics."

Of more moment to this enquiry is Wordsworth's capacity critically to anticipate and to read the scene of crossing in Freudian therapy. Against the intervening voice of therapeutic authority Wordsworth implicitly pits the power of imaginative "usurpation" that, whatever its relation to the will, breaks through the discourse of anteriority and confinement to found a new language on the farther side. To speak more encompassingly, if the limits of contemporary language are, as I argued in the Introduction, in many ways the limits of Freud's tropes, then Wordsworth's passage enjoins the image-making power (the power of Satan, Eve, the narcissist, the speculator, and the poet) as the means of renewing language and life. At the same time, this observation raises Freud's normative language to the level from which a renewed poetic discourse must arise: "Those images that yet / Fresh images beget," as Yeats has it.

One lesson of the Simplon Pass sequence, at least as I understand it, is that although most people will assume the discourses that culture offers or imposes upon them, there are others who will not. Such people aspire to speak a different language and, perhaps, to live a different sort of life, despite the forces that oppose them. Milton's scene at the pool is rewritten at the Simplon Pass, but so too is Freud's therapeutic scene. Wordsworth here shows us how the discourse of a supernal deity or of an invisible analyst might be displaced in the interest of one's own particular quest for self-determination.

The Simplon Pass sequence concentrates Wordsworth's aspirations for *The Prelude* as a whole: it is a microcosm of the poem's overall design. In it Wordsworth provides a condensed image of his ambitions. The proof of success that he offers is the poem itself. For anyone compelled to submit to harsh norms of any sort, Wordsworth's poem provides an image of possible human resistance.

IV

And yet there may be a certain injustice in what I have said so far; the contrast I have established between Freud and Wordsworth might be too stark, overdrawn. For I have purposely chosen what is perhaps Wordsworth's most aggressive text on the theme of imagination. The poet is never more recklessly Romantic than at the Simplon Pass. Rather than closing the comparison here, I want to try to see how the imagination is conceived in a few other moments in the poet's work. Can Wordsworth do consistently what Freud did not, unbind his Romantic impulse from the bureacratic or normative? Is the Simplon Pass an isolated moment, or does it provide the pattern for Wordsworth's major poetry? This further enquiry into Wordsworth also allows us to extend our reflections on psychoanalysis and to see more clearly the part played by the therapist in the analytical drama. We have come to understand the way that the patient can be fixed by the Freudian exchange, but what about the doctor? Is the physician himself, whose psychological health is supposed to exemplify that to which the patient can aspire, genuinely free?

The affirmation in the paean to imagination of "hope that can never die" connects the passage indirectly, but illuminatingly, I think, to what is probably Wordsworth's first great poem, "The Ruined Cottage." (F. R. Leavis, in fact, believed it to be his greatest.)[30] The version of the poem that I consider here was completed in 1798 but not actually published until Jonathan Wordsworth included it in the volume entitled *The Music of Humanity* in 1968.[31] The hope at issue in "The Ruined Cottage" is that of Margaret, who seems quite literally to perish from hope's excess. Despite years of disappointment, Margaret cannot surrender her hope that her husband, who has been forced by economic disaster to leave home and enlist in the army, will eventually return to her.[32] Margaret pines away and dies because she cannot detach herself from the past; she yearns incurably for the complete restoration of what is gone, for what over time becomes her own version, one might suggest, of "the glory and the dream."

Armytage, who knew Margaret, tells the story to a young man, Wordsworth's stand-in on some level, and throughout his narrative of Margaret's sorrows one senses that Armytage's feelings for the young woman were, and perhaps are, potentially comparable to those she sustained for her husband.[33] I say "potentially" because the Wanderer struggles in telling the tale, as he appears to have struggled when he witnessed Margaret's gradual decline, not to surrender to self-ruining sorrow:

> You will forgive me, sir,
> But often on this cottage do I muse

---

[30] See Leavis's *Revaluation: Tradition and Development in English Poetry* (London: Chatto and Windus, 1936), pp. 154–202. The "revaluation" comes specifically on p. 179.

Coleridge also estimated "The Ruined Cottage" highly, taking it to be one of Wordsworth's best performances. He described it as "the finest poem in our language, comparing it with any of the same or similar length."

[31] All quotations from "The Ruined Cottage," cited by line number in the body of the text, are from *The Music of Humanity* (London: Thomas Nelson and Sons, 1969).

[32] See Jerome McGann's account of the way Wordsworth works gradually to elide the social content of the text, placing emphasis instead on private narratives; the point is accurate in that every major figure in "The Ruined Cottage" comes, in time, to signify some aspect or potential aspect of Wordsworth's own subjectivity. See *The Romantic Ideology: A Critical Investigation* (Chicago: University of Chicago Press, 1983), pp. 82–86.

[33] See Peter J. Manning, "Wordsworth, Margaret, and The Pedlar," *Studies in Romanticism* 15 (1976): 195–220, especially p. 210.

As on a picture, till my wiser mind
Sinks, yielding to the foolishness of grief.

(116–19)

In book 10 of *The Republic* Plato argues for banishing art from his ideal
state not only because it imitates mere imitation but also because it stim-
ulates the emotions to overthrow the rule of logos. Art is, to Plato, a fem-
inizing influence. It is at the aesthetic moment, when the cottage becomes
"a picture," that the Wanderer feels his powers of control threatened. His
"wiser mind" sinks like the sun, the sign of mastering, masculine reason.

Notice how in the above lines—as at many of the points of maximum
intensity in the narrative—the Wanderer addresses the younger man as
"sir."[34] It is as though the Wanderer needs to evoke the stability of class
boundaries, and also perhaps of masculine solidarity, at the moments
when his "wiser mind" is threatened by a feminine impulse to mourn. His
narrative is, moreover, extremely attentive to the fate of the physical
boundaries of Margaret's cottage. The decay and collapse of those
boundaries works often as a synecdoche, not only for the decay of the
property as a whole but also for Margaret's personal decline.[35] It is difficult not to hear a certain anxiety in the Wanderer's voice when he speaks
of the breakdown of walls, the incursion of weeds into the garden, the
overgrowing of the path, and the way that sheep were allowed to couch
"even at her threshold" (336).

This sensitivity to the fate of material boundaries points up the Wanderer's concern, evident all through his tale, about boundaries of a more
abstract sort, such as those between self-control and grief, masculinity
and femininity, reason and passion, knowledge and art. The Wanderer is
not, as some critics have thought, an unfeeling, icy personage; he recognizes that the second term in each of these pairs has a certain undeniable
place in every human life. But he is also determined that the borders that
contain the potentially refractory powers of femininity, grief, passion,
and a certain sort of art within him are going to stay intact.[36] His peda-
gogical objective in the poem is not only to show his younger listener how
this sort of bordering is achieved but also to challenge and reconfirm his
own resources of defense. One might even say that Armytage strengthens
himself by transferring the burden of his perplexity to the young man,

---

[34] See ll. 96, 116, 252, 362, 375.

[35] See *Music of Humanity*, p. 130.

[36] The status of the border or liminal zone is central to Jonathan Wordsworth's reading
of the poet. See *William Wordsworth: The Borders of Vision* (Oxford: Clarendon Press,
1982).

Christopher Ricks reflects usefully on borders in both a thematic and formal sense in his
essay "William Wordsworth 1: 'A Pure Organic Pleasure From The Lines' " in *The Force
of Poetry* (Oxford: Clarendon Press, 1984), pp. 100–101.

whose attractions to disabling grief the Wanderer will be compelled to
discipline. Thus Armytage will externalize his own inner state and gain,
by way of an exercise of instruction, a form of interior control, a dynamic
that may not be unfamilar to those who teach. I return to this line of
thinking shortly, but first some basic observations are in order: we need
a larger sense of what the figure of Armytage would have meant to
Wordsworth.

The Wanderer bears a family resemblance to a whole line of characters
that seems to have fascinated the poet—stoical, solitary, self-reliant old
men of the earth who inhabit a blurred zone between life and inorganic
form, figures, presumably, whose early love of Nature has induced her to
take them very gradually back to herself in their later years. Armytage is
far more vital than, say, the Old Cumberland Beggar or the leech-gatherer in "Resolution and Independence," yet he is unmistakably related to
them in Wordsworth's imagination. Many readers probably feel, as I do,
a little chilled by these characters, who seem to be unwitting recipients of
the curse of Tithonus, but Wordsworth in certain moods is cheered by
them.[37]

These figures, as Wordsworth indicates in "Resolution and Independence," move him in part because they illustrate a way that one might
survive the dashing of high Romantic hopes. Like the leech-gatherer, Armytage is an implicit answer to the question of how a spirit that is prone
to making the kinds of demands on experience that Burns and Chatterton
and Margaret make could go on living after fate has denied them what
they desire most. Wordsworth seems to know that there is something in
his own make-up that is akin to Margaret and to those poets whose capacity for early joy leads them to despondency and madness. But he is
also determined, no matter what befalls him, to go on living. In a figure
like Armytage, whose passions are so circumscribed that he sometimes
seem to be one who, as Lacan would put it, desires to be without desires,
Wordsworth would have seen a model of wise self-sufficiency. The Wanderer represents a position into which the poet might withdraw if the
worst befell him—or which he might assume in advance to head danger
off. Yet though the self-created (and self-creating) boundaries that defend
Armytage may be one answer to Wordsworth's difficulty, they are not an
answer with which he can be fully content.

The evidence for this discontent lies in the poetry. Wordsworth—like
any number of ambitious young men—takes a peculiar pleasure in assum-
ing the voice of venerable figures of wisdom. And he is admirably elo-

---

[37] Michael Cooke describes this state of stoical remove as a Wordsworthian ideal in *The
Romantic Will* (New Haven, Conn.: Yale University Press, 1976), pp. 201–16.

quent when he speaks through Armytage, as a few particularly well-wrought lines clearly show:

> "I see around me here
> Things which you cannot see. We die, my Friend,
> Nor we alone, but that which each man loved
> And prized in his peculiar nook of earth
> Dies with him, or is changed, and very soon
> Even of the good is no memorial left."
>
> (67–72)

Despite the solecism "We die, my Friend," the verse is persuasively elegiacal; the cadences convey a measured dignity and resolve. Yet as accomplished as the lines no doubt are, there is also something inert and overworked about them. Armytage here, as at other points in the poem, seems less to be talking than reading a lengthy engraving. Moreover, the sensibility conveyed in the lines is almost prototypically neoclassical, such that the passage suffers from the flaw that Dr. Johnson found in so many able but undistinguished performances: it gives us very little that is new. Adopting Armytage as an ideal may be a step toward self-preservation, but it clearly does not unlock the kind of innovative poetry that Wordsworth aspired to write.[38]

If one searches "The Ruined Cottage" for a fresher and more arresting voice, one naturally comes to Margaret. Inhabiting her sensibility releases an impressive force of passion and verbal resource in Wordsworth, much in the way that identifying himself with flawed but vital creators did in Browning:

> "I perceive
> You look at me, and you have cause. Today
> I have been travelling far, and many days
> About the fields I wander, knowing this
> Only, that what I seek I cannot find.
> And so I waste my time: for I am changed,
> And to myself," said she, "have done much wrong,
> And to this helpless infant. I have slept
> Weeping, and weeping I have waked. My tears
> Have flowed as if my body were not such
> As others are, and I could never die.
> But I am now in mind and in my heart
> More easy, and I hope," said she, "that heaven

[38] Leavis is thus right to say that Wordsworth "sought the Wanderer's 'equipoise' just because of the 'piteous revolutions' and the 'wild varieties of joy and grief' that he had so disturbingly known" (*Revaluation*, p. 178), but this is only part of the story.

Will give me patience to endure the things
Which I behold at home."

(347–61)

One could not easily, in my view, overpraise this passage, and it succeeds
at least in part by being what Wordsworth says in the famous Preface that
he wants all of his poetry to be, seemingly spontaneous, simple in its diction, urgent, compelling without being sensationalistic.[39] Yet the voice of
Margaret is not at all Wordsworth's characteristic voice: it is far too sudden and unpremeditated. As Leavis rightly says, "It has to be admitted
that the present of [Wordsworth's] poetry is, for the most part, decidedly
tranquil and that the emotion—anything in the nature of strong excite-
ment or disturbance—seems to belong decidedly to the past."[40] Margaret's voice, one might say, is the voice within Wordsworth's "proper"
voice, the voice that is remembered, pursued, and mourned, but never
completely acquired. Or rather, Margaret's voice is the negative form—
the despondent inverse—of the joyous voice that Wordsworth both wants
and does not want fully to possess.

Some relationship to the intensity of feeling that Margaret represents is
critical to what one would recognize as truly Wordsworthian poetry; yet
the dangers of becoming Margaret, of making her voice uninhibitedly his
own, are palpable to Wordsworth. She is something of a taboo figure in
Frazer's sense, one who emanates both power and danger. Might one
speak of her elaborate distancing within the text—her lines are mediated
by Armytage, whose words pass through the young man, then Wordsworth the author—as a "civilized" form of counterspell against totemic
contagion? For whatever the disease is that afflicts Margaret, it seems
capable of being "transferred": Armytage says that Margaret's child has
"from its mother caught the trick of grief" (410); and there is a point of
severe anxiety at which the Wanderer, sitting with Margaret, hears sighs
and cannot tell "whence they came" (387). Are they hers, his, theirs? Or
do they derive from some unbounded region that no available pronoun
can quite fix?

Margaret's grief is potentially destructive of the boundaries that enable
one to live the well-proportioned stoical life for which the narrator re-
veres Armytage. One danger of her sort of mourning (and perhaps of the
kind of love that leads one to it) is, I think, that it may force upon one a
sense of the arbitrariness of certain socially constructed boundaries, particularly the boundaries of conventional gender identity.[41] Margaret's

---

[39] *The Poetical Words of William Wordsworth* ed. Ernest de Selincourt, 5 vols. (Oxford:
Clarendon Press, 1944), 2:383–404.

[40] Leavis, *Revaluation*, p. 176.

[41] See D. A. Miller's remarks on homophobia and the "transference" of femininity in his

presence threatens to feminize the Wanderer, just as hearing her story will threaten the masculinity of the narrator. (Kenneth Johnston, a fine reader of the poem, speaks with no perceptible irony of the "narrator's helpless, unmanned response.")[42] If Margaret is in some sense "the poet in the poet," then it seems fair to conjecture that what is most authentically original and Romantic in Wordsworth involves a negative force of dissolution, one that threatens not only the boundaries imposed by various conventions but also life itself.[43] Yet it is a force that Wordsworth clearly cannot do without.[44]

These difficulties work their way into a critical knot by the end of "The Ruined Cottage" when, after Margaret's tale has been recited, the younger man turns aside "in weakness":

> I stood, and leaning o'er the garden gate
> Reviewed that Woman's suff'rings; and it seemed
> To comfort me while with a brother's love
> I blessed her in the impotence of grief.
>
> (497–500)

Impotence, an "unmanned response": surely the issue of symbolic neutering contributes to the crisis here. But still there is something to hold onto; as Jonathan Wordsworth sensitively observes, the young man "is comforted by the garden gate on which he leans—because it offers a standard of normality, something ordinary that is still going on."[45] Soon the young man's stay and prop, his border, will be Armytage, who intervenes, vocally, upon his sad speculations:

> "My Friend, enough to sorrow have you given,
> The purposes of wisdom ask no more:
> Be wise and cheerful, and no longer read
> The forms of things with an unworthy eye."
>
> (508–11)

---

remarkable book *The Novel and the Police* (Berkeley and Los Angeles: University of California Press, 1988), pp. 152–56.

[42] See *Wordsworth and "The Recluse"* (New Haven, Conn.: Yale University Press, 1984), p. 44.

[43] See J. Hillis Miller's remarks on this tendency to destabilization in Wordsworth in *Linguistic Moment*, pp. 61–63. Miller sees this drive as always somehow overcoming the poet's more conventional allegiance to form. My own perspective emphasizes an unresolved and unresolvable dialectic.

[44] The kind of ambivalence that Margaret evokes in the poet may in this case be responsible for the tendency Coleridge found in Wordsworth of "feeling *for*, but never *with*," his characters. For a more general critique of the limits of Wordsworthian sympathy, see David Ferry's *The Limits of Mortality: An Essay on Wordsworth's Major Poems* (Middletown, Conn.: Wesleyan University Press, 1959).

[45] *Music of Humanity*, p. 99.

The humanely authoritative voice intrudes upon a rapture different from, but connected to, that of Narcissus, and recalls comparable interventions in Milton and Freud. As Freud teaches us, self-ruining melancholia derives from the loss of the narcissistically invested object and is the fate of those who love "in the feminine manner."[46] Margaret will not let go, and the young man faces a similar danger. But not relinquishing, refusing detachment, may also be a prerequisite for becoming a poet in the Romantic vein: one who has a "disposition to be affected more than other men by absent things as if they were present,"[47] to cite Wordsworth's own well-known description of the poetic temperament; one whose dispositions of feeling challenge the socially insinuated ethos of safe investment and predictable return; one whose radical ebb and flow affront the ideology of the stable subject and the institutional practices that arise from the "creation" of subjects. But unlike the hymn to imagination and hope in *The Prelude*'s sixth book, "The Ruined Cottage" records the sufferings to which the Romantic spirit is prone.

Yet there appears to be a cure. Armytage's strategy is to induce the disease of melancholia in his friend by way of a fiction and, that done, to go on to provide a remedy. The young narrator, one can speculate, would not have responded as strongly as he did to Margaret's tale if the proclivity for over-strong attachments, for being "affected more than other men," was not highly developed in him. Armytage educates him, not by ministering directly to this tendency, but by using a narrative to produce a displaced set of symptoms. In other words, Armytage brings on a form of transference illness. As Freud writes, the transference assumes "all the features of the illness; but it represents an artificial illness which is at every point accessible to our intervention. It is a piece of real experience, but one which has been made possible by specially favorable conditions, and it is of a provisional nature" (12:154).

I said that the young man must have appeared to Armytage to be particularly susceptible to the disease of overattachment; but be that as it may, the Wanderer's narrative skill also confers upon him, by his own admission, a dose of the same sort of malady. The Wanderer infects and, presumably, "cures" the narrator in order also to minister to his own defenses. In *The Golden Bough*, a book that Freud admired, Frazer describes the primitive method of healing by transferring the malady to inanimate objects, to animals, and to other men. The last section on the subject discusses "the Transference of Evil" as a European social practice.[48]

---

[46] I take up this issue in the next chapter.

[47] Wordsworth's *Poetical Works*, 2:393.

[48] See Sir James George Frazer's *The Golden Bough*, 7 vols. (New York: St. Martin's Press, 1911), 6:1–59.

Wordsworth's text, then, encourages one to pose some questions about the analyst's true role in the therapeutic exchange. To what degree is therapy a ritual in which the therapist projects her own wayward impulses onto the person of the patient, there to discipline them by the use of an authoritative voice that both is and is not her own? Is the patient's role in therapy as unmediated id or unconscious established, at least in some measure, to force the doctor into a confirmation of her own ego or superego? Is what Freud called the "counter-transference" then constituted at least in part by the analyst's drive to apprehend the patient as a figure of pure desire, along with her collateral resistances against doing so? In other words, might not therapy be, in at least one of its dimensions, a ritual of askesis for an aspiring secular clerisy? If these questions do have some bearing, one might also ask in whose interest the therapeutic process is really conducted. The answer then would be that it is perhaps in the physician's interest, but that it is more certainly in Freud's. For Freud, one ought to remember, found the greatest threat to the continuity of psychoanalysis in the tendency of his disciples and heirs to rebel. What "The Ruined Cottage" teaches us most centrally about Freud, I think, is the extent to which the therapeutic procedure, as it is outlined in the papers on technique, works to discipline in analysts (and not just in patients) the activity that worried Freud the most, what he thought of as "speculation," which is very close, if not identical, to what a Romantic like Wordsworth would call—"through sad incompetence of human speech"—imagination.

·   ·   ·

But the issues to which Freud makes us attentive in Wordsworth are in their way more disturbing. To begin with, one might, setting out from this brief reading of "The Ruined Cottage," redescribe some important moments of Wordsworth's career in terms of the question, How shall I go on living, protecting myself from self-destroying "melancholia," but also go on writing the poetry that matters, poetry that has some access to the spirit of Margaret? This redescription would be a difficult task, in that Wordsworth's urgency over the question compels him time and again to rewrite and to complicate the dialectic whose contours—no more than that—I located in "The Ruined Cottage." Among many other things, one would have to consider the way that the poet's sister Dorothy, invisible until the final verse paragraph of "Tintern Abbey," is suddenly invoked as a guarantor, lest the myth of memory fail and the poet's genial spirits decay.[49] Memory becomes for Wordsworth, under the influence of Cole-

---

[49] Richard Onorato remarks on Dorothy's indeterminate status in the poem in *The Char-*

ridge and particularly his "Frost at Midnight," the faculty that can mediate between child and man, preserve poetic force while relieving the poet of the burden of having to coincide completely with the vulnerable and dangerous Romantic self. But the failure of the religion of memory is already written into the poem in the need to turn to Dorothy, a figure both attached to (so safely possessed by) and outside of (so not in danger of destroying) the poet. From this perspective, too, one might see a poem like "A slumber did my spirit seal" as an effort to preserve contact with the feminine while externalizing it, this time through a sort of scapegoating. When "she" is "Rolled round in earth's diurnal course, / With rocks, and stones, and trees," the fatal muse is present but dispersed, accessible but not mortally close.[50] It is the poet now who both hears and sees with the acuity that Lucy once possessed.[51]

These remarks are meant to be only elementary and provisional ones; clearly the dynamic is extremely complex, and to read the poems I have mentioned and other relevant ones would be a long, exacting task. But if my remarks thus far do little justice to the unfolding subtlety of Wordsworth's text, they do begin to disclose a certain affinity among Milton and Freud and Wordsworth. Each seems to have a disposition to project his own image of creative and transgressive force onto a female figure, such that one might speak of the place occupied by Eve, the narcissist, and now Margaret, Dorothy, and Lucy and, on the other side, of the place taken by the poet authorized by God, the therapist, and now the Wanderer, the leech-gatherer, and the man who possesses the "philosophic mind."[52] (One might think also of Freud the self-inventor and the normative representation of the individual subject from the reading of the Oedipal passage.) This observation is perhaps too compressed; it occludes too many differences among the authors, but it usefully challenges the rather stark contrast I drew earlier between Wordsworth's hymn to

---

acter of the Poet: Wordsworth in "The Prelude" (Princeton, N.J.: Princeton University Press, 1971), p. 82.

[50] Thus F. W. Bateson seems to me to be astute, if too narrowly focused, when he reads the Lucy poems as symbolic exorcisms of the poet's love for his sister. See Wordsworth: A Reinterpretation (London: Longman's, 1954), especially pp. 153ff.

[51] Frances Ferguson reads the Lucy poems as a progress in which the poet develops a more demystified sense of "the object" and of "poetic language." Her emphasis on issues of epistemology provides an alternative to approaches like mine that press the subject of imagination. See Wordsworth: Language as Counter-Spirit, pp. 173–94.

[52] Thus Lionel Trilling's question as to whether the ode is about growing old or growing up still seems the right one to ask; it is Trilling's undialectical affirmation of "the philosophic mind" that needs, in its turn, to be questioned. The classic essay, "The Immortality Ode," appears in The Liberal Imagination, pp. 129–59.

imagination and the ethos of the therapeutic scene. Wordsworth is na-
kedly and aggressively self-venturing at the Simplon Pass, challenging any
number of symbolic and social accommodations. Yet another perspective
on his work reveals him to be, at least at times, intricately self-defended
in a manner that brings to mind the dialectic between the normative and
the Romantic Freud.

Wordsworth's distinctions ought not to be discounted: his discourse
remains contingent; he has little impulse to generalize or institutionalize
his dramas of self-engendering in the way that Freud does; and Wordsworth, at least in the early moments of his career when he is writing Margaret's story and the tale of the female vagrant, allows the woman a voice,
one that reveals the poet's own dependency on the feminine. Freud's female patients, on the other hand, are for all purposes silenced in his text.
Moreover, one continually feels the pathos involved in Wordsworth's ambivalent relations with the feminine, while Freud can say very little about
women that is not infused with an anxious disdain. In response to Freud's
derisive "What does a woman want?" one might suggest that, first of all,
she wants not to be fixed within the Freudian allegory.

Yet the continuities between Freud and Wordsworth remain troubling,
particularly for a critic who set out with a conviction about the large
distinctions to be made between Freud's ethos and that of the major Romantic poets. In the Conclusion I return to the issues that arise from the
parallels found in this chapter. For now, though, it will pay to continue
the enquiry into the ideology of the narcissistic ego and consider a further
Romantic alternative.

My approach in this chapter has been to some degree structural. That
is, I have emphasized the positions and exchanges that make up the therapeutic encounter as Freud describes it, and I have considered Wordsworth in terms of his ability to engage, to shift, and to transform certain
constituent parts of received literary forms. In associating Margaret's self-
ruining love with the condition that Freud stigmatized as narcissism, I
began to pay some attention to the modes of energy that are involved in
Wordsworthian creation. But we still lack a full sense of how Freud
thought that energy (or libido, as he would call it) was distributed in and
by the narcissistic ego, particularly when that ego comes into contact with
therapeutic authority. How shall one characterize the disposition of force
that accompanies obedience to the psychoanalytical norm? What sort of
energy makes for resistance? And what are the costs to others and to oneself of engaging either kind of force?

To answer these questions I turn to "Mourning and Melancholia," the
concluding text in the series that begins with "On Narcissism" and runs
through the papers on therapy and technique. In contrast to Freud's great

essay on grief and loss, the next chapter poses the work of Emerson. Emerson was, from his earliest writing onward, fascinated by the question of force. His work was a continual enquiry into how one might attain personal creative power despite the inhibiting claims of grief. The dialogue between Emerson and Freud will clarify the normative designs of the narcissistic ego and lend further insight into the Romantic alternatives.

Chapter Four

THE WORK OF MELANCHOLIA:
"MOURNING AND MELANCHOLIA,"
1917

GERTRUDE: Thou know'st 'tis common, all that lives must die,
Passing through nature to eternity.
HAMLET: Ay, madam, it is common.
—Shakespeare, *Hamlet*

FREUD'S creation of the narcissistic ego is not completed in the 1914 essay, or in the intramural pieces on therapy and technique that surround it. If erotic life (and eros is never considered by Freud in isolation from the issue of authority) is our most central and determining life, then it is not enough to theorize the ways that the ego constitutes others as objects. The action of de-cathexis or detachment may be yet more critical: if we are not always in the act of falling in love, we are invariably in the process of losing something that we have loved, or of experiencing our own love's decline. What Freud calls "the labors of grief" (*Trauerarbeit*) are, as Wordsworth knew probably better than anyone, going on continually.

Freud's reflections on loss and grief become interpretable, it seems to me, when placed within the context provided by Emerson, whose own reflections on mourning traverse the body of his work. The pages that follow show how this issue became as crucial as it did for Emerson and then proceed to put him into a dialogue with Freud on the dynamics of loss.

. . .

There coexist in *Nature*, Emerson's first book, two contending urges that continue up to a certain point and in highly transformed guises to self-divide, and in doing so to vitalize his prose. The "Transparent Eyeball" passage is the crossroad at which they, perhaps for the first time, stage a full encounter. "Coherence in contradiction expresses the force of a desire," says Derrida,[1] and the scene in question presents a significantly coherent contradiction, which one might describe in basic terms as a desire to preserve continuity while practicing disjunction.

The most concise expression of Emerson's "anxiety of continuity," to

---

[1] *Writing and Difference*, p. 279.

use Northrop Frye's phrase, occurs in the "Language" chapter of *Nature*. There he writes the by-now-famous equation:

> Language is a third use which Nature subserves to man. Nature is the vehicle of thought, and in a simple, double, and threefold degree:
>
> 1. Words are signs of natural facts.
> 2. Particular natural facts are symbols of particular spiritual facts.
> 3. Nature is the symbol of spirit.[2]

Emerson means in his third observation that Nature is *potentially* the symbol of spirit, but our corruption by what he calls "secondary desires,—the desire of riches, of pleasure, of power, and of praise" (p. 22) has brought a fall from a former, harmonious state in which man spoke nature. If this is so, the poet-prophet's task must be to integrate the "particular" natural and spiritual facts until nature and spirit reveal themselves as the harmonious totality they potentially are.[3] A redeemed language will presumably be the medium for the American "marriage" of the mind and the "goodly universe."[4]

Those terms are Wordworth's, of course, and Emerson derives his early organicism from Coleridge and the Wordsworth who writes at Coleridge's behest in his more programmatic poetry, such as the *Recluse* fragment. It was this piece that drove Blake to his expostulation against the mind and nature "fitting and being fitted" and, according to Crabb Robinson, incited the bowel complaint that nearly killed the poet. Blake's wrathful marginalia address Wordsworth as "your lordship," suggesting that the kind of political conservatism and love for the status quo that eventually came out in the Lake District poets was the underside of their early, "revolutionary" organicism. Although, as we have seen, Wordsworth is only ambivalently a poet of beautiful accommodations, Coleridge's appetite for totality and continuity shows up on nearly every page of his prose.[5] As a young man Emerson steeped himself in *Aids to Reflection* and the *Biographia*, finding there a religion of nature that seemed apposite to the New World experience but also enough displaced theol-

---

[2] Ralph Waldo Emerson, *Essays and Lectures*, ed. Joel Porte (New York: The Library of America, 1983), p. 20. All references to Emerson's prose works are to this edition and appear in the body of the text.

[3] See Kenneth Burke's essay on the Emersonian sublime in *Nature*, "I, Eye, Ay—Concerning Emerson's Early Essay on 'Nature,' and the Machinery of Transcendence," in *Language as Symbolic Action* (Berkeley and Los Angeles: University of California Press, 1966), pp. 186–200.

[4] See Charles Feidelson's *Symbolism and American Literature* (Chicago: University of Chicago Press, 1953), pp. 142–50, for comments on Emerson's organicism.

[5] The classical treatment of Coleridge's visionary organicism is I. A. Richards's *Coleridge on Imagination* (New York: Norton, 1950).

ogy to keep him in transitional contact with the Puritan tradition.[6] At any number of points in the *Biographia*, Coleridge seems to prefigure Emerson's more conventional aspirations for achieving a totalizing vision. A passage like this one, in which Coleridge describes the "esemplastic power" of the imagination would have spoken forcefully to the Emerson of the 1820s and early 1830s:

> This power . . . reveals itself in the balance or reconciliation of opposite or discordant qualities: of sameness, with difference; of the general, with the concrete; the idea, with the image; the individual, with the representative; the sense of novelty and freshness, with old and familiar objects; a more than usual state of emotion, with more than usual order; judgement ever awake and steady self-possession, with enthusiasm and feeling profound or vehement; and while it blends and harmonizes the natural and the artificial, still subordinates art to nature; the manner to the matter; and our admiration of the poet to our sympathy with the poetry.[7]

This image of the poet as a synthesizing god, rendering all difference into harmony by a willed blending of the variorum of sense, feeling, and thought, might have served as an emblem of imaginative possibility for the young Emerson. One could see as a god sees, without impiety yet without having to submit to a transcendent power either.

Coleridge's ideal, which in many ways motivates Emerson's first book, participates in what one might call "the metaphysical dream." That dream is to find a language that represents the world as it truly is from some Archimedean vantage. As Richard Rorty puts it, "The notion that our chief task is to mirror accurately, in our own Glassy Essence, the universe around us is the complement of the notion, common to Democritus and Descartes, that the universe is made up of very simple, clearly and distinctly knowable things, knowledge of whose essences provides the master-vocabulary which permits commensuration of all discourses."[8] Emerson's urge is similarly to uncover "essences" by aligning words, natural facts, and spiritual facts; like every dreamer of the "metaphysical dream," he wants to get what is out there—nature—under control. To render "all things transparent" and to reveal our own "glassy

[6] See Gay Wilson Allen's *Waldo Emerson* (New York: Penguin, 1981), pp. 160–61; also "From Coleridge to Emerson" in F. O. Matthiessen's *American Renaissance, Art and Expression in the Age of Emerson and Whitman* (New York: Oxford University Press, 1941), pp. 133–40; and Sherman Paul's *Emerson's Angle of Vision* (Cambridge, Mass.: Harvard University Press, 1952), pp. 40–48.

[7] *Biographia Literaria*, ed. James Engell and Walter Jackson Bate, *The Collected Works of Samuel Taylor Coleridge*, 16 vols., Bollingen Edition (Princeton, N.J.: Princeton University Press, 1983), 7:2. 16–17.

[8] *Philosophy and the Mirror of Nature* (Princeton, N.J.: Princeton University Press, 1979), p. 357.

essence" is to achieve a universal dominance. The posture is in many ways defensive and attempts to identify the subject with external forces outside the reach of time and chance. To the extent that the "metaphysical dream" is motivated by a fear of being overwhelmed in a chaos of disordered sensations, its articulations tend to be violent and compulsive. There is an anxious, jarring rush in the passage from Coleridge to force as many opposites together as possible. Something in the insistently temporal rhythms of writing resists representations of totality, though, and that conflict between conceptual design and the recalcitrance offered it by language may account for much of what is singular in Coleridge's style. Yet there is another sort of violence, less defensive and more visionary, submerged in Coleridge.

Perceptible in the early Emerson, and active sporadically throughout Coleridge, is a sense that the secondary or poetic imagination comes to birth through a violent rejection of the givens of experience. It turns against the echo in the mind of the "infinite I Am" and is driven to "dissolve, diffuse and dissipate" (perhaps in imitation of Dis) the primary order. Sometimes this urge to visionary dissolution rises in Coleridge with a surprising vehemence, as when in "Dejection" he launches into what sounds like the midst of a daemonic epic: "Thou mighty Poet, e'en to frenzy bold! / What tell'st thou now about?" Coleridge asks the wind, calling for inspiration. And he is answered by a compelling, dark muse: "Tis of the rushing of an host in rout, / With groans, of trampled men, with smarting wounds."[9] From the prospect of such an epic Coleridge retreats in disarray, invoking an image of a helpless child lost upon a moor. The child is a version of Coleridge, a figure far too innocent to dare the kind of poem that unexpectedly ruptures his verse letter.[10]

Emerson's own disjunctive urge is, through most of *Nature*, almost as mildly accommodated as his Coleridgean organicism; he calls it a "noble doubt" as to whether "nature outwardly exists." Less subtle than Coleridge, though still inspired by him, Emerson raises his doubt in conventional Cartesian terms:

> To the senses and the unrenewed understanding, belongs a sort of instinctive belief in the absolute existence of nature. In their view, man and nature are indissolubly joined. Things are ultimates, and they never look beyond their sphere. The presence of Reason mars this faith. The first effort of thought tends to relax this despotism of the senses, which binds us to nature as if we were a part of it, and shows us nature aloof, and, as it were,

[9] *The Complete Poetical Works of Samuel Taylor Coleridge*, ed. Ernest Hartley Coleridge, 2 vols. (Oxford: Clarendon Press, 1912), 1:367.
[10] I am indebted here to Walter Jackson Bate's comments on the poem. See his *Coleridge* (New York: Macmillan, 1968), pp. 106–10.

afloat. . . . If the Reason be stimulated to more earnest vision, outlines and surfaces become transparent, and are no longer seen; causes and spirits are seen through them. The best moments of life are these delicious awakenings of the higher powers, and the reverential withdrawing of nature before its God. (p. 33)

This begins to move away from the kind of totalizing vision that depended on a pure reciprocity between subject and nature. Emerson's ambition to dissolve contours and surfaces is a retrospective commentary on the "Transparent Eyeball" passage that emphasizes all of its most radical drift. Reason's power to break relations with the given, a power that later will become crucial to Emerson, receives one of its first discursive expressions here. But I want to defer fuller consideration of Emerson's contending drives—on the one hand to organicism, transparency, harmony, and comprehensive mastery, and to disjunction, negation, and imaginative self-recreation on the other—until we have looked thoroughly at the Transparent Eyeball passage.

.   .   .

Emerson's first major scene of symbolic self-making begins with an entry into a peculiarly American liminal space: "Crossing a bare common, in snow puddles, at twilight, under a clouded sky, without having in my thoughts any occurrence of special good fortune, I have enjoyed a perfect exhilaration. I am glad to the brink of fear"(p.10). There is a conjunction here, as there often is in Wordsworth, between the literal episode—crossing a common—and the figurative structure of the passage, a symbolic transition to another version of self. It is twilight, the space between nightfall and day; Emerson is walking over the common and is "under a clouded sky," inhabiting the space between earth and firmament, when he is brought quite suddenly to a liminal brink, "to the brink of fear." A New England common is a space between nature and culture. It belongs to everyone and yet to no one. To be alone on the common, as Emerson feels he is here, is to be a representative figure but also, oddly, to experience an extreme isolation. Emerson enhances the sense of borderline dissociation by deferring the personal pronoun until near the end of first sentence, suspending his own presence syntactically and so inviting the reader to immerse herself in the threshold sensations.

Yet what is it that brings Emerson "to the brink of fear"? Is it, perhaps, a Wordsworthian sense that he will have to pay for his pleasures, a belief that "As high as we have mounted in delight / In our dejection do we sink as low"? I think not. The peremptory shift into the present tense indicates that the fear is too sudden to be the product of calculation. Emerson's abruptly heightened sense of self would seem to signal the beginning of a symbolic act of self-translation. So the Wordsworthian "I" is similarly precipitated when his sudden meeting with a blind beggar propels him out of his own fluctuating mid-space.[11] Yet something much different happens in *Nature*. Emerson is transported suddenly away from the common and into the woods:

> Crossing a bare common, in snow puddles, at twilight, under a clouded sky, without having in my thoughts any occurrence of special good fortune, I have enjoyed a perfect exhilaration. I am glad to the brink of fear. In the woods too, a man casts off his years, as the snake his slough, and at what period soever of life, is always a child. In the woods, is perpetual youth. Within these plantations of God, a decorum and sanctity reign, a perennial festival is dressed, and the guest sees not how he should tire of them in a thousand years. In the woods, we return to reason and faith. There I feel that nothing can befall me in life,—no disgrace, no calamity, (leaving me my eyes,) which nature cannot repair. (p. 10)

Why does Emerson make the sudden transition from being "glad to the brink of fear" on the common to a vision of renovated childhood in the woods? I would speculate that, among other things, Emerson is committed here to demonstrating the superiority of American visionary possibilities to those available in England. Just by going to the woods Emerson can restore himself to the childhood glory that Wordsworth, strain as he does, can never entirely recapture in "Intimations." Whereas Wordsworth has to trade the "glory and the dream" for the "years that bring the philosophic mind," Emerson, who lives amidst the pure possibilities of a New World, tries to convince us and himself that "perpetual youth" is always accessible. The image of the sloughing snake may be a virile laugh at Wordsworthian and English delicacy. Wordsworth cannot identify himself with such crude figures of instinct, and that, the passage suggests, is part of what inhibits his possibilities for real change.

Yet I think that Emerson may be overestimating himself here: the free space of nature into which he is transported is manifestly continuous with religious conventions. Emerson's woods are an outdoor cathedral where decorum and sanctity "reign" and elicit "reason and faith." His diction suggests that he is still within a rather stereotypical kingdom where displaced parental forms hold sway over the respectful child.

Emerson's inability authentically to supply an alternative to the English Romantic mode is manifest in the way he completes the passage. His figure of self-recreation is at least partially derivative, a fact Emerson's

[11] See Wordsworth's 1850 *Prelude*, 7.619–49.

American critics seem to have left unremarked. Nourished by his sojourn in the woods, Emerson returns to the scene on the common:

> In the woods, we return to reason and faith. There I feel that nothing can befall me in life,—no disgrace, no calamity, (leaving me my eyes,) which nature cannot repair. Standing on the bare ground,—my head bathed by the blithe air, and uplifted into infinite space,—all mean egotism vanishes. I become a transparent eye-ball; I am nothing; I see all; the currents of the Universal Being circulate through me; I am part or particle of God. (p. 10)

The passage is far more cautious than it initially appears to be. Notice first how the famous "I" / "eye" pun preserves the integrity of character or conventional selfhood at what appears to be a moment of maximum risk. The pun sustains self-continuity just where Emerson proclaims the most radical dislocation and metamorphosis.[12] More centrally, Emerson here retreats to one of the received discourses he was attempting to overcome in the interest of having "a poetry and philosophy of insight and not of tradition, and a religion by revelation to us, and not the history of theirs" (p. 7). There can be little primary "insight" from a vision that derives so directly from Wordsworth. "Tintern Abbey" was one of the poems the young Emerson knew best, and he could perhaps have repeated from memory the lines about the "serene and blessed mood":

> In which the affections gently lead us on,—
> Until, the breath of this corporeal frame
> And even the motion of our human blood
> Almost suspended, we are laid asleep
> In body, and become a living soul:
> While with an eye made quiet by the power
> Of harmony, and the deep power of joy,
> We see into the life of things.[13]

To cast the burdens of selfhood by becoming the eyeball that renders all things transparent may be an appealingly grotesque modification of Wordsworth's tranquil vision, but it is only that. The American newness—if it existed at all—required something without an immediate precedent to sum it up.

Why is Emerson here unable to provide it? Why does he fall into the received terms of the metaphysical dream when he is striving hardest for originality? Perhaps the most accurate fundamental answer to these questions is that Emerson fails because he is unable to figure the antagonist

[12] For another reading of the passage's diction see Richard Poirier, *A World Elsewhere: The Place of Style in American Literature* (New York: Oxford University Press, 1966), pp. 66–67.

[13] Wordsworth, *Poetical Works*, 2:260.

against which he contends. At the moment when he shifts into the present tense and calls himself "glad to the brink of fear," Emerson seems to be very close to contact with the forces that most inhibit him. But he retreats from the encounter in the all-too-effortless move to the woods. The transformation becomes difficult to credit in that Emerson achieves it against no perceptible opposition. His inability to summon a negative counterforce, and in figuring his worst fears attain a renewed self-knowledge, may inhibit him from arriving at a genuinely fresh image of renovated self.

What is Emerson avoiding? What would his antagonist have looked like if he had been able to call it up? Here one can only speculate, but Emerson leaves many clues. The discovery that allows Emerson to return to the bare common is that nothing can befall him in life, except for blindness, which nature cannot repair. Thus Emerson's proper antagonist may be associated with the possibility of irreparable harm. And that harm, I suggest, threatens to come to Emerson from the permanent loss of those persons and things he loves. The Transparent Eyeball passage is surrounded by references to grief: "In the presence of nature," Emerson writes, "a wild delight runs through the man, in spite of real sorrows. Nature says,—he is my creature, and maugre all his impertinent griefs, he shall be glad with me" (p. 10). And later, "Nature is a setting that fits equally well a comic or a mourning piece" (p. 10). Emerson's is, I suspect, a mourning piece, and the despondency from which his sudden epiphany raises him is probably brought on, in experiential terms, by the deaths of his wife Ellen and his dearest brother Charles not very long before.

More generally, for the passage has caught the imagination of too many readers to be merely autobiographical, Emerson's grief is over the passing of time and the concomitant narrowing of possibilities. Emerson is afraid that more mourning will cripple him creatively and humanly. His solution is to elevate himself above time and chance in the defensive image of the eye that is "part or particle of God," and thus beyond mortal loss. In this exalted state, Emerson says, "The name of the nearest friend sounds then foreign and accidental: to be brothers, to be acquaintances,—master or servant, is then a trifle and a disturbance" (p. 10). In other words, he is so far estranged from others that their loss will not affect him. Emerson's hope is that he will be able to reproduce this state of secure alienation at will. Thus in the journal passage from which the scene derives he warns himself to sustain the feeling "(which in your lifetime may not come to you twice,) as the apple of your eye."[14] Yet there is

<hr/>

[14] See the journal entry for March 19, 1835, in *The Journals and Miscellaneous Notebooks of Ralph Waldo Emerson*, ed. William H. Gilman et al., 16 vols. (Cambridge, Mass.: Belknap Press of Harvard University, 1960–1982), 5:18–19.

a fear, too, that this state may be finally inadequate. He closes the chapter noting that "there is a kind of contempt of the landscape felt by him who has just lost by death a dear friend" (p. 11). The figure that Emerson avoids on the brink of his midspace, then, and which he can only evoke obliquely, would have been associated with death and death's power to break the creative spirit by binding it to what Freud will call "the work of mourning." Emerson tries, figuratively, to shelter himself from loss, rather than imaging and overcoming it in some unexpected yet finally "inevitable" way.

But the description I have offered thus far is too narrowly focused. Emerson's perplexity matters because it accords with a pervasive American difficulty. A country committed from its inception to reinventing itself unpredictably and fruitfully needs to create a new relationship to the past. Yet the problem that Emerson evokes on the first page of *Nature* remains unsolved at the book's close: "Why should not we have a poetry and philosophy of insight and not of tradition?" The aim is to be released from the hold of the past, whether it be sustained through mourning for our own loved ones or through an excessive deference to cultural tradition, which is to Emerson another form of mourning. And Emerson has achieved a great deal by divining the centrality of the issue and by responding to it, even if incompletely, in what was probably his most powerful piece of writing to that time.

But Emerson achieves something more in *Nature*. The sudden spatial shifts in the "Transparent Eyeball" passage, from common to woods to common, show traces of his future disjunctive mode, which he later described as "the shooting of the gulf . . . the darting to an aim." His assertion, later in the book, that the ruin or the blank that we see when we look at nature is in our own eye (p. 47) may rather slavishly repeat the "blank eye" of Coleridge's "Dejection."[15] But it also prefigures the perception of the gap between the self and the inert universe of things that Emerson used to provoke his own powers of self-reliance in the later texts.

II

Christopher Cranch's cartoon version of Emerson as a massive eyeball balanced on spindly legs illustrates the precariousness of his visionary posture. It wasn't mobile or sinewy enough, and its easy susceptibility to witty caricature pointed up its own lack of saving wit. The American situation was too tenuous to support the illusions of mastery in the metaphysical dream. It is hard to speculate on all the reasons for Emerson's

[15] *Complete Poetical Works*, 1:364.

shift from visionary to rhetorician in the late 1830s. But most simply one
might say that Emerson was enough of a pragmatist to leave his visionary
mode behind because it simply did not work. He could not assume the
posture at will (as his journal entry indicates), and even if he could, it was
too feeble as a defense against mourning and too derivative poetically.

In the essays of 1841 the Emersonian resistance to mourning becomes
aggressive and constant. Emerson is by then committed to unbinding
himself from "deadening" forms through the exertion of a force he alter-
nately calls spontaneity, intuition, genius, and "that gleam of light which
flashes across [the] mind from within." He gives up the defensive image
of the transparent eye, which is a figure of substantial, all-inclusive selfhood, and claims that true life lies in the inspired moments in which one
is propelled from one state of being to another. Where there is no such
power, there is no life.[16] The textual equivalent of this inspired movement
is the passage from one sentence to the next, so that Emerson's antagonist
is not only everything he has received from culture and from others, but
his own previous utterance and in fact everything he has thought and said
before.[17] Thus in a certain sense all that is part of the not-me and large
territories of the self, and perhaps even the notion of selfhood, qualify for
Emerson as antagonists.

One can enlarge the significance of Emerson's strategy of perpetual unbinding by seeing it as a fresh attempt to achieve what he failed to get in
the Transparent Eye passage, a plausible defense against the crippling
power of loss. Unsuccessful in his past efforts to rise above the claims of
grief, the Emerson of "Self-Reliance" devises an imaginative method for
cutting himself loose from what is behind him, a method that Nietzsche,
an attentive reader of Emerson's, would come to describe as "the will's ill
will against time and its 'it was.'" Emerson's declaration of prophetic
independence, "Self-Reliance," is what all of his work from then on
would be, a refusal to mourn.

Considered in its broadest, Emersonian sense, to mourn is to misplace
one's energies in customs, conventions, usages, and laws that oppress the
soul because they are, for all purposes, dead. We tend habitually outward,
to overestimate culture, great men, and, most destructively, the wealth of
the past. The object of life, as Emerson sees it, is to redeem our grief over
what we are not and have not, "to bring the past for judgment into the
thousand-eyed present, and live ever in a new day" (p. 265). In this en-
larged sense, all of the self-inflicted repressions against which Emerson
inveighs in "Self-Reliance" and the essays of the 1840s are assimilable to

---

[16] See Julie Ellison's remarks on Emersonian transitions in *Emerson's Romantic Style*
(Princeton, N.J.: Princeton University Press, 1984), pp. 162–65, 175–94.

[17] On this urge in Emerson see Richard Poirier's fine essay "The Question of Genius,"
Raritan 5 (Spring 1986): 77–104.

the category of mourning. Envy, imitation, reticence, craven consistency, prayer, regret, in short, conformity in all of its guises is evidence of our fallen urge to give our bounty to the dead.

Characteristically, Emerson deploys the language of misdirected grief to figure spiritual bondage:

> The objection to conforming to usages that have become dead to you is, that it scatters your force. It loses your time and blurs the impression of your character. If you maintain a dead church, contribute to a dead Bible society . . . I have difficulty to detect the precise man you are. And, of course, so much force is withdrawn from your proper life. (p. 263)

And later in the essay he writes: "Why drag about this corpse of your memory, lest you contradict somewhat you have stated in this or that public place?" (p. 265). Emerson excoriates our tendency to "lament the past" (p. 270) and our "mortifying" social smiles (p. 264). One of his more memorable fables about the soul's resurrection is that of the sot, "dead drunk," who wakens to his princely estate (p. 268). To mourn is to carry on a mere death-in-life: "imitation is suicide" (p. 259). And the dark figures that haunt the essay—the "stranger" who says "with masterly good sense precisely what we have thought and felt" (p. 259); the "fatal shadows" of the essay's epigraph; the corpse of memory dragging behind us; the giant who stalks the unself-reliant traveler (p. 278)—may be manifestations of the deathly spirit that Emerson had been unable to summon in the critical passage in *Nature*. To mourn is to succumb to the stranger, who is the Emersonian equivalent of Blake's Spectre, of Keats's Identity, and of the intrusive man from Porlock who halts Coleridge's composition of "Kubla Khan."

Yet Emerson doesn't just preach against mourning. He offers a philosophy of perpetual motion by which one can call up whatever circumstances threaten to bind, even before they have closed their grip, and do away with them. This strategy of ceaseless self-creation, which, it should be added, is always accomplished through the systematic destruction of the existing self, is the subject of this fine passage from "Compensation":

> Every soul is by . . . intrinsic necessity quitting its whole system of things, its friends, and home, and laws, and faith, as the shell-fish crawls out of its beautiful but stony case, because it no longer admits of its growth, and slowly forms a new house. In proportion to the vigor of the individual, these revolutions are frequent, until in some happier mind they are incessant. . . . And such should be the outward biography of man in time, a putting off of dead circumstances day by day. . . . But to us, in our lapsed estate, resting, not advancing, resisting, not coöperating with the divine expansion, this growth comes by shocks. (pp. 301–2)

To Emerson the mind always seeks to record its transformations in some outward form, be it a religious rite, a social usage, or a literary text. Our chief sorrow derives from the tendency to inhabit those forms as though they were ultimate truths. The spirit flashes and burns, and we, hungry for stabilities, make of the ashes that remain a faith. To begin dwelling in received forms is, for Emerson, to enter the house of mourning.

Yet the ability to produce a false sense of ultimates in one's reader is inseparable from poetic genius. The test of visionary power for Emerson is the capacity to force an impression on the reader, to establish her character. That is, the sublime poet is one who can unloose so compelling a force of tropes that the reader takes them for literal revelation and lives them out. She is made over in "the image of the imagery," in Kenneth Burke's phrase. "Speak your latent conviction," writes Emerson, "and it shall be the universal sense." The reader constituted by Emerson's "universal sense" will find the received vocabulary inevitable; she will have involuntary recourse to it in moments of crisis. The poet attempts to "interpret" his crises; he sees them as occasions for metaphor making. The reader, believing that she can "solve" hers, retreats to an anterior discourse that she hopes will provide her with mastery over the situation.

Emerson knows that even as he preaches self-reliance he is dispensing a series of figures for the enfranchised spirit on which his readers may rely. (The paradox might recall Freud's dual versions of the Oedipal passage, normative for us, sublime for him.) Emerson is not bothered by this apparent difficulty. What does matter to him is his own tendency to substantialize his text, becoming its inert reflection—(a) mere cold type. Thus the effort of the creative mind is initially negative. It must reimagine its true poverty, its clinging to forms, as the motive for self-reinvention.

Yet the stakes for turning perpetually against the given are more than aesthetic, for when we fail to do so, our "growth comes by shocks." Unexpectedly, fate intervenes to deprive us of an unacknowledged prop and to shame us by exposing our dependencies. Mourning then enters its painful and debilitating phase, though it has from the beginning scattered our force. Aggressive perpetual motion is the only cure: "Life only avails, not the having lived. Power ceases in the instant of repose; it resides in the moment of transition from a past to a new state, in the shooting of the gulf, in the darting to an aim. This one fact the world hates, that the soul *becomes*" (p. 271). Life thus faces us with two choices: leap or be shoved. And the Emersonian leap, a self-willed free-flight, is by far the better option. Yet if our tendency is groundward, defensively piling on dead forms until we become, as Spenser's Redcrosse is once, entirely vulnerable from the weight of our own protective armoring, by what means do we rise and shoot the gulf, cut ourselves loose from the binding labor of grief?

Eloquence is Emerson's chief weapon against mourning. His true units of composition in the early essays are his sentences, "barbed and winged" as O. W. Firkins, the author of a distinguished book on Emerson, called them.[18] The Emersonian utterance, at its most formidable, has a dual purpose: it is a barbed irony and a metaphor conducive to flight. The ironic charge severs a draining attachment. It locates an unconsciously maintained idealization ("a dead church . . . a dead Bible society"), or an easy reduction, and undoes it with a rhetorical thrust. But coeval with this detachment is an injunction to make a new commitment, to return the proper energies of the spirit to the self or to fresh objects that are truly conducive to power. Each effective utterance affirms availing life and purges the having lived.

To Emerson the spirit is most vital in the midspace—"in the moment of transition from a past to a new state"—when energies have been withdrawn in a sudden curtailment of mourning, but before the new investment has been made. Then is the "shooting of the gulf . . . the darting to an aim." It is this state of empowered suspension that reveals how "the mind is lord and master—outward sense / The obedient servant of her will."[19] Yet to Wordsworth, whom I quote here, these instances will be rare "spots of time." The Emersonian injunction is that one find in every passing moment the "renovating virtue," which means that a rhetoric of perpetual crisis dominates his early essays.

Yet the midspace, as Emerson knew to his sorrow, is not eternal. We are so constituted—our influxes of power being temporary—that we must seek new forms in which to reside. The location of these forms is the metaphorical objective of the Emersonian pronouncement. Metaphor puts one thing in the place of another, completes the crossing, and closes the gap. The objective of Emersonian metaphor is the uncovering of values that are eternal within us, but from which circumstances have led us away. Emerson turns himself and his readers back to reinvest his own properties: "that plot of ground which is given him to till"; his own endowments: for "the power which resides in him is new in nature"; and his own inspiration: "that gleam of light which flashes across his mind from within" (p. 259).

This ritual of sacrificing a former self to invent oneself anew, condensed into a sentence length symbolic action, leads of course to life lived as a larger irony, one of incident. The fresh deployments that appeared once as a salvation will become, in time, as deadening as those they replaced. We will begin to mourn them, too, and that grief will need violently to be curtailed. Nietzsche was, perhaps, thinking of Emerson when he called

[18] *Ralph Waldo Emerson* (Boston: Houghton Mifflin, 1915).
[19] Wordsworth, 1850 *Prelude*, 12.222–23.

the tendency to turn perpetually against the past "the spirit of revenge" or "the will's ill will against time and its 'it was,' " and he found it incompatible with his projected *Übermensch*. Nietzsche imagined that the kind of perpetual motion that Emerson commended would result in obsessive repetition as one set of terms and commitments was replaced by the next, ad infinitum. This repetition could itself become as deadening as the stasis or compulsive mourning it sought to overcome. Nietzsche's solution to the problem posed by "the spirit of revenge" was that one might learn to affirm repetition by willing the eternal recurrence of the same and in so doing triumph over resentment against the past.[20] Yet the doctrine of the eternal recurrence seems to be almost fully anticipated in "Circles," which records Emerson's own shrewd reading of his new, rhetorical mode. He sees himself tied to the wheel of recurrence, and so he proclaims that embracing inevitable repetition keeps the spirit vital:

> For it is the inert effort of each thought, having formed itself into a circular wave of circumstance,—as, for instance, an empire, rules of an art, a local usage, a religious rite,—to heap itself on that ridge, and to solidify and hem in the life. But if the soul is quick and strong, it bursts over that boundary on all sides, and expands another orbit on the great deep, which also runs up into a high wave, with attempt again to stop and to bind. But the heart refuses to be imprisoned; in its first and narrowest pulses, it already tends outward with a vast force, and to immense and innumerable expansions. (pp. 404–5)

Here Emerson prefigures not only Nietzsche but the Wallace Stevens who writes that "the man-hero is not the exceptional monster, / But he that of repetition is most master."

III

The reader will perhaps recognize the compatibility between Emerson's injunction that the spirit be mobile and freely extemporizing and the ethos that seems implicit in Freud's 1914 formulation of the narcissistic ego. Remember that, beginning with the essay "On Narcissism," Freud conceives of the ego as itself constituted by libidinal investment. Thus there is no firm distinction between the energy that is the ego and that which "invests" or "occupies" objects in the world. It follows, then, that the subject's allocation of libido, which is finite and constant, is depleted by every external investment. But self-enclosure is not a solution: "a strong egoism is a protection against falling ill, but in the last resort we

---

[20] See *Thus Spoke Zarathustra*, trans. Walter Kaufmann (New York: Viking Press, 1954), pp. 137–41, 198, 220–21.

must begin to love in order not to fall ill, and we are bound to fall ill if, in consequence of frustration, we are unable to love" (14:85). From this pronouncement comes Philip Rieff's formulation of the Freudian ethic: "The therapy of all therapies, the secret of all secrets, the interpretation of all interpretations, in Freud, is not to attach oneself exclusively or too passionately to any one particular meaning, or object."[21] The ethic is as characteristic of Emerson as it is of Freud.

Yet Emerson differs significantly from Freud in his implicit denial that the erotic component is constitutive of every human engagement. The Emersonian soul exists somewhere beyond the vicissitudes of erotic experience; or, perhaps more accurately, power always subsumes eros in Emerson. Yet it is the Freudian dilemma of having made poorly comprehended investments, and then paying for them with an attenuation of his proper force, that Emerson attempts to free himself from by way of symbolic action. His assurance that imagination—an influx of power that is made manifest through a surprising piece of eloquence—can sever commitments and redeploy force is, of course, surpassingly naive in Freudian terms. Freud's most firmly held perceptions about the mortal state involve the grim resolve with which we conserve our libidinal positions. Even when reality testing has shown the object to be lost, Freud observes, the psyche will not function in its own economic interests and quickly choose another. Rather, we disassociate ourselves from the world and undertake the labor of grief (*Trauerarbeit*). The early Emerson, Freud would say, under-estimates the stubbornness of the psyche, its cruel inertia. To think that a flash of rhetorical judo, which turns the bulk of fate against itself, can set one instantly free sorely underestimates how much the strength of one's first crucial attachments lingers on into what is called adult life and adult love.

We might think of the later Emerson as someone who develops just this kind of Freudian sense of the inadequacies of a condensed dialectic of liberation. The Emersonian "refusal to mourn" may indeed disappear in 1842, the year his young son Waldo died, but it is not replaced by acquiescence to "the beautiful Necessity." Instead Emerson devises a new spiritual strategy of self-recreation, one whose process is more arduous out of a deepened sense of the conservatism of the drives. Yet the goal of the quest remains unchanged: it is to reinvent the self by liberating the energies that allow one to respond to fresh experience. In a sense the effect of Emerson's shift in strategy reaches as far ahead as to a nonreader, Freud. (Perhaps it is more accurate to say, as I indicated in the Introduction, that Freud read Emerson indirectly, through Nietzsche.) For if Freud provides the terms for the limits of the early Emerson's methods, Emerson will

[21] Rieff, *Triumph of the Therapeutic*, p. 59.

allow us to undo one of Freud's most guarded idealizations, the normative "work of mourning."[22]

The critical consensus, of course, is that 1842 marks the turning point in Emerson's career, his "lordly man's down-lying." Stephen Whicher, whose *Freedom and Fate* remains the most influential book on Emerson, conceives that Emerson's Romantic aspirations perish on the crossroads of his boy's death.[23] Henceforth Emerson teaches submission to Fate and her iron laws, turns his podium into an altar to "beautiful Necessity" and dispenses the sacraments of circumstance. This final submission to Fate—the normative Freud would call it a sane acquiescence to the Reality Principle—occurs against considerable resistance: something in Emerson still refuses to be conquered. A week after Waldo's death, Emerson writes to his friend Caroline Sturgis: "Alas! I chiefly grieve that I cannot grieve; that this fact takes no more deep hold than other facts, is as dreamlike as they; a lambent flame that will not burn playing on the surface of my river."[24] Then there is the withering passage from "Experience," published in 1844:

> Grief too will make us idealists. In the death of my son, now more than two years ago, I seem to have lost a beautiful estate,—no more. I cannot get it nearer to me. If tomorrow I should be informed of the bankruptcy of my principle debtors, the loss of my property would be a great inconvenience to me, perhaps, for many years; but it would leave me as it found me,—neither better nor worse. So it is with this calamity: it does not touch me: some thing which I fancied was a part of me, which could not be torn away without tearing me, nor enlarged without enriching me, falls off from me, and leaves no scar. It was caducous. (p. 473)

Yet the grief for Waldo's death, most of Emerson's critics affirm, eventually makes its full weight known through a delayed reaction. At the time of the boy's death, Emerson put aside his journal (lettered J), saving it for his recollections of his son. He returned to the journal in April to begin

---

[22] In his excellent book *The English Elegy, Studies in the Genre from Spenser to Yeats* (Baltimore, Md.: The Johns Hopkins University Press, 1985), Peter Sacks uses "Mourning and Melancholia" as a means of arriving at a poetics of elegy. But he uses Freud too uncritically, I think, taking at face value the distinction drawn between melancholia and mourning.

[23] *Freedom and Fate: An Inner Life of Ralph Waldo Emerson* (Philadelphia: University of Pennsylvania Press, 1953). Others who more or less concur with Whicher on the trajectory of Emerson's career include Jonathan Bishop in *Emerson on the Soul* (Cambridge, Mass.: Harvard University Press, 1964); Harold Bloom in *Figures of Capable Imagination* (New York: Seabury Press, 1976), pp. 46–64; and Joel Porte in *Representative Man: Ralph Waldo Emerson in His Time* (New York: Oxford University Press, 1979).

[24] *The Letters of Ralph Waldo Emerson*, ed. Ralph L. Rusk, 6 vols. (New York: Columbia University Press, 1966), 3:9.

"Threnody," the elegy for Waldo that was completed and published in 1846. There, the received understanding goes on, one sees the authentic toll of Emerson's loss. Until this point he cast himself in the image of Hegel's *belle âme*, lacking "the power of alienation, the power to make himself a thing and support being." In *The Conduct of Life*, published the year Lincoln was elected president, 1860, particularly in the seminal "Fate," this story continues; one can see how Emerson has adapted himself to the new position, the inert buttressing of alien being. He recognizes his place in the world and understands that fate, not spirit, is the dominant force in his and every life.

Yet the crucial passage from "Experience" on Waldo's death may not signal a refusal of grief, but that the spiritual labors of mourning have been in some way completed. Emerson's shocking figuration of his loss in material terms—of a beautiful estate, bankruptcy, property, debt and enrichment—darkly anticipates Freud's own economic tropes for the psyche.[25] (The European Freud, however, prefers liquid assets to Emerson's real estate.) In an excellent essay on Emerson's "Experience," Sharon Cameron attempts to mitigate the ostensible cruelty of the "Experience" passage. She writes that "the vulgarity of alluding to these losses as if they were comparable is meant to replicate the vulgarity of experience's obliviousness to any niceties of human perception. The man who must sacrifice not simply his child but also his belief that the sacrifice has special meaning replicates the failure of discrimination by which he sees himself victimized."[26] Yet Emerson is rarely so elaborate an ironist; his chief attribute is, rather, metaphorical power, which is part of what made him mean what he did to writers as diverse as Thoreau, Whitman, Dickinson, and Nietzsche. To have achieved this vocabulary in which grief is so severely objectified may represent the fact that, for Emerson, the loss has been surpassed, and that, in Freud's terms, "the ego has become free and uninhibited again." Yet this is but an isolated moment. The entire drama of self-surpassing is recorded in the text of "Threnody."

"Threnody" is a Wordsworthian poem whose concerns and strategies of Romantic argument owe their first debt to the "Intimations" ode. Emerson's burden is the burden of all of the imaginative dualists, poets of loss, from Milton to Wordsworth, Keats, and Coleridge: what to make of a diminished thing. Emerson, in "Threnody," is diminished not only by the loss of his boy but by the failure of his own earlier hopes—not his

[25] On Emerson's "economics" see Michael T. Gilmore's "Emerson and the Persistence of the Commodity" in *American Romanticism and the Marketplace* (Chicago: University of Chicago Press, 1985), pp. 18–34; also see Richard Grusin's " 'Put God in Your Debt': Emerson's Economy of Expenditure," *PMLA* 103 (January 1988): 35–44.

[26] See "Representing Grief: Emerson's 'Experience,' " *Representations* 15 (Summer 1986): 15–41; this quotation is from p. 22.

hopes to become a poet of the first order, for this he has accomplished (though, as he says, his poetic voice is a hoarse and rugged one most itself in prose), but his hopes to transform his rude nation, to be the true prophet of American life. Those aspirations have, along with his dear son, faded into the light of common day, leaving memory:

> The gracious boy, who did adorn
> The world whereinto he was born,
> And by his countenance repay
> The favor of the loving Day,—
> Has disappeared from the Day's eye;
> Far and wide she cannot find him;
> My hopes pursue, they cannot bind him.[27]

These lines are from the beginning of the poem; but before long the departed Waldo merges with his father's own lost aspirations:

> 'Tis because a general hope
> Was quenched, and all must doubt and grope.
> For flattering planets seemed to say
> This child should ills of ages stay,
> By wondrous tongue, and guided pen,
> Bring the flown Muses back to men.
> Perchance not he but Nature ailed,
> The world and not the infant failed.
> It was not ripe yet to sustain
> A genius of so fine a strain,
> Who gazed upon the sun and moon
> As if he came unto his own,
> And, pregnant with his grander thought,
> Brought the old order into doubt.

(p. 134)

The "old order" still stands firm in 1846 despite Emerson's efforts to turn America's children into prophets. "Threnody" embraces that failure along with Waldo's death and pursues both losses through their every effect, much the way Wordsworth works through his grief at the necessary loss of the "visionary gleam" up to the turning of "Intimations." The irony of both poems is a massive irony of situation, the negative gap between expectation and event. And it is this overwhelming irony that permits Wordsworth and Emerson to suspend local qualification or the kinds

[27] Quotations from "Threnody" are from *The Complete Works of Ralph Waldo Emerson*, ed. Edward Waldo Emerson, 12 vols. (Boston: Houghton, Mifflin, 1903–1904), 9:130. Henceforth they are cited by page number in the text.

of specific ironies that are commonly manifest in tonal ambiguities and to write with a full, uninhibited force of feeling. This is the painful freedom of the elegist, who even attenuates his grief to preserve the right to speak in an idiom of originary force. For tonal irony may be nothing more than evidence of the abiding awareness that it all has happened before and will again. Thus in the Romantic elegy an achieved eloquence redeems grief somewhat, preventing a too-thorough identification with the dead. "The intellect . . . converts the sufferer into a spectator," Emerson writes in his essay on tragedy, "and his pain into poetry. Hence also the torments of life become tuneful tragedy, solemn and soft with music, and garnished with rich dark pictures" (p. 1295).[28]

The double labor of grief in "Threnody," for Waldo and for the Waldo the author himself was before becoming a name, becoming "Emerson," might be approached by way of a great paragraph of Freud's in "Mourning and Melancholia":

> In what, now, does the work which mourning performs consist? I do not think there is anything far-fetched in presenting it in the following way. Reality-testing has shown that the loved object no longer exists, and it proceeds to demand that all libido shall be withdrawn from its attachments to that object. This demand arouses understandable opposition—it is a matter of general observation that people never willingly abandon a libidinal position, not even, indeed, when a substitute is already beckoning to them. This opposition can be so intense that a turning away from reality takes place and a clinging to the object through the medium of a hallucinatory wishful psychosis. Normally, respect for reality gains the day. Nevertheless its orders cannot be obeyed at once. They are carried out bit by bit, at great expense of time and cathectic energy, and in the meantime the existence of the lost object is psychically prolonged. Each single one of the memories and expectations in which the libido is bound to the object is brought up and hyper-cathected, and detachment of the libido is accomplished in respect of it. Why this compromise by which the command of reality is carried out piecemeal should be so extraordinarily painful is not at all easy to explain in terms of economics. It is remarkable that this painful unpleasure is taken as a matter of course by us. The fact is, however, that when the work of mourning is completed the ego becomes free and uninhibited again. (14:244–45)

This passage contains two quite radical implications, one of which Freud, in his desire to enforce certain distinctions between "mourning" and "melancholia," conceals from his readers and perhaps from himself. The

---

[28] David Porter's reading of the elegy judges that "it lacks emotional authority and convincing particularity." My own valuation is obviously a great deal higher. See Porter's " 'Threnody': The Hidden Allegory" in *Emerson and Literary Change* (Cambridge, Mass.: Harvard University Press, 1978), pp. 30–44.

first implication is submerged in Freud's compound *Trauerarbeit*, the "work of mourning." To figure mourning as "work" is to issue, however subtly, an ethical injunction that one undertake mourning economically, proceed to work thoroughly but without waste, cut the failed investment, suspend losses. One might call this an "ethic of substitution." Freud here, as throughout his text, asserts the priority of the erotic aim over the erotic object. Freudian grief derives not from the loss of some unique and irreplaceable person or thing but from the drive's temporary failure to locate a source of satisfaction. Mourning, for Freud, works its way toward an implicit realization of the arbitrariness of the object, its constitution by the drive in the image of earlier imagos. (Proust eloquently expresses this "realization" when, after the death of Albertine, the narrator observes that "the truth is that the woman has only raised to life by a sort of magic spell a thousand elements of affection existing in us already in a fragmentary state, which she has assembled, joined together, bridging every gap between them, it is ourselves who by giving her her features have supplied all the solid matter of the beloved object.")[29] If the object is invariably a cliché or revenant, as Freud describes it elsewhere, it cannot demand a prolonged psychic allegiance. It is this tacitly achieved sense of love as a function in the service of the ego, as a "protection against falling ill" (14: 85), that signals the closure of healthy mourning.

Emerson fully anticipates these thoughts in the symbolic action of "Threnody." Although his loss is too grievous to convert to gain in the space of a single utterance, with a rhetorical flourish, the objective remains an expeditious freeing of the energies of the self, their orderly withdrawal from a bankrupt object. (Recall the broker's rhetoric in the central passage from "Experience.") Here, though, Freud's darker insight comes into play. Freud has equated the "work of mourning" with summoning up and hyper-cathecting the lost object. Yet, this would be closer to a formula for falling in love, engraving the image deeper. The insight that Freud avoids is, I take it, that the object is brought up, born into the psyche, in order to be dismissed, done away with, slain by the subject. This labor of grief, for Freud and for the Emerson who in "Threnody" calls up a sequence of images of his boy in order, symbolically, to slay each one, is most brutally and compellingly described by Nietzsche. It is the labor of transforming "thus it was" into "thus I willed it." The method here is not, as it was in the early works, to sunder deadening commitments with a single stroke of invention. It is, rather, inventively to

---

[29] *Remembrance of Things Past*, trans. C. K. Moncrieff and Frederick A. Blossom, 2 vols. (New York: Random House, 1927), 2:736. The entire section entitled "Grief and Oblivion" (pp. 675–773) would be useful to compare to Emerson and Freud.

reproduce the actions of fate, and in the inspired reinvention or representation of the "it was" to make the past, symbolically, into a function of one's own imaginative will. By repeatedly representing the birth and death of the lost object, the poet becomes imaginatively identical with Fate. " 'Tis paltry to be Caesar / Not being Fortune," says Shakespeare's Cleopatra, yet the sacrifice for becoming, in one's own mind, Fortune is humane grief for what has been loved and lost.

This understanding of the dynamics of loss will perhaps leave us less perplexed by the moment of turning in "Threnody" in which an appallingly revised version of the Over-Soul intervenes:

> The deep Heart answered, "Weepest thou?
> Worthier cause for passion wild
> If I had not taken the child"

> (p. 135)

Surely the "deep Heart" is crucially Emerson's, but it is also the agent of Fate, that which has "taken the child." The symbolic action of the poem, representation and sacrifice of the image, makes the poetic imagination identical with Fate, an identification that Emerson, unlike Freud, is willing to acknowledge and to sustain in the interest of his abiding project, the acquisition of power. And in Emerson the power that matters most is always the power to reinvent the self at the expense of whatever conformity impedes quickened life. As James Cox writes, "Getting over the deaths of loved ones is no tired or traditional 'spiritual' vision for Emerson precisely because it is a literal breathing in, or inspiration, of the death in life."[30] Thus the death of Waldo is mastered, assimilated in "Threnody" to the imagery of self-surpassing that crowns the pivotal essay, "Circles":

> And know my higher gifts unbind
> The zone that girds the incarnate mind.
> When the scanty shores are full
> With Thought's perilous, whirling pool;
> When frail Nature can no more,
> Then the Spirit strikes the hour:
> My servant Death, with solving rite,
> Pours finite into infinite.

> (p. 137)

[30] See Cox's brilliant essay, "R. W. Emerson: The Circles of the Eye," in *Emerson: Prophecy, Metamorphosis, and Influence*, ed. David Levin (New York: Columbia University Press, 1975), pp. 57–81. The quotation is from p. 72. On Emerson and mourning, see also B. L. Packer, *Emerson's Fall: A New Interpretation of the Major Essays* (New York: Continuum, 1982), pp. 50–54.

What force now takes responsibility for having broken the circle that was constituted by Waldo's life? The answer is as disturbing as it is unavoidable.

Freud defends himself against such broodings not from any tenderheartedness but, I think, as a maneuver for protecting the therapeutic process, or rather that aspect of the process in which the therapist establishes her authority over the subject under treatment. To justify this statement, though, I have to move more deeply into the text of the essay on loss. Ostensibly "Mourning and Melancholia" is an attempt to understand the "neurotic" condition of "melancholia" (or what one would now call severe depression) by comparing it to its closest analogue in "normal" experience, "mourning." The stakes increase somewhat, though, when one realizes that the 1917 piece is actually the continuation, and perhaps the completion, of "On Narcissism."[31] Where the earlier work had reflected on the vicissitudes of object choice and object investment, the 1917 piece takes up the question of de-cathexis, the process whereby the subject gives up an erotic object. Thus "Mourning and Melancholia" quickly becomes less a treatise on a particular neurotic condition than a more generalized meditation on erotic life, which for Freud is our most centrally determining life. Freud sets out by characterizing melancholia as a special instance of mourning:

> The distinguishing mental features of melancholia are a profoundly painful dejection, cessation of interest in the outside world, loss of the capacity to love, inhibition of all activity, and a lowering of the self-regarding feelings to a degree that finds utterance in self-reproaches and self-revilings, and culminates in a delusional expectation of punishment. This picture becomes a little more intelligible when we consider that, with one exception, the same traits are met with in mourning. The disturbance of self-regard is absent in mourning; but otherwise the features are the same. (14:244)

This disturbance of self-regard is, Freud goes on to point out, the result of an ambivalent investment in the object, which in turn indicates "that the object-choice has been effected on a narcissistic basis" (14:249). Such a conflict of heightened ambivalence makes for an internal strife absent from "the work of mourning," which Freud characterizes as normative.

Even from these brief descriptions, it becomes clear that "Mourning and Melancholia" participates in, and elaborates, the extended dualisms that cut across "On Narcissism." One may locate these two new terms, "mourning" and "melancholia," within the twin constellations of tropes with which Freud attempts to reinvent himself (and us, his purported sub-

---

[31] Strachey points this out in his introductory notes to "Mourning and Melancholia," 14:240.

jects) in the 1914 piece. Accordingly, the tendency to mourn falls in with what Freud broadly characterized as the scientific temperament. The scientist is one who invests objects "anaclitically"; is capable of making judgments based on disinterested observation; is susceptible to rational authority; recognizes his true place in the order of things; employs language instrumentally; stands beyond superstition in all its forms. The scientist is essentially masculine, a master, a "purveyor of truth," as Derrida puts it. And this is, of course, the image of the normative Freud. To it one may now add the tendency to mourn the lost object and accept substitution and the exigencies of an efficient psychic capitalism that encourages one to cure rather than to interpret and refigure one's situation. "Melancholia" joins the narcissistic character traits: commitment to the "thaumaturgic power of words" and the "omnipotence of thoughts"; delusions of power, originality, and self-generation; the tendency to resist authority; the penchant for speculative excess. The exemplars of narcissism include, in Freud's estimation, women (particularly beautiful women), children, homosexuals, primitive peoples, and Jung and all the conquistadors and parvenus who put speculation before observation or, one might say, literature before science, for it is the literary artist who, to Freud, summarizes and concentrates many of the qualities of the "narcissist." Numbered covertly in the litany of narcissists ought, of course, to be Freud the Romantic artist, who in "On Narcissism" authors his most speculative, mythopoeic text in his fifteen-odd years of psychoanalytic writing. The Romantic Freud is the Freud who silently aligns himself with femininity and who refuses to be restrained by any authority whatsoever, including the authority exerted by images of his own most conservative self.

Yet this is only to redeploy and to sharpen what has come before. I want now to approach the text of "Mourning and Melancholia," keeping in the forefront Kenneth Burke's interpretive question: "What is the writer trying to do for himself by way of symbolic action in this particular text?" Let me begin, then, by suggesting that in "Mourning and Melancholia," as in "On Narcissism," Freud is reflecting indirectly but continually on the therapeutic situation. The 1914 essay speculates on the establishment of the transference; "Mourning and Melancholia" considers the closure of therapy and the fate of the internalized authority of the physician. One might suppose that if "narcissism" accounts for a faulty transference relationship, so then "melancholia" is a diagnosis for the patient's inability to sustain the effects of analytical intervention. The melancholic is the patient who, once what appears to be a transference has been established, cannot "work it through" in a way that perpetuates the physician's authority after analysis has been "terminated."

Consider Freud's description of the genesis of melancholia:

An object-choice, an attachment of the libido to a particular person, had at one time existed; then, owing to a real slight or disappointment coming from this loved person, the object-relationship was shattered. The result was not the normal one of a withdrawal of the libido from this object and a displacement of it on to a new one, but something different, for whose coming-about various conditions seem to be necessary. The object-cathexis proved to have little power of resistance and was brought to an end. But the free libido was not displaced onto another object; it was withdrawn into the ego. There, however, it was not employed in any unspecified way, but served to establish an *identification* of the ego with the abandoned object. Thus the shadow of the object fell upon the ego, and the latter could henceforth be judged by a special agency, as though it were an object, the forsaken object. (14:248–49, emphasis Freud's)

Consider, for a moment, the applications of this paragraph to the therapeutic process. If the "object-choice" is indeed the analyst, then one might imagine that the "real slight or disappointment" in question refers to the narcissistic wound inflicted by what Freud calls "the first communication." The function of this first, critical intervention is, one might recall, to begin to dissolve the transference by "giving the resistance a name" (12:155). Yet, if this reading is correct, the "first communication" marks the crisis point in therapy, recapitulating as it does the Freudian moment at which the father intervenes with the Oedipal prohibition. In therapy, one might hypothesize, the first critical utterance will begin to undo the patient's illusions about his relations with the physician. The idealized version of the analyst, established through transference, will be modified in the moment that she asserts herself as a figure of critical authority. Then will begin the labor of grief in which the patient works through "each single one of the memories and expectations in which the libido is bound to the object" (14:245). One might guess that every interpretive thrust by the physician will release yet another false memory or excessive expectation "until the work of mourning is completed" and the ego, to avoid a complete break with the past, revises itself to resemble the image of the lost object. Freud describes such a process in *The Ego and the Id*:

When it happens that a person has to give up a sexual object, there quite often ensues an alteration of his ego which can only be described as a setting up of the object inside the ego. . . . It may be that this identification is the sole condition under which the id can give up its objects. At any rate the process, especially in the early phases of development, is a very frequent one, and it makes it possible to suppose that the character of the ego is a precipitate of abandoned object-cathexes. . . . It must, of course, be admitted from the outset that there are varying degrees of capacity for resistance, which decide the extent to which a person's character fends off or accepts the influences of the history of his erotic object-choices. (19:29)

The therapeutic point becomes clear. To terminate analysis by way of the work of mourning is to remake the ego, and perhaps the super-ego, in a form that resembles the image of the lost object, the physician, and all that she, as a representative of the therapeutic ethos, embodies. Mourning is a way of sustaining and consolidating authority, of sacrificing whatever there might be of originality to the urge to maintain some continuity with one's past self, and of conforming to a revised standard biography.

In the case of the melancholic, one might surmise, the "first communication" or "narcissistic wound" inflicted in therapy is the beginning of an internal contest in which the object is to throw off a received version of the self. To the melancholic, the "narcissistic wound" consists in the sudden realization that what he had conceived of as his own at least provisionally autonomous being has, without his awareness, begun to be rewritten in the image of the Freudian construct, the "narcissistic ego." Freudian melancholia ought to be understood as a form of exorcism in which the patient turns against himself in the interest of achieving a less comprehensively constructed or determinate being. In the idealized condition of "mourning" the patient desexualizes the imago, making himself over in its image and conforming to the analyst's narrative version of events.

Yet a stronger resistance against intrusion, an Emersonian resistance, attempts to slay the ingested other—which is of course a form of self-slaughter, or self-scapegoating—rather than merely naturalize him. "Desexualization" is, from this perspective, failed exorcism, the feebler resistances of a self that at bottom desires to be reconstituted by institutions and cultural forms beyond itself, of a self that longs, in Foucault's terms, for status as a "subject." Emerson thus prefigures and undermines the Freudian category of "normal mourning," affirming instead the rather cruel activity of self-recreation, "melancholia." Toward the close of the 1917 essay, having failed to draw a clear distinction between mourning and melancholia, Freud becomes franker about what is at stake in the latter:

Just as mourning impels the ego to give up the object by declaring the object to be dead and offering the ego the inducement of continuing to live, so does each single struggle of ambivalence loosen the fixation of the libido to the object by disparaging it, denigrating it and even as it were killing it. . . . The ego may enjoy in this the satisfaction of knowing itself as the better of the two, as superior to the object. (14:257)

This is the struggle, not to be constituted by the lost object, that Emerson undertakes in "Threnody," and that Freud, as a proponent of the authority of the psychoanalyst and of psychoanalysis in general, finds most troubling. The insight that Freud finally evades is that "mourning" is a normative fiction: pragmatically there will always be two forces at work, the conservative disposition to preserve the received version of the self, propped on powers not its own, and the contrary drive to do away with this newly consolidated form in the interest of a certain indeterminacy. Perhaps Romantic poets are those in whom simultaneous tendencies to mourning and to melancholia are unusually heightened. Emerson's hatred of the internalized past is as extreme and intricate as Wordsworth's deference to it, yet both feel the opposing tendency: Wordsworth is drawn to apocalyptic dissociations, Emerson to visions of preserved totality.

But what of the therapist? How shall one describe the energies that he deploys in the psychoanalytical exchange? Here it may be that one ought to see the violence of the "first communication" and of the vocal interventions that follow as aimed toward exorcising the internalized image of the patient. That is to say that the physician's attempts to undo the patient's "narcissistic" investment in him also act to undo the counter-transference. Thus the therapist's interventions are exercises in melancholic disengagement designed to free himself from any strong attachment he might have developed to the patient. This would not be a particularly self-inventing form of melancholia, however, because its procedures and ends would be entirely predictable. Scripted by Freud, the analyst's melancholia would be repeated in the course of every full-term analysis.

Given this reading of "Threnody" and of the analytical exchange, one might go on to conceive of Emerson's last great essay, "Fate," which reputedly is the bitter proof of his final acquiescence to the principle of reality, in more radical terms. Perhaps Emerson, having internalized Fate in "Threnody," proceeds in the essay to submit Fate itself to the work of melancholia. Like "Threnody," "Fate" moves toward a massive turning, a dialectical swing at its midpoint, where Emerson can rise up and say that "Fate has its lord; limitation its limits" (p. 953), and leave us in little doubt as to who that lord might be. This turning is achieved rhetorically by a sequence of refigurings of Fate until the agency becomes, imaginatively, a function of Emerson's powers of verbal invention. Through the first half of the essay, Emerson shows how Fate can be summoned forward, figured, and dismissed, slain, as it were, in the gap between sentences, then brought freshly to life at the whim of the creator. One would not be wrong to equate this rhythm of willful creation and destruction with the rhythm of melancholia. Consider a representative affirmation of limits from the opening section of the essay: "In different hours, a man represents each of several of his ancestors, as if there were seven or eight

THE WORK OF MELANCHOLIA

of us rolled up into each man's skin,—seven or eight ancestors at least,— and they constitute the variety of notes for that new piece of music which his life is" (p. 947). Surely this is close to anticipating Freud's remark that the ego is "a precipitate of abandoned object-cathexes, and that it contains the history of those object-choices" (19:29), and yet the inventiveness of the image, the spirited transformation of the ancestors into notes, would make of Emerson the finer composer, the master of mastery. To proceed in this way, by a kind of rhetorical imperialism, is, in Stevens's phrase, to be stripped of every fiction except one, with Emerson's imagination taking the part of that fiction, the "absolute-Angel." For to trope against Fate is to deprive oneself of defenses; in Freud's terms it is to attempt to use the imagination to demystify the Reality Principle, and the experiential results are likely to be disastrous.

Yet perhaps that only adds to the grandeur of the turning passage in "Fate":

> Thus we trace Fate, in matter, mind, and morals,—in race, in retardations of strata, and in thought and character as well. It is everywhere bound or limitation. But Fate has its lord; limitation its limits; is different seen from above and from below; from within and from without. For, though Fate is immense, so is power, which is the other fact in the dual world, immense. If Fate follows and limits power, power attends and antagonizes Fate. We must respect Fate as natural history, but there is more than natural history. For who and what is this criticism that pries into the matter? Man is not order of nature, sack and sack, belly and members, link in a chain, nor any ignominious baggage, but a stupendous antagonism, a dragging together of the poles of the Universe. (p. 953)

Freud would perhaps stigmatize this exhilaration as mania, the exultation that follows upon an achieved work of melancholia; whereas mourning ends in tranquility, melancholia terminates in a manic burst of newly accessible force. Freud describes the onset of mania as follows:

> [A] large expenditure of psychical energy, long maintained or habitually occurring, has at last become unnecessary, so that it is available for numerous applications and possibilities of discharge. . . .
> . . . In mania, the ego must have got over the loss of the object (or its mourning over the loss, or perhaps the object itself), and thereupon the whole quota of anticathexis which the painful suffering of melancholia had drawn to itself from the ego and 'bound' will have become available. (14:254–55)

If this is the case with melancholia, however, why does mourning, which follows the same economic development, not end in comparable triumph? "I find it impossible to answer this objection straight away"

(14:255), Freud responds. Pursuing the question further, Freud, with characteristic honesty, comes to the conclusion that mania can only result from the termination of an interior struggle:

> Just as mourning impels the ego to give up the object by declaring the object to be dead and offering the ego the inducement of continuing to live, so does each single struggle of ambivalence loosen the fixation of the libido to the object by disparaging it, denigrating it and even as it were killing it. . . . The ego may enjoy in this the satisfaction of knowing itself as the better of the two, as superior to the object. (14:257)

In our terms, of course, mania would follow upon just such a relative triumph over the attempt to impose a narrative that would solidify and stabilize "identity." What the melancholic resists is having a "nature" attributed to herself, even if embracing that "nature" is likely to be "effective" therapeutically. The sense of power over one's own suffering that accepting the analytic narrative can confer is, for some patients, evidently unacceptable, because it means giving up the sense of future possibility (and future risk) that goes with nonconsolidated being. Yet if Freud is right, the freedom of melancholic self-undoing will only be a temporary one. As he remarks, "The manic subject plainly demonstrates his liberation from the object which was the cause of his suffering, by seeking like a ravenously hungry man for new object-cathexes" (14:255). And so the cycle begins again.

Perhaps we have ourselves come full circle. Recall that in a speculative moment of the first chapter I drew some analogies between Freud's situation in the wake of his father's death and the situation of Shakespeare's Hamlet, who, I said, sustained his powers of imagination by deferring revenge and prolonging his grief for his father. In that attenuation of sorrow, perhaps, Hamlet found the energies that allowed him to achieve something like a Nietzschean perspectivism. From Freud's point of view, Shakespeare owed his ability to write his "supreme masterpiece," *Hamlet*, to the sentiments aroused by his father's death. Now, having read "Mourning and Melancholia" in conjunction with Emerson, one can perhaps be more precise—although no less speculative—about the nature of the grief that for Freud, for Emerson, and, if one may include a fictional character, for Hamlet, contributes to Romantic creation.

It is not that melancholia, with all of the attributes associated with it, is somehow the essence of the Romantic imagination. No one ought to cultivate melancholia in the hopes of becoming a poet of the sublime. Rather, the category of melancholia may provide the best Freudian analogue for the energy that motivates, or accompanies, a certain kind of Romantic invention. The impulse to disassociate oneself from binding commitments—to shoot the gulf—will of course always be tempered by some desire to preserve and renew the past. Were that not the case, the text would simply be incoherent. To use the clinical terms for a moment, those many Romantic texts that are in central ways elegiacal will work out a dialectic between mourning and melancholia. It may be a distinguishing mark of a great deal of Romantic poetry, in fact, that in it the conflict between these tendencies is heightened to an unusual degree.

In his most extreme moments, Emerson seems to possess comparatively little of the desire for continuity. He succeeds as nearly as anyone in unbinding a Romantic drive from normative commitments. To Emerson in certain moods all of humanistic culture probably looked like nothing more than a communal act of mourning. In Freud's assault against Jung and the vision of continuity that Jung represented, one sees, perhaps, a form of self-destroying self-invention with analogues to Emerson's own most aggressive procedures. Conceivably, it is the normative dimension of Freud's thought that disguises his own more violent designs in texts such as "On Narcissism." For most of us, for the patient in search of a cure, for the normative analyst, for the reader who wants to be steadied and assured by the text, the way of incorporation is best. But for Emerson at his most aggressive, and perhaps sometimes for Freud, vitality can only arise from the inner struggle to do away with that which one most loves.

Conclusion

FREUD IN THE FUTURE

At the close of David Lodge's academic romance, *Small World*, the mild quester, Persse McGarrigle, brings light and life to the parched kingdom of the MLA Convention by posing to the aged Fisher King (named Arthur Kingfisher) and his colleagues on an important panel a simple question: "What follows if everybody agrees with you?"[1] What, in other words, are the practical consequences of what you have said? Nothing could be more satisfying, or mystifying perhaps, than for me, given my own critical orientation, to identify here at the end of the book with a questing pragmatist. But every volume of academic criticism, whatever its approach, should probably turn on itself and speculate on the consequences of its findings, even as the author is aware that such consequences might not be his to comprehend or to control. In fact, given the number of readers many scholarly books succeed in getting, it's fair to speculate that, in worldly terms at least, one's book may simply have no consequences at all.

This book bears on a few areas: on Freud's writing and Freudian therapy, on Romantic poetry, and, indirectly, on the practice of contemporary literary criticism. My objective overall was to contribute to the reading of Freud, so on that issue my thoughts on the consequences of the book begin. The reflections on Wordsworth and Emerson from the perspective of the "new" version of Freud developed here came later and were, for all purposes, a secondary design. The polemic, for it was that, on the issue of contemporary criticism was latent throughout the writing of the book, but perhaps the more insistent for being so. First then to Freud: what consequences do these pages have for an overall view of Freudian writing and Freudian therapy?

Reflecting on the possible effects of his challenge to Freud's seduction theory, the redoubtable Jeffrey Moussaieff Masson predicted havoc in the psychoanalytic industry. "They would have to recall every patient since 1901," he said. "It would be like the Pinto."[2] Lines this good should be prophetic, I suppose, but naturally Masson's was not. No patient seems to have applied for a refund on the grounds that her seduction as a child

[1] *Small World* (New York: Warner, 1984), p. 362.
[2] *In the Freud Archives*, p. 19.

hadn't been at all imaginary; no analyst called back her discharged anal-ysands for a therapeutic overhaul. Surely I am not myself in a position to claim that I have "debunked" psychotherapy and that the "recall" of faulty products should now begin.

What this book *has* done, I think, is to provide a sense of what costs might be entailed in submitting to Freud's therapy and his writing. The second, third, and fourth chapters showed at some length how Freudian therapy—at least as it is described in the papers on technique—has as its unspoken and perhaps unconscious objective the creation of a certain sort of subject, or self. When the voice of the therapist intervenes (like the voice of Milton's God, like Adam's voice calling Eve back to him, like Armytage's at the climax of "The Ruined Cottage" it recapitulates the (mythical) intervention of the father's voice at the moment of Oedipal crisis. The father's role, as Freud dramatizes it, is inevitably a brutal one, for he delivers the "castration threat." Naturally, if there is to be psycho-logical health, that cruel indwelling voice must be tempered, must be re-vised. And that revision is the task of the therapist or, more exactly, of his voice as it descends to the patient from above. But to say that the voice belongs to the therapist is not quite right either; the voice descends to him through Freud, who himself usurps it from the literary tradition.

This puts our reflections on the dramatic structure of therapy rather crudely, but not inaccurately. My point was that Freud's construction of the narcissistic ego was such that for that ego to be healthy it would very likely need his intervention, his cure. We, as narcissistic egos, need Freud about as much as Narcissus needed the warning voice (which he never heard) and Eve, in a normative construction of Milton, needed the celes-tial voice. We can acquire that salutary intervention, then, by entering therapy or by reading Freud in a particularly acquiescent way, becoming his patient readers, something that I of course think our culture has done in a wholesale way.

But the analyst does not for his part stand outside the game, judging it like an impartial official, handing down rulings and interpretations. For if his intervening voice is not quite his own, then therapeutic authority is not fully his own either. If the therapist is prone, perhaps compelled, to project his own urge to speculate onto the patient, and then to discipline it, thus reaffirming his scientific purity, then psychotherapy confines him too inside the Freudian construction. (An analyst reading these pages might conclude that I am as confined within the arbitrary values of Mil-ton and Emerson as she is within Freud's. Perhaps teaching and criticism are my rituals of "self-creation," rituals whose powers of determination I am in no position to understand.) Both analyst and patient have their respective "borders" reconfirmed, or set into place. They become Freudian subjects.

The fourth chapter's reflections on the dynamics of the therapeutic exchange also showed how analysis confirms the ethos of mourning. Having been encouraged to love the analyst as though he were her own reflected ("narcissistic") image, the patient then faces the choice of preserving the analyst's voice and values through an act of "mourning," or of striving against them in an internal version of Potlatch, which aims at the destruction of what the psyche has come to love and possess. And this destruction is undertaken in the interest of nothing more than a certain indeterminacy of self. To submit to the ethos of mourning is to submit to the necessity for a standard—and Freudian—construction of one's biography. What's lost then, of course, is the power to tell your own stories about yourself, to relate many different kinds of fictions, rather than adopting one for the continuity and security it may provide.

The reading of therapy—that is, of the normative Freud at his most aggressive—in this book is tied to a pair of assumptions with which the reader may wish to contend. The first is that, contra Freud, there is no absolutely accurate representation of the self, no representation that the human subject must ultimately receive to be truly understood. Every representation of the self has to be judged pragmatically, which in this case means, among other things, judged politically. One needs to ask what it is good for, what kind of behavior it's conducive to, what acts it enables and delimits. The belief that trope is the only form of access to "the self" stems, naturally, from a literary prejudice. It may well be that part of what attracts people to literature is a sense that the most important matters in life are not those that one can arrive at consensus upon, or, *pace* Wittgenstein, that one is compelled to pass over in silence, but the ones that have to be described and described again, always with the knowledge that every account will fail to encompass the complexities one perceives. My resistance to the finality of any version of selfhood is, naturally, a Romantic commonplace; one may find it in Keats and Shelley and Blake, and one may find it challenged in any form of thinking, be it Marxist, Freudian, or deconstructive, that argues for the power of circumstances over the possibilities of creative will.

The second assumption that readers, and particularly readers who are professional analysts, may wish to challenge is my sense that what I say about Freud is relevant to psychoanalysis as it is now practiced. Even if what I observe about the relations between the construction of the narcissistic ego and Freud's instructions for the conduct of analysis happens to be true, someone might respond that therapy has come a long way since Freud. Therapeutic technique has changed. To this challenge I cannot speak with any immediate knowledge; I have neither practiced nor undergone analysis. But without offering a survey of contemporary psychoanalytic writings, I can say this much. Psychoanalysis is, as I have stressed repeatedly, modeled on the structure of the family and—Freud makes this analogy available in *Group Psychology and the Analysis of the Ego*—modeled on the structure of a primitive tribe. There are rites of initiation; there is inheritance; there are coherent generations. This kind of structure stresses continuity in the strongest possible ways. The primitive peoples who so fascinated Freud perpetuated their cultures through rituals that, as I pointed out in the third chapter, have more than a little in common with the rituals of psychoanalysis. One of Freud's strongest drives from 1914 until his death in 1939 was to guarantee that the institutions and practices of psychoanalysis would reproduce themselves. A look at the familial, not to say tribal, structure of the analytic profession today, as Janet Malcolm describes it in *Psychoanalysis: The Impossible Profession*, confirms the success of Freud's enterprise. " 'He was a very brilliant and charming old man—an Austrian Jew of the first generation of analysts after Freud,' " says Aaron Green, the psychoanalyst Malcolm profiles in the book, of his analyst. " '*His* analyst had been Sándor Ferenczi, and he idealized him. There was a bust of Ferenczi in his consultation room, together with one of Freud, who had analyzed Ferenczi. I could thus trace my analytic lineage back to Freud.' "[3] A remark like this encourages me to think that our understanding of Freud's writing on therapy and technique may have some bearing on psychoanalysis in its contemporary form.

The critique of Freudian self-creation offered in this book focuses overall on what Freudian therapy and, probably more important, Freudian writing cost the literary imagination. I think a certain uncritical reading of Freud, a passive reception of his authoritative voice, is for all purposes comparable to the therapeutic reception of the analyst's intervening voice. Freud, all through his work, busily evokes the crisis of cultural authority that only he can resolve. In *Civilization and Its Discontents* he repeatedly owes our unhappiness to the pressures of denial that grow stronger, not only as each individual life progresses but also, because the super-ego is in some inexplicable manner hereditary, simply as time passes. The moral is that we as readers, we as a society, will need Freud's voice to cultivate and transform the super-ego more tomorrow than we do today—and today we need it a great deal. But the cost is not small. Drawn to Freud, perhaps, by intimations of his Romantic daring, we find ourselves confined within his normative enclosures. There is a price for attempting to solve one's dilemmas rather than using them as motives for remaking.

---

[3] *Psychoanalysis: The Impossible Profession* (New York: Knopf, 1981), p. 50.

This book has, I hope, made that cost palpable. But it is a cost that many people will, and perhaps ought to, assume. The normative guidance that Freud gives can probably provide a remedy—or at least a timely relief—for sufferings that are quite real. Freud praised psychoanalysis once for its power to transform misery into common everyday unhappiness, and anyone who has ever been miserable knows that such a transformation is not inconsequential. Freud the normative thinker understood how brutally painful life could be in a culture that was becoming as spiritually vacuous as the West was. If Freud's "intervention" does not produce poets, it may have the effect of reclaiming lives that would otherwise have been wasted.

No one who has been absorbed by literature can turn calmly away when asked what human good all his work amounts to when compared to the labors of even the most modest healer. "Sure a poet is a sage; / A humanist, physician to all men," Keats proposes to Moneta, but she never confirms the view. Freud was, to stay a moment with Keats, one for whom, at least at times, the miseries of the world were miseries and wouldn't let him rest. And that has probably been true of few poets, and fewer critics. Perhaps Eve would have ended in morbid self-absorption, a version of the fate of Narcissus, rather than in imaginative freedom if she had not been compelled to repudiate her fiction-making powers completely. Perhaps, the psychoanalyst might argue, something similar would be true for all of us if we were deprived of the Freudian education that culture administers so generally. My own view on this matter is clear; I hope that I have put readers in a better position to develop their own.

It is also worth pointing out that the first step for any "speculator"— any poet—is to comprehend the normative vocabularies in which she finds herself enmeshed. Without a full sense of what qualifies as the standard wisdom, one will never be able to arrive at novelty, which must be both different from, and continuous with, what is given by culture. Most of what we need to possess is standard wisdom, and of that Freud is now a crucial source. So I am not advocating the abandonment of Freud; rather, I would like to see him read more actively and inventively, for only then will we be able to move honorably beyond him. Thus one objective of this book is to help free up the kinds of imaginative energies that might take us past Freud. Poets, to modify Blake, reason and compare (that is, criticize their predecessors in the art) and create simultaneously. One function of criticism—Matthew Arnold seems to me to be to the point in this—is to facilitate that critical reflection and help make the context more conducive to poetry.

My enjoining the task of continuing to read Freud with energetic resistance and with due admiration brings forward another question. Though the writings examined here are crucial ones, they are only a fragment of Freud's work: would the rest of his corpus respond to a reading guided by the dialectic I have proposed between the normative and the Romantic Freud? Overall I think that it would. The approach proved effective in considering some of the more austerely "scientific" of Freud's texts, the papers on therapeutic technique, texts that would seem to offer the most resistance to a "literary" approach. I have little doubt that overtly mythological works such as *Group Psychology, Civilization and Its Discontents, Beyond the Pleasure Principle*, and *Moses and Monotheism* would, on close examination, show Freud the inventor playing off Freud the figure of cultural and scientific authority.

In his recent essay "Withholding the Missing Portion: Psychoanalysis and Rhetoric," Stanley Fish uses some critical terms that are comparable, if not assimilable, to my own. A brilliant reading of the celebrated Wolfman case, the essay calls attention to Freud's continual practice of

> discovering at the heart of the *patient's* fantasy the very conflicts that he himself has been acting out in his relationships with the patient, the analysis, the reader, and his critics. In all of these relationships he is driven by the obsessions he uncovers, by the continual need to control, to convince, and to seduce in endless vacillation with the equally powerful need to disclaim any traces of influence and to present himself as the passive conduit of forces that exist independently of him.[4]

What Fish brings forward here is Freud's habit of projecting his own imperial impulses somewhere else, the better to affirm his disinterestedness. Fish locates the split between the scientific Freud ("the passive conduit of forces that exist independently of him") and Freud the rhetorician, whose greatest satisfactions lie in what Fish calls "the pleasure of persuasion."[5] The rhetorician seeks absolute mastery, a position outside the game from which he can also dominate it. My account focuses on the masterly authorial self who is created by way of the kind of rhetorical maneuvers Fish describes; Fish's emphasis is on the action of the rhetoric itself. But our perceptions are comparable. I chose to emphasize the issue of selfhood rather than that of rhetoric because Freud's conceptions of the self have had far more cultural influence than have his powers as a rhetorician. In Fish, though, there is further confirmation for the dialectic that

---

[4] Stanley Fish, *Doing What Comes Naturally: Change, Rhetoric, and the Practice of Theory in Literary and Legal Studies* (Durham, N.C.: Duke University Press, 1989), p. 540.
[5] Ibid., p. 543.

this book has used, and I am encouraged to think that such a dialectic might be brought to bear in the future on other writings of Freud.

. . .

What about the consequences of this book for an understanding of the Romantic impulse? What should one make of the concurrences—and the distinctions—between Freud's Romantic, or self-creating, drive and the urges toward self-reinvention in Emerson and Wordsworth? Actually finding a Romantic impulse in Freud was my first surprise in reading him critically. At the start I was convinced that, as Philip Rieff and others had argued, we had entered a phase of life characterized by "the triumph of the therapeutic." A Freudian orientation toward experience, an orientation one might describe as detached, ironic, self-enclosed, and apolitical, seemed to be ascendant. It also appeared that procedures and discourses associated with Freud were coming to be used to underwrite social practices that had, as their end, what Foucault has identified as "the creation of subjects." If during the period of its first appearance Freud's was a language of liberation—and I have no doubt that it was—it had somehow been assimilated by the institutions that most actively induce conformity. Part of becoming a patient, a prisoner, a student, a citizen was being described time and again in terms derived in part from Freud's. Freud had become an embodiment and defense of the softly tyrannical norm.

But in reading such works as *The Interpretation of Dreams* and "On Narcissism," I found another Freud as well, a Romantic Freud devoted to symbolic self-regeneration, to the invention of fresh ways of seeing things that seemed to contend, at least for him, against normative standards. This naturally was a literary Freud, one who proved Shoshana Felman's observation that "literature . . . is the unconscious of psychoanalysis; that the unthought-out shadow in psychoanalytical theory is precisely its own involvement with literature; that literature in psychoanalysis functions precisely as its 'unthought'; as the condition of possibility and the self-subversive blind spot of psychoanalytical thought."[6] It seemed to me, at the beginning of this project, that pointing to the literary properties of Freud's work could help to undermine a lot of the values and practices that the authority of "Freud the scientist" helps to legitimate. My first hope was that Freud's Romantic impulse might be a useful form of resistance against Freud's own and other urges for social conformity. The Romantic Freud, I believed, could inspire hope for a culture hospitable to a wider variety of subjectivities.

I wanted to call attention to this "self-creating" Freud by pointing to

6 "To Open the Question," p. 10.

the analogies between him and Emerson and Wordsworth, arguably the two most influential of the Romantic writers. It seemed to me that in the Romantics one found a form of writing that exceeded, as far as this might be possible, not only the conventions for representing the self that existed when they wrote, but even many of those that are currently in place. I also saw in the symbolic self-makings of Emerson and Wordsworth a more general kind of hope. Though both writers were self-obsessed and overtly resisted the intrusion of historical issues into their work, I thought that their drive to displace given vocabularies might serve to encourage human resistance to outmoded social practices and institutions, to the "lucrative patterns of frustration," to use Auden's phrase. Frost says that poetic education—but he might also have been speaking of the activity of writing literary criticism—is the process of finding out how far-reaching a particular metaphor might be, of learning what situations it illuminates and where it fails. My initial perception was that the Romantic rebirth metaphor, as put into practice by Freud as well as by Emerson and Wordsworth, might have a long collective reach. I suspected it might be a way of thinking about the self and its possibilities for change that a lot of people could use.

But actually reading the works critically impinged on this hypothesis. The literary artists who for so long had been disciplined by criticism (criticism in many ways beholden to Freud) might, as it were, answer back to Freud: they might show how Freud's normative terms had been called into cultural eminence to circumscribe literary creations, and they might show, by analogy, how sublime a self-inventor Freud himself was. But in this dialogue other less-welcome facts came into focus.

It became evident, first of all, that my effort to draw a strict distinction between a normative and a Romantic Freud would not stand up. Freud achieved his self-rewritings through a complex practice in which it was necessary to represent the woman, the patient, and the narcissist in a variety of delimiting ways. The male scientific authority evoked in "On Narcissism" needed to project his own urge to speculate onto the "narcissist" so that the reader would locate it there, and not in Freud himself. Freud's stigmatizing the narcissist, women, and all other speculators gave him the freedom to speculate himself, and the right to affirm his own standing as a reliable empirical authority over and against speculators. Freud is both man and woman, scientist and poet, authority and creator, but to the detriment of every reader who is identified with the second term in any of these pairs. Without the derogatory fiction of the narcissist, Freud the Romantic self-creator would not be possible. Without the figure of the "normal" subject, confined by Oedipal repression, Freud's overcoming of the paternal literary tradition and his possession of the oracle would not be such a dramatic self-making gesture. As affecting as Freud's sojourn in

a space of pure possibility during the year in which he grieved for his
father was, the turn to the generalized truth of the Oedipal complex that
followed was in many ways disheartening. At a certain point Freud could
not extemporize freely on his own identity without defending the results
by concealing them within a general theory about the basic identity of all
men and women everywhere.

Still, what about the poetic alternative? Surely Emerson and Wordsworth were not so elaborately self-defended. But the Romantic reading of
Freud brought on a Freudian rebuttal that revealed some unexpected affinities. One had to see, for instance, that the logic of scapegoating was at
work, not just in *Oedipus Rex* and *Hamlet* and in Milton's depiction of
Eve and Satan, where one expected to find it, but in Wordsworth's relations to the women and children represented in his work and in Emerson's turnings against himself and whatever other attachments inhibited
his vitality, including his remembered image of Waldo. It would be possible, I suppose, to believe that there exists a movement, from Sophocles
through Shakespeare, Milton, the Romantics, and Freud, in which the
symbolic act of self-overcoming, turning "thus it was" into "thus I willed
it," grows gradually more imperial and remorseless. Analogies would be
conceivable between this trend and the development of an ever more aggressive Western culture, one less tolerant of human differences and more
determined to impose its monologic. One might refer then to Hazlitt's
view that "the language of poetry naturally falls in with the language of
power"[7] or extend Stephen Greenblatt's diagnosis of Christopher Mar-
lowe to apply to Emerson and Wordsworth: perhaps their acts of resistance not only conjure up the order they seek to undermine but at times
have been conjured up by that very order.[8]

But this would deny too many significant facts. I continue to believe
that Emerson and Wordsworth represent impressive alternatives, albeit
problematic ones, to Freudian accommodations. Keep in mind that both
writers are largely uninterested in generalizing or institutionalizing their
terms. Wordsworth speaks at the close of *The Prelude* of teaching others
to love what he and Coleridge have loved, but the poem is overwhelm-
ingly about the growth of an individual and particular mind. The injunction of *The Prelude*, and much of the rest of Wordsworth's poetry, is that
so different are we from one another that every man and woman would
write a much different poem of self-becoming. It is for all purposes a
Wordsworthian hope that Keats adopts at the beginning of *The Fall of
Hyperion* when he says that "Every man whose soul is not a clod / Hath

---

[7] See Hazlitt's lecture on *Coriolanus* in *The Complete Works of William Hazlitt*, ed. P. P.
Howe, 21 vols. (London: J. M. Dent and Sons, 1930), 4:214–21.

[8] See *Renaissance Self-Fashioning* (Chicago: University of Chicago Press, 1980), pp. 209–
10.

visions, and would speak, if he had loved, / And been well-nurtured in his mother tongue." As idealizing as these lines may be, the idealization is one that modern poetry, the poetry of the inner self, might not have been able to develop without.

Wordsworth's turning against figures like Margaret and Lucy in the interest of the stability of his own selfhood is surely disturbing. But Wordsworth's representation of women is distinct from Freud's in a number of ways. Wordsworth openly attributes the source of his poetic voice to Margaret. She is there in the text, speaking more in the idiom to which the poet says he aspires than does Wordsworth when he assumes his "proper" voice. Freud, on the other hand, makes every move possible to disassociate himself from femininity: almost compulsively he confers upon himself characteristics that are precisely opposite to those he claims to find in women as a group. Wordsworth conveys an awareness of his bond with women that Freud, for his part, will not express. The woman is to Wordsworth foreign and a threat but also a part of himself, the part for which he sustains the most awe, the sublime imagination. One feels Wordsworth's pain when he turns against Lucy in the poetic sequence on her life and death, whereas the Freud who writes the disturbing case of Dora sometimes seems morally anaesthetized. Recall too that part of what first distinguished Wordsworth's poetry, and earned it considerable mockery, was its representation of characters who had conventionally been excluded from high art. This is a commonplace, naturally, but one worth remembering at a time when a pervasive ideological critique reprimands the Romantics for not being progressive enough, for not being enough like ourselves.

Emerson may have taken the time to say that institutions are the lengthened shadow of a single man, but the shadow that Emerson casts on the present is far too shifting and amorphous to guide any kind of institutionalized practice. Like Wordsworth, Emerson is a prophet of individualism, though he feels that a person is likely to be most herself at the moment of transition and of the withdrawal of energies from existing things—that is, when she's pure energy, potentia, when she's closest to being nothing at all. It is very hard to consolidate and administer a dogma on the basis of a practice that, in certain phases, enjoins the undoing of all stabilities and holds everything "titular and ephemeral," including the self.

Emerson's rebellion against character, or stability of self, by way of melancholic self-undoing and the fracture of received narratives about who and what one is, makes violence into a method and reveals, perhaps, the ruthless attitude one must have to all commitments to be devoted to the Romantic ethos of self-recreation. It might appear that such an attitude would threaten the social sense, or what Northrop Frye would call "the myth of concern." But if this reading of Emersonian melancholia demonstrates anything, it is that suffering is entailed for no one more than he who turns against himself in this brutal way. Melancholia is surely a form of self-laceration, one that few of us will be able to bear. Those who do will not have much chance of significantly undermining the larger social fabric composed of the many who are inclined to preserve continuities of all sorts.

There may also be some indirect benefits to the Emersonian mode. As Norman Mailer, the contemporary writer in America who probably most resembles Emerson, says in his version of "Self-Reliance," "The White Negro": "In widening the arena of the possible, one widens it reciprocally for others as well, so that the nihilistic fulfillment of each man's desires contains its antithesis of human cooperation."[9] By contrast the melancholia of the analyst, in which he exorcises his patient's internalized image with each "communication," is undertaken in a far different spirit. His melancholia is programmatic, circular: it has happened before, and so he knows its dynamics. It is not, in other words, conducive to what Mailer would call an "existential situation," which he defines unpretentiously enough as one in which your defenses are dissolved and you don't know what will happen next.

Part of what has made criticism suspicious of writers like Emerson and Wordsworth, at least over the past decade or so, is their infatuation with power. Naturally this suspicion is related to what critics perceive as the misuse of power in and by our own culture. I am not opposed, as some are, to making the past subject to the concerns of the present. If criticism is a form of metaphor making, seeing the past in terms of something that it both is and is not, then it is legitimate to use the poets to mediate our own thoughts about the difficulties in which we find ourselves.

I think, though, that ethical critics of a historicizing bent often read too literally, establishing facile equivalences between the language of poetic power and that of imperial triumph. Blake, who detested war as much as anyone, still uses as his image for the redeemed imagination a depiction of battle. At the close of *The Four Zoas*, Urthona rises up "to form the golden armour of science / For intellectual War The war of swords departed now / The dark Religions are departed & sweet Science reigns." Blake's affection for "mental fight" and William James's commendation of "the moral equivalent of war" are two of the many available examples of pacifists using the imagery of strife as a trope to illuminate other situations that require vast efforts. War can be purged of violence; it can become spiritual. The passions unleashed in battle are not passions we want to lose all access to: that anyway might be the moral imparted by Blake and James, and by Kenneth Burke when he uses as the epigraph for

---

[9] *Advertisements for Myself* (New York: G. P. Putnam's Sons, 1959), p. 316.

his tetralogy on symbolic action the phrase *ad bellum purificandum*, toward the purification of war. The point here is that to come upon images of strife in literature is not necessarily to have run into morally reprehensible ideology. Nor, on the other hand, should the possible social relevance of any writing be dismissed too easily out of a belief that "this is merely fiction." A careful reading of the work is always called for, a kind of reading that, in the case of Wordsworth and Emerson, could not leave one in a state either of simple accord or of facile condemnation.

The suspicion of power that in part motivates Jacques Derrida's deconstructive practice has, in my view anyway, been taken to an extreme. For if the deconstructor comes to believe that every positive utterance must smack of repressive mastery, then he is likely to be self-limited to playing the role of the spirit that only denies. In fact, the ethos of deconstruction sometimes seems compatible with the melodramatic position that Nietzsche identified as super-historical, the position from which one "could feel no impulse from history to any further life or work, for [one] would have recognized the blindness and injustice in the soul of the doer as a condition of every deed."[10] A certain impotence, Nietzsche suggests, will inhere in an approach that views every unironic investment, be it in words, persons, or causes, as a form of fetishism. Perhaps deconstruction, along with a good deal of the "demystifying" criticism that it has helped to engender, is bound permanently to the Romance of the negative.

It is not surprising that the misuse of power by the institutions of the West has led in the past few years to a rejection of many of the tenets of the Romantic faith in self-creation. But the Western abuse of political power does not give one sufficient reason to think of power itself as an absolute evil. If power, which is perhaps comparable in some ways to what the Romantics wanted, has been misused, this may be in part because it has been badly assigned. The writers discussed here all teach that change requires the use of positive force, and even if their own Romantic self-moldings were not in every way admirable, I still find much to celebrate in their energy, invention, and boldness. In other words, the consequence of these pages, at least for me, has not been to disconfirm the Romantic endeavor. Romanticism is a tradition, but a tradition of change and independence; it wills to overcome itself. Nothing will better liberate culture from the oppressive aspects of the Romantic project than more (Romantic) invention.

So I do not number among the consequences of this book any imperative comparable to the one that deconstruction issues that we strive to

[10] See *The Uses and Abuses of History*, trans. Adrian Collins (Indianapolis, Ind.: Bobbs-Merrill, 1978), p. 10. For a more developed version of this critique of Derrida see my essay "The Ethics of Deconstruction" in *Michigan Quarterly Review* 27 (Fall 1988): 622–43.

become post-Romantics. Romantic writers who do not fit well term for term with Freud, such as Shelley, Blake, and Whitman, might have provided a stronger alternative to the accommodations of psychoanalysis, and those writers on whom I focused differ from Freud on crucial points that ought not to be overlooked. I hope that, more than questioning the validity of the Romantic endeavor, these pages have given grounds to ask some questions about the authenticity of academic literary criticism in its current form.

· · ·

Surely Freud is not the first demystifying critic that we know of in the Western tradition. That honor must go to Plato, who himself says that the war between poetry and philosophy was already old in his day. Even in the nineteenth century, both Nietzsche and Marx preceded Freud in proposing critical modes that helped the interpreter to read against the grain of the text, to tell a story about it that the author could not have. Yet Freud has probably contributed more than any other figure to making contemporary academic literary criticism the expanding enterprise that it is.

As I observed in the Introduction, a number of seminal Anglo-American critics in the 1930s and 1940s were freshly inspired by what they learned from Freud. Such significant books as Wilson's *The Wound and the Bow*, Empson's *Some Versions of Pastoral*, and Trilling's *The Liberal Imagination* come directly out of their authors' engagements with psychoanalysis. What Freud gave to the ambitious critic was the possibility for a new kind of relation to the texts he wrote about. No longer did one have to be content with merely celebrating the great works or, if one were in a daring frame of mind, arguing that this or that one had been overvalued. Now one had the freedom of analysis. The critic could see into the text, penetrate to its moment of genesis, describe the factors that had brought it to birth and made it what it was. It was possible, in other words, to read literature as the analyst reads the patient. Neither Marx nor Nietzsche gave critics so compelling an analogy for their work. Trilling and Empson used Freud with care, aware of what the reductive power now available to them could end up costing literature. Numerous other Freudian critics have struggled for comparable restraint.

Still, with the ascendancy of Freud's work, everything changed in literary studies. The balance of power between critic and artist was dramatically altered. Even a mode of criticism as deferential to the literary work as the New Criticism was in certain ways made possible by Freud. The stroke against the primacy of the author that Wimsatt delivered when he attacked "the intentional fallacy" was surely abetted by the Freudian sense that, because of the action of the unconscious, no one, no matter how adept, ever has full control of her own meanings.

Not only did Freud help to establish a new relation between critic and text, he also licensed a fresh expansion of critical activity. One of the lessons Freud dispenses most frequently, from *The Interpretation of Dreams* to "Analysis Terminable and Interminable" forty years later, is that interpretation is by nature an open-ended activity. There are no limits to the number of illuminating associations one may attach to a dream, or a slip of the tongue, or to losing an object. Then one must turn and interpret one's interpretation. So it is now with the criticism of the arts. As George Steiner puts it, "In a most graphic way, this automatism of secondary and tertiary discourse, this formal and empirical interminability as we see it in psychoanalytic pursuits of meaning, is illustrative of all [present day] interpretive and critical treatment of the aesthetic."[11] The difficulty is not only that the work is eventually suffused in commentary, but that it comes to be thought of as an act of commentary itself, not much different from the criticism that takes it as a "pre-text." Can a dream claim superiority to the interpretation that illuminates it? Once that question has been posed, the next step is to ask the same thing, however implicitly, about the work of art.

From the change in the balance of power that derives in so many ways from Freud a number of things have followed. Contemporary writers are, more and more frequently, being directed by the subliminal injunction that they compose texts that are "readable," "interpretable," susceptible to being taught. In order for one's work to live, it must solicit the energies of the academy. More and more the artist, who may also be a professor, is drawn to doing the kind of work that will survive because it can answer the hermeneutic concerns of the moment. The difficulties that arise from this situation are considerable, for we expect the best contemporary art to be always out ahead of established critical vocabularies, compelling us to invent new terms in order to live in the present that the artwork has both invented and found. I am not predicting the death of literature at the hands of Freudian-inspired criticism, or anything comparably apocalyptic. Art will not be suffocated by imperial modes of reading, but it may have to switch its locus of generation. There is a good chance, I think, that much of what is most vital in imaginative writing in the next few decades will be coming to us from far outside the culture of the Western university.

But perhaps the major damage is taking place among our students. Inspired in large measure by Freud's "contribution" to criticism, we are conveying to them forms of thinking that grant illusory power over the

[11] *Real Presences*, p. 47.

works they study. We can condescend to those works, make them the objects of a discipline, know them in much the way that Freud "knew" the human subject. This kind of will to power over texts is distinct from the kind enjoined by the classical competition. We are not encouraging students to take the prize for tragedy away from this great man or that. Rather, we are suggesting that a certain critical exercise, one undertaken in Freud's spirit, can give them power over the past. But analytical power of this sort is a false and dishonorable power. It is dependent, at least in part, on the illusions that this book has, I hope, succeeded in exposing.

If Freud himself is in his major dimension a literary writer, and not the scientist that he claimed to be, then neither Freud's work nor the myriad forms of criticism that rely on it can grant one a position outside of, or superior to, great writing. Freud can legitimately inspire in us the power to attempt to write imaginative texts that emulate or surpass his own. But, when he is accurately understood, he can no longer be a source of analytical power over major art. Thus part of the effort of the book has been to induce doubt about the authority of certain ambitious forms of contemporary literary theory. How much this skepticism ought to be applied to my own reflections, readers will of course decide for themselves.

Yet I do not want to end with a negative turn, for the overall impulse of this book has been hopeful. It looks forward to that point in the future when we have freed ourselves from the imposition of Freud's normative terms and have ceased deploying them ourselves. We will then be in a better position to be moved by his originality and courage. Perhaps at that point Freud will be an ally, rather than the antagonist that our own weakness has made of him.

INDEX

Printed in Great Britain
by Amazon